NEW LIFE AT GROUND ZERO

New York, Home Ownership, and the Future of American Cities

Charles J. Orlebeke

The Rockefeller Institute Press
Albany, New York
Distributed by The Brookings Institution Press

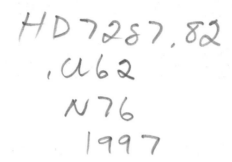

Cover Design by Emil Antonucci
Cover Photos by Camilo J. Vergara

Rockefeller Institute Press, Albany, New York 12203-1003
© 1997 by the Rockefeller Institute Press
All rights reserved. First edition 1997
Printed in the United States of America

The Rockefeller Institute Press
The Nelson A. Rockefeller Institute of Government
411 State Street
Albany, New York 12203-1003

Library of Congress Cataloguing-in-Publication Data

Orlebeke, Charles J.
    New life at ground zero : New York, homeownership, and the future
of American cities / Charles J. Orlebeke. -- 1st ed.
        p.   cm.
    Includes bibliographical references (p.   ) and index.
    ISBN 0-914341-52-9 (cloth). -- ISBN 0-914341-51-0 (paper)
    1. Home ownership--New York (state)--New York 2. Community
development, Urban--New York (State)--New York.   I. Title
    HD7287.82.U62N76   1997
    363.5'83'097471--dc21
                                                        97-27654
                                                        CIP

ISBN: 0-914341-52-9 Cloth
      0-914341-51-0 Paper

To Faith

CONTENTS

FOREWORD

harles J. Orlebeke and I have worked together for a long time. Both of us have experience as what political scientist Richard E. Neustadt calls "inners and outers," in that our careers have included both appointive positions in government and, in our case, academic positions outside of government. We first met late in the 1960s, when I was executive assistant director of the U.S. Office of Management and Budget and Orlebeke was executive assistant to George Romney, Secretary of the U.S. Department of Housing and Urban Development. From 1969 through 1971, we worked on the same issues, saw each other often, and exchanged ideas frequently. After that, we collaborated on several national evaluation studies of federal programs.[1] During this later period, Orlebeke was a faculty member and, at various times, urban affairs dean at the University of Illinois at Chicago.

Now fast forward to 1992 when I first learned about the New York City Housing Partnership. I was intrigued by accounts by Kathryn Wylde, formerly president of the Partnership, of its activities in neighborhoods in New York City. With colleagues, I visited several sites to learn more about the Partnership. At the time, the Partnership had constructed about seven thousand housing units, mostly middle-income

---

1 Over the years, Charles J. Orlebeke has participated in four evaluation studies we worked on together. The four studies include a field evaluation of the public service employment component of the Comprehensive Employment and Training Act (CETA), a study of all federal aid to ten big cities (including Chicago), a study of the effects of the Reagan administration's cuts and changes in federal grants-in-aid, and most recently the Rockefeller Institute assessment of the implementation of the Empowerment Zone/Enterprise Community program.

owner-occupied units or duplexes rather than multi-family rental properties. These units are located in clusters all over the city, some of them part
of the renaissance of the South Bronx.

We often hear about the urban downside and do not know enough
about what works, so it seemed like a good idea to take a close look at
the work of the Housing Partnership. As I thought about who could undertake such a project and write it up with the kind of *panache* that
doesn't always (I am understating) characterize academic research, I
thought immediately of Charles Orlebeke, who is a superb writer and not
a New Yorker (which I thought would be good in this case), having spent
his academic career in Chicago. I approached Orlebeke about studying
the New York City Housing Partnership with the idea that the resulting
book would have a broad audience. We spent a considerable amount of
time talking about how such a project could be organized, and eventually
it was arranged for him to interview people, visit sites, and study documents in order to write this book, which was reviewed anonymously by
outside readers.

As the project came to its conclusion, I asked Orlebeke to provide
me with notes on his experiences that I could use to write a foreword. He
produced a fascinating personal essay, which it was decided should be
drawn from in his own voice, describing his experience in and out of
government working on urban and housing issues. The author's preface
which follows includes a discussion of the inspiration for this study and
acknowledges the key informants Orlebeke met along the way. Our hope
is that the book will be of interest to students of government and urban
policy and to a broader audience of people who care about the well-being
and prospects of America's cities.

Richard P. Nathan
August 1997

PREFACE

I n the summer of 1992, Richard P. Nathan suggested to me that the New York City Housing Partnership was transforming neighborhoods on a surprising scale, and that this achievement deserved close study. He urged me to look at what the Housing Partnership had been doing and then let him know if I was interested in pursuing a project that the Nelson A. Rockefeller Institute of Government might sponsor, and that could have some appeal to the general reader as well as to academics and policy addicts like ourselves. Since I had recently completed with colleagues a project for the MacArthur Foundation on community development corporations in Chicago, the prospect of studying a somewhat different model of neighborhood-based development in New York City was compelling.

My personal engagement with urban devastation and its consequences goes back to the 1967 Detroit riot, when I was working as an assistant to George Romney, Governor of Michigan. Detroit saw the worst of the urban riots of the 1960s: four days of arson and looting quelled only after Romney asked President Johnson to send in federal troops. I was posted to Detroit for the first few months after the riot, acting mainly as organizer and liaison between the Governor and the office of Detroit Mayor Jerome Cavanagh. Led by Romney and Cavanagh, the city's civic leaders formed the New Detroit Committee, an early example of a city-wide "partnership," wherein labor chieftains and CEOs of the big automakers sat side-by-side with young street gang leaders.

In 1968 Richard Nixon was elected President, and his somewhat surprising choice for Secretary of Housing and Urban Development was

Governor Romney, who asked me to come to Washington to be his executive assistant and, later, Deputy Under Secretary for Policy. With civil unrest and desolated neighborhoods the dominant images on the domestic policy landscape, Romney's HUD in the first Nixon term was in many ways the agency's most activist period up to that time or since: More than a million units of federally subsidized housing were produced, and the first experiments with housing vouchers were launched. In addition, a bundle of federally conceived development programs, including Urban Renewal and Model Cities, were discarded in favor of the Community Development Block Grant, which transferred control over money and program choices to the nation's mayors. The Community Development Block Grant, among its other virtues, would become the mother's milk for hundreds of community-based development groups that were springing up to begin the arduous process of reclaiming the territory that had been laid waste. It was, in my judgment, then and now, a policy shift in the right direction.

By 1975, the fear of more urban riots had subsided, but a new kind of urban crisis, with New York City at its center, was threatening. My return to HUD as an Assistant Secretary, thanks to an invitation from Secretary Carla Anderson Hills, followed a two-year stint in academe and coincided approximately with the middle of the New York City fiscal crisis, an event that seemed to point to a general downward cycle in cities caused by middle-class outmigration, loss of industry, and the rising cost of public services for the impoverished population left behind. The fiscal crisis prompted our commitment of a big chunk of HUD's research budget to scholars who constructed "urban distress indices" in an effort to answer the question "How many New Yorks?" Meanwhile, President Gerald Ford, who was facing an uphill campaign against Georgia Governor Jimmy Carter, decided to create a special Cabinet Committee on Urban Development and Neighborhood Revitalization chaired by Secretary Hills and staffed by my Office of Policy Development and Research. The Cabinet Committee's report, released by Ford shortly before the election, called for better targeting of federal grants to distressed cities, for increased tax incentives to stimulate housing rehabilitation and neighborhood redevelopment, and for special countercyclical grants to cities with high unemployment. President Jimmy Carter would later adopt many of its ideas, and some were enacted.

Ford's defeat in 1976 sent me back to the University of Illinois at Chicago, and from then on I pursued my interest in urban policy as an academic, frequently as a field researcher on national evaluation projects. The key question addressed by such research is whether a new program or policy initiative is really working as its political authors intended. (The Clinton administration's Empowerment Zone program is a current example of a program that is being looked at this way.) The field research method combines data analysis of program results with interviews of people at the local level who are operating the program, or who are affected by it.

The New York City Housing Partnership presented a somewhat different kind of research challenge: a homegrown initiative of neighborhood renewal without direct federal sponsorship that seemed nevertheless to be making significant headway. What was going on? As a HUD official in the 1970s, I had been familiar with the rampant devastation of entire neighborhoods in the South Bronx, Brooklyn, and Harlem. Those vivid images were still lodged in my head as I set out on a breakneck tour of these same places with Housing Partnership CEO Kathryn Wylde at the wheel of her beat-up Honda, her right arm waving in all directions at hundreds of bright new townhouses, block after block — many already occupied by homeowners and many more at various stages of construction. As she whipped around corners, Wylde provided blunt, rapid-fire commentary on a gallery of characters — including politicians, community and civic leaders, bankers, builders, and bureaucrats — who were either fostering this amazing rebirth or getting in the way.

I had no good explanation for what I was plainly seeing. The picture of families buying new homes by the thousands in those neighborhoods clashed sharply with both popular and expert notions of what had been happening in New York City and in the nation's cities generally. After all, many influential social scientists and policy analysts had seen nothing but continuing bad news in the 1990 census numbers: more middle-class migration to the suburbs, increasing urban poverty and racial concentration, loss of jobs, and declines in housing availability and affordability, all of which fit nicely with the conventional political judgment that cities had been left to rot by Ronald Reagan and George Bush. Against this bleak backdrop, either the Housing Partnership's born-again neighborhoods were merely an improbable and isolated success story that beat very long odds, or perhaps they were a relatively early installment of a larger, hopeful story of American cities on the rebound. Nathan and I discussed these reactions in a preliminary way, and I agreed to take on the project.

I owe Dick Nathan much more than the idea and the opportunity for undertaking this book. Throughout the long process of researching and writing, I profited greatly from his generous encouragement, his provocative and insightful ideas on the state of domestic policy in America, and his critical reading of early drafts as the book was taking shape. In particular, Nathan challenged me to make the book more than a New York story — to attempt a broader assessment of the important ways that the urban policy environment had changed since the 1960s and 1970s. The outcome of that exploration is laid out in the last two chapters.

Most of the material for this book was gathered from mid-1993 through 1995. I made several trips to New York City, usually for about a week at a time, to conduct interviews, attend meetings and events, rummage through documents, and observe the Housing Partnership operation at close range. At the outset I had the benefit of two wide-ranging interviews with David Rockefeller, who as leader of New York City's business community had conceived the idea of the Housing Partnership and then played the key role in its formation and first several years of operation. I thank Marnie Pillsbury and Peter Johnson for help in arranging these meetings and for providing a stack of documents from the Rockefeller archives relating to the inception of the Housing Partnership. They, along with former Rockefeller advisor Warren Lindquist, provided helpful perspective on Rockefeller's role as civic and corporate leader in New York City since World War II. In addition to Kathryn Wylde, I interviewed several people who had worked closely with Rockefeller in the formation and early years of the Housing Partnership, including Edgar Lampert, E. Virgil Conway, John C. Nelson, Frank Macchiarola, and Richard Parsons.

For unlimited access to Housing Partnership materials and staff, and for a multitude of other courtesies extended to this interloper from Chicago, I am indebted especially to Kathryn Wylde, president and CEO of the Housing Partnership until September 1996, when she became the first CEO of the New York City Investment Fund. An especially rich source of information was Wylde's personal chronological file going all the way back to her early days at the organization in 1982. Wylde was a prolific generator of detailed and candid memoranda and correspondence, and I spent many productive hours going through large black looseleaf notebooks. Wylde's colleagues on the Housing Partnership staff were also uniformly cooperative and forthcoming. Gale Kaufman and Steven Brown, Housing Partnership vice-presidents, who occupied the offices adjacent to Wylde's, were especially generous with their time in responding to my stream of questions and requests for information. Other Housing Partnership staff and consultants who provided both information and valuable perspective included Patricia Colon, Connie Hackett, Olive Idehen, Jody Kass, Sheila Martin, Sonia Martinez, Diane Nowlin, Brian Smalley, Karen Sunnarborg, Elsie Crum, and George Calvert. Thanks also to administrative staff members Hilda Gonzalez, Mary O'Donnell, Miroslabia Vega, and Donald Valentine, who helped facilitate my visits by scheduling meetings and interviews, taking messages, finding workspace, and photocopying piles of documents.

Throughout the course of this research, many officers and board members of the Housing Partnership and its parent organization, the New York City Partnership, provided information and offered suggestions related to my task. Thanks are due to Jerry Speyer, John P. Mascotte, Barry Sullivan, Fred Wilpon, Robert Kiley, Bill Green, Donald Jacob, David Jones, Ellen Sulzberger Straus, Thomas Osterman, and Veronica White. Many others who were not connected to the Partnership organizations also provided valuable insights, including Louis Winnick, Susan Motley, Bernard McGarry, Martin Levine, Harold DeRienzo, Stanley Newman, Gale Schechter, Scott Goldstein, Jack Schwandt, John Metzger, and Michael Lappin.

As recounted in this book, completion of Housing Partnership projects is the outcome of a long and complex balancing act involving many interested "partners." The persons already identified helped illuminate various aspects of this process. In addition, I would like to thank three former commissioners of the New York City Department of Housing Preservation and Development — Anthony Gliedman, Abraham Biderman, and Deborah Wright (formerly with the Housing Partnership) — and other city housing officials who served at various times, including Kathleen Dunn, Jody Kass (currently with the Housing Partnership), Meredith Kane (later a *pro bono* legal consultant for the Housing Partnership), Jerry Salama, and Mark Willis. I am also indebted to leaders and staff of neighborhood organizations, usually community development corporations, which served as community sponsors for Housing Partnership projects — in particular, Joseph Holley from Northeast Brooklyn Housing Development Corporation, David Pagan from Southside United Housing Development Fund Corporation ("Los Sures"), Ralph Porter from MBD Community Housing Corporation, Yolanda Rivera from Banana Kelly Community Improvement Association, Judi

Stern-Orlando from Astella Development Corporation, the Reverend Calvin Butts from Abyssinian Community Development Corporation, and Dr. V. Simpson Turner, Sr., and the Reverend V. Simpson Turner, Jr., from Mt. Carmel Housing Corporation. For providing a banking perspective, I owe thanks to E. Virgil Conway, Mary Cosgrove, David Daly, and Carol Parry. Many builder/developers of Housing Partnership projects were helpful in explaining the challenges of building houses in New York City; they include Alan Bell, Harold Bluestone, Desmond Emanuel, Kenrick Jobe, R. Randy Lee, Leslie Levi, Gerson Nieves, Joseph Schupler, Felipe Ventegeat, and Emerson Welch. Finally, thanks are due to the many purchasers of New Homes whom I encountered in my research, especially Doris Bembury, Mary Boswell, Phyllis Brown, Patricia Irving, Eli Martinez, Maryanne Manousakis, and Elsa and George Ortiz.

Three research assistants, Wendy Yaksich, Jennifer Olmstead, and Mark Dwyer, worked with me at various times and were enormously helpful, particularly in searching out background material on New York City history, politics, and planning issues. I would also like to thank Silvia Becerra, who handled the word processing chores for this book with skill and patience.

A first draft of this book was circulated to Professors Michael Rich and Todd Swanstrom and to other anonymous reviewers. Each offered detailed and perceptive comments and suggestions, and I am indebted to them all for their diligence and candor. I also thank the editor of the revised manuscript, Robert Cohen, whose careful and wise scrutiny made this a better book. Michael Cooper, publications director at the Rockefeller Institute, prepared the manuscript for publication and was wonderful to work with. His assistant, Michele Charbonneau, handled the final word processing and a million other details. The title of this book was suggested by a line in a January 1997 *Atlantic Monthly* article by Alexander von Hoffman: "There is new life in the ground zeroes of urban America" (*Good News!*, p. 35). With that I agree, and I would like to thank von Hoffman for graciously assenting to my appropriation of his apt image.

Charles J. Orlebeke

1

A GROUNDBREAKING
IN BROOKLYN

On December 8, 1983, in the Windsor Terrace neighborhood of Brooklyn, David Rockefeller with ceremonial shovel in hand, broke ground for seventeen houses to be built on a bleak and littered vacant lot once occupied by the Pilgrim Laundry. Lined up with Rockefeller, the chairman of the New York City Partnership, were Governor Mario Cuomo, Mayor Edward I. Koch, U.S. Senator Alfonse D'Amato, Brooklyn Congressman Charles Schumer, Brooklyn Borough President Howard Golden, Housing Partnership president Kathryn Wylde, and an assortment of City Council members, state legislators, city and state officials, bankers, corporate executives, community leaders, newspaper reporters, and television crews.

Mingling with the big shots were several dozen ordinary New York families who had put their names into a lottery, hoping for a chance to buy one of those seventeen two-family houses when they were completed. The nearby St. Rocco's Roman Catholic Church had supplied a green wire-mesh drum normally used for bingo games. One by one, Rockefeller, Koch, Cuomo, and other dignitaries gave the drum a spin and reached in for the winning names. Cheers erupted from around the crowd as the names were called out — Conlon, Gillespie, Markovinovic,

Lehpamar, Pasternak, McEldowney, Van Cook, Galluccio, Benson. All the names in the drum went on a list in the order they were pulled. The first seventeen families on the list would have two weeks to put down a deposit of $10,000 or step aside for the next family.

Elsewhere in 1983, without ceremony or celebration, the nation's homebuilders started more than a million houses for the ownership market, mainly in suburbs and small towns. Why all the fuss over Windsor Terrace's handful of houses? The reason is that new home construction and eager buyers in such a place were surprising, unexpected; they bucked the conventional wisdom that city neighborhoods like Windsor Terrace had only one way to go: down. As Channel Two's Jennifer McLogan put it on the six o'clock news: "Something new is going to be growing in Brooklyn, and the neighborhood excitement is contagious. Today, they brought in shovels to Windsor Terrace, and the residents even joined in the digging. . . ." Windsor Terrace was news because it hinted that the long odds against neighborhood comeback could be beaten — if the right people were ready to dig in. But long odds they were.

Nearly two years had passed since David Rockefeller, the then recently retired head of the Chase Manhattan Bank, and Mayor Ed Koch first announced that New York City's private and public leadership would join in a "partnership" to build thousands of houses for the city's working families. Despite the surface good will displayed at that announcement, the road to Windsor Terrace had been strewn with political and bureaucratic potholes. Those seventeen houses were worth celebrating and made a modest media splash, but the real question was whether the ballyhooed "public-private partnership" could sustain any kind of momentum in the years ahead. Susan Motley, then a member of the New York City Planning Commission now with the John D. and Catherine T. MacArthur Foundation, recalls that "few knowledgeable people in New York really expected the Housing Partnership to go very far — maybe a project or two and that would be it." And not long after Windsor Terrace, Rockefeller himself said, "When we announced the Housing Partnership in January, 1982, some of my colleagues suggested that my retirement as a banker may have coincided in some ways with the onset of terminal lunacy." David Daly, a Chase Manhattan Bank vice-president, recalls the first incredulous reaction of bankers to Rockefeller's idea: "You want to build *what*? You want to build *where*?"

People who questioned Rockefeller's sanity in launching the Housing Partnership had reason to do so. Urban scholars George Sternlieb and

James W. Hughes wrote in 1976 that "the levels of complexity of all elements of [New York City] surpass those of any other population center in the United States. And nowhere is this more clearly evident than in its housing supply system." Writing a dozen years later, architect John Ellis observed that "New York may be the most difficult city in the United States in which to build housing, let alone 'affordable' housing. The process is complicated to begin with, and there are so many things that *can* go wrong that almost inevitably, some will. In addition, the high cost of land, infrastructure, and construction relative to the residential market create [*sic*] a need for public subsidies in a variety of forms, each of which bring further complications." A state legislator, commenting in a context unrelated to housing — namely, the city university system — noted simply: "In a city as complicated as New York, you aren't going to get things through in a pure way."

How the New York City Housing Partnership managed to beat the odds, and build housing that people would line up to buy in some of the nation's worst neighborhoods, is the story this book seeks to tell. Like all good stories, this one has its memorable characters, its conflicts, and its. unlikely plot twists. As such, the Housing Partnership story stands on its own as an account of a signal achievement in an unlikely place. But I will also argue later in the book that it is part of a larger national story about cities that is not being told. Scholarly writing about cities abounds with the bleak statistical tracking of discouraging trends, with the failed interventions of government, and with laments over the cities' descent into political oblivion. Surely these accounts should not be casually waved away, but I believe there is more going on in cities.

The establishment of the Housing Partnership was an early chapter in a more hopeful story that challenges the conventional view of American cities as the sorely wounded victims of implacable economic trends, social chaos, and political neglect. In addition to citywide organizations such as New York's, thousands of neighborhood-based community development corporations have sprung up — many in the last ten years — to contest the forces of decline. Banks and corporations are pouring billions of dollars of private investment into central-city housing and commercial development. Despite cuts in federal aid to cities, a critically important package of federal programs and urban investment incentives remains in place. A huge stock of vacant urban land, much of it publicly owned, is available for creative re-use. A wave of new immigrants is energizing neglected and failing neighborhoods in many cities. Finally, urban home ownership is making a comeback in the most unexpected places — not just in New York City, where the movement is most advanced, but in many other central cities as well. Cities, as they always have historically, are striving to adapt and to remake themselves; in the 1990s and beyond, I will argue, this is becoming a lively — perhaps, even optimistic — quest.

New York City — Graveyard of Good Intentions

Novelist Saul Bellow once wrote of New York City: "What is barely hinted at in other cities is condensed and enlarged in New York. New York is stirring, insupportable, agitated, ungovernable, demonic." New York's immense size, its multitude of racial and ethnic rivalries, its complex political structure, and its many-layered bureaucracies put it in a class by itself as a hard place to get anything done. Even the pious altruism of a Mother Teresa can fail to budge the system.

When Manhattan lawyer Philip K. Howard wrote his 1995 bestseller, *The Death of Common Sense*, a book on "how law is suffocating America," he picked a New York City case as his leading example. Mayor Koch and Mother Teresa, the story goes, had agreed that her order of nuns, the Missionaries of Charity, would establish a homeless shelter in the South Bronx by converting abandoned city property at the order's expense. In 1988 the nuns spotted two fire-damaged buildings which the city agreed to turn over for a dollar apiece. Mother Teresa's group committed $500,000 to the renovation project. "Although the city owned the buildings," Howard writes, "no official had the authority to transfer them except through an extensive bureaucratic process. For a year and a half the nuns, wanting only to live a life of ascetic service, found themselves instead traveling in their sandals from hearing room to hearing room, presenting the details of the project and then discussing the details again at two higher levels of city government. In September 1989 the city finally approved the plan and the Missionaries of Charity began repairing the fire damage." Later, the nuns and the city bureaucracy hit an impasse on the issue of installing elevators in the four-story buildings — a city building code requirement. The nuns objected both on religious grounds — they would not use such modern conveniences as dishwashers and elevators — and on cost grounds, as the elevators would cost an additional $100,000 or more which the sisters thought could be better spent on "soup and sandwiches" for the homeless. City officials insisted that they could not waive the elevator requirement. Mother Teresa had met her match; reluctantly, her group pulled out and the project folded.

Like Mother Teresa, the Housing Partnership would find that nothing is easy in New York City. The city's "constellation of political-bureaucratic mega structures" has ways to slow down or smother completely all but the most stubborn and resourceful operators. As Peter D. Salins and Gerard C. S. Mildner have commented: "In the world of New York politics, a deal is never a deal, but a new basis from which to bargain."

In an interview for this book, R. Randy Lee, a lawyer and veteran homebuilder who has worked on several Housing Partnership projects, reacted bluntly to the entangling mesh of building regulations: "Don't ever expect government to be logical. There's no balance left. Every requirement, every demand has the same weight. No one is willing to stand up and say, 'This is ridiculous.'"

New York, with its population of 7.1 million, is more than twice the size of the next largest American city, Los Angeles. The tourist's view of New York City — the island of Manhattan with its Central Park, Empire State Building, United Nations headquarters, and all the rest — takes in only about 7 percent of the city's total land area. Four out of five New Yorkers live in the four "outer boroughs": the Bronx, Brooklyn, Queens, and Staten Island. Each of the five boroughs has a powerful sense of identity and considerable political power — there is an active "secession" movement in Staten Island and similar rumblings in Queens.

Overlaying competition among the five boroughs is New York's racial and ethnic diversity: a steadily declining white population, which stood at about 40 percent in 1990; a growing black population (27 percent), swelled by in-migration from Atlantic islands such as Barbados and Jamaica; a large Puerto Rican population (12 percent) and a similar number of non-Puerto Rican Hispanics, including many recent migrants from Central and South America; and the fastest growing minority, Asians, which increased by 67 percent between 1987 and 1991 and make up about 7 percent of the city's population. Each of these broad groupings masks a multitude of subgroups, each with their own distinct identity, heritage, and aspirations. More often than not, ethnicity also corresponds to pieces of urban territory, with inevitable skirmishes at the boundaries as the groups that are increasing in size seek to break through previously established borders.

New York's inter-borough rivalry and polyglot population, coupled with extremes of wealth and poverty, make for a highly complex and contentious political culture. The two most recent mayoral contests were racially charged squeakers. In 1989 David Dinkins, a Democrat who had been Manhattan borough president, defeated Republican Rudolph Giuliani, a former federal prosecutor, with 51 percent of the vote. In 1993 the two met again, but this time Giuliani won with 50.7 percent. Borough presidents, also elected by popular vote, can significantly influence development decisions affecting their boroughs.

Below elected officials, who come and go, is a sprawling city bureaucracy with hundreds of separate power centers, each of which may have something to say about whether a project goes forward and under what conditions. And they often take their time deciding. New York City also has a system of fifty-nine community boards, established in 1975 as a vehicle for local residents to review development proposals before they are acted on by the City Planning Commission. Although their role is advisory, the community boards are a factor in the approval process — and, if nothing else, can prolong the process by months.

New York is also, by American standards, an old city; large parts of the city have been built and rebuilt several times in the last three hundred years, leaving behind buried rubble, toxins, and occasional archaeological treasures from the past. Tearing down and rebuilding was not a particularly big deal prior to 1970, when New York's planning czar, Robert Moses, could single-handedly carve out expressways, create large parks and cultural monuments, and clear land for tens of thousands of housing units in a single area. But the 1970s and 1980s brought in a period of regulatory activism that introduced a host of restrictions intended to protect the environment from excessive air, water, and noise pollution; to properly dispose of toxic wastes; to protect historically significant buildings and neighborhoods; and to advance social goals, such as affirmative action and access for the disabled.

As each safeguard was put into place, a bramble of regulations and implementing bureaucracy grew up around it. And although each was intended to serve a laudable public purpose, the cumulative effect has been to add layer upon layer of review, stretching out the time between concept and construction and swelling the total cost. One would think that putting up a few townhouses on a vacant lot would be a straightforward, simple matter. Not in New York. A modest project on a "fast track," with all parties cooperating, typically takes a year to move from site approval to groundbreaking. Two or three years of processing are not uncommon; many projects take much longer. As Edward J. Logue has commented: "It takes a minimum of three years to complete a project that could and should be completed in one." Logue, who headed the New York State Urban Development Corporation in the early 70s, and later was president of the South Bronx Development Organization, said in 1985 that a "basic characteristic of [New York] city development for twenty-five years" is "the diffusion of authority and responsibility [so] that one finds little sense of urgency. It all adds up to delay and more delay, and that builds up costs."

After groundbreaking and during construction, many further bureaucratic detours often lie ahead before the city government finally certifies that a house is ready to be moved into. Take Windsor Terrace: A host of environmental and regulatory hassles bedeviled the project following the groundbreaking celebration in December 1983. Windsor Terrace's jubilant but increasingly impatient new home buyers were not able to move in until 1986.

In the early 1980s, the New York City Housing Partnership had more to confront than the city's ugly politics and bureaucratic idiocies. Memories of New York's crippling and humiliating fiscal crisis of the mid- and late-70s were still fresh. The exodus of industries and middle-class families in the 60s and 70s had created vast stretches of wasted land: derelict industrial sites; the shells of vacant apartment buildings, gas stations, and storefronts; and empty lots of all sizes, overgrown with weeds and strewn with a miserable collage of cast-off furniture, auto parts, and plastic sidewalk toys. In particular, the South Bronx and parts of Brooklyn had become legendary symbols of the worst of urban war zones, so infamous that busloads of foreign tourists would be taken there to snap pictures of the rubble. Ronald Reagan, the new President elected in 1980, had visited the South Bronx during his campaign, but it soon became clear that his plans did not include a rescue of America's cities.

Against this backdrop, the Housing Partnership's agenda of building homes for sale in those very neighborhoods seemed far-fetched. It was assumed that families wanted to leave the city at their first opportunity, not plunk down $10,000 — perhaps a life's savings — for a house on a bombed-out block in the South Bronx, Brooklyn, or Harlem. As Julius Mehrberg, a partner in the homebuilding team that built Windsor Terrace, told a Housing Partnership conference in 1984: "If you had told me five years ago that people would pick a lottery number and line up to buy a house from me, I would have laughed at you." But they did.

The Elusive Idea of Partnership

"Partnership" has become the warm and fuzzy buzzword of American politics. It seems to lack any distinctive political coloration: No one owns the term politically, and no one, so far as I know, has come out against it.

The New York City Housing Partnership fits into the broad category of "public-private partnership," a policy concept that came into vogue after the activist period of national urban policy faded in the late 1970s. When President Jimmy Carter proposed an ambitious "national urban policy" in 1978, he called it "A New Partnership" of the federal government, state and local governments, the private sector, and community groups. Neither the policy nor the theme caught on. But Carter's successor, President Ronald Reagan, with his themes of "less government" and more private initiative, did much to popularize the idea of public-private partnerships. In 1982 Reagan told a New York City Partnership meeting that "his administration wanted to create partnerships between the public and private sectors in every community."

The idea still flourishes in the 1990s. In November 1990, thirty-five big-city mayors met in New York City for an "urban summit" and "called for increased public and private partnerships to address critical issues facing urban America." No specifics were offered. More recently, Newt Gingrich, the Speaker of the House of Representatives, unwittingly latched on to Jimmy Carter's term, telling a group of governors meeting in Washington that he liked the term "new partnership" to describe what he hoped would be the future relationship between the federal government and state and local governments. Later that day, President Bill Clinton used the same term in speaking to the same group. "The American Community Partnerships Act of 1995" was the name given by the Clinton administration to its proposed restructuring of the Department of Housing and Urban Development.

The core of the public-partnership concept is promising; it suggests that the public and the private sectors have common interests, so they should work together cooperatively, rather than separately or at odds. In attacking a problem, both sides have things to contribute: Both command pools of money and people of talent. They have distinctive roles, however. Only the public sector can claim the endorsement of the popular will and wield such legal powers as taxation, spending public money, zoning, and eminent domain; whereas the private sector, driven as it is by the bottom line, is inherently more efficient and less encumbered by competing political demands and entrenched bureaucracies. The private sector better understands how to get things done and is more attuned to people as customers. The "reinventing government" movement is an attempt to transfuse these features from the private to the public sector.

When one moves beyond these generalities to a specific context, the term "public-private partnership" becomes more elusive. For all the talk of public-private partnerships, there persists a fundamental incompatibility between the two sectors. The private sector, civic and altruistic impulses notwithstanding, expects to make a reasonable profit when it sits down to deal with government — and defining "reasonable" is often not easy. The private sector also expects agency bureaucracies to march to the music of partnership played when elected officials and corporate leaders made their speeches and held their press conference. But press conferences do not override the volumes of laws, regulations, and procedures that are firmly in place, nor do they dislodge the guardians of that structure, who view themselves as agents of a collective public will empowered to protect citizens from the plundering instincts of private interests. Each public-private initiative will need to confront these difficulties sooner or later. And even when both sides do so in a spirit of commitment and good will, the multitude of administrative details involved in program implementation can defeat all but the most talented and resourceful managers. Thus, David J. Ricker, a former banker now working in the public sector, refers to "public-private partnership" as a "euphemistic" term that masks inherent conflicts. Ricker writes: "Identifying the nature and scope of public investment in a given transaction, relating it to appropriate private investment and formulating a conclusion is the final conundrum of implementation which finally determines whose, and what project will proceed toward its stated goals." The "conundrum of implementation" would, in fact, be the principal challenge taken up by the Housing Partnership.

David Rockefeller and Ed Koch — Wary Partners

This book is about how the notion of "public-private partnership" played out in New York City when the city government headed by Mayor Ed

Koch and the city's organized business community, led by David Rockefeller, decided to join in a "housing partnership."

This was itself an unlikely collaboration. Koch, the former liberal Democratic Congressman and then a popular mayor, was thin-skinned, voluble, and witty; Rockefeller, the long-time banker, civic leader, and urbane citizen of the world, was unflappable and courtly. Koch believed that Rockefeller did not like him and stereotyped him as a Jewish politician from Brooklyn even though Koch's political base since 1956 was in Manhattan — he had, in fact, been Rockefeller's own Congressman. In that role, Koch took pains to make clear that he was not overawed by his famous constituent. He liked to describe his Congressional district with the line: "In the north I have David Rockefeller, in the south I have sixty-five thousand Hispanics — in effect the richest man in the country in the north and the poorest people in the country in the south. And he thinks his one vote cancels out theirs, but with me it doesn't." Applauding his own cleverness, Koch added, "Not a bad line, and I used it a good deal. It happened to be true."

An incident in late 1969 gave Koch an opportunity to demonstrate that he was not afraid to take on Rockefeller. On December 22, 1969, the *New York Times* broke a story saying that President Nixon had, on December 9, invited a group of business leaders with commercial interests in the Arab nations "to discuss with him 'the political situation in the Middle East.'" Rockefeller, who had met with Egyptian president Gamal Abdel Nasser, was among those briefing Nixon. This was a time when the Arab nations had broken off diplomatic relations with the United States following the 1967 Arab-Israeli war, and when the United States was supplying weapons to Israel while the Soviet Union was supplying the Arab side.

The gist of the *Times* story, which was based on versions of the meeting leaked by anonymous "administration officials" — not the business leaders — was that Nixon was warned about declining U.S. influence among moderate Arab leaders because of its strong pro-Israel policies. The group reportedly urged the President to "act immediately to improve its relations with oil-producing and other Arab states."

Koch went ballistic. He wrote a letter to the *Times* and also wrote Rockefeller, demanding that he confirm or deny the accuracy of the story. Then Koch made a thousand copies of his letter and handed them out at subway stations, inviting people to send their own letters to Rockefeller and tell him what they thought of his desire to weaken Israel. A few weeks later, Rockefeller, through an intermediary, asked for a meeting with Koch. As Koch recounts the meeting in his book *Politics*, Rockefeller comes off as evasive and defensive — so clueless that he opened the conversation by telling Koch that his best friends at school were Jewish. Koch portrays himself, on the other hand, as fearless and incisive, cornering Rockefeller into admitting that he had counseled Nixon to tilt more toward the Arab side. Koch wrote: "I lean forward and I say to him, 'Change your position.' He was clearly startled. I said, 'I have to go, Mr. Rockefeller. I'll be making a statement about this on television over the weekend.' He looked even more startled."

Whether that's exactly the way it went, who can say. Recalling the incident with the hint of a wince, Rockefeller seems more puzzled than anything else about Koch's combative reaction to a simple plea for greater understanding of the Arab position in the Middle East powderkeg. With an above-the-battle smile, Rockefeller says now, "We did not get off to the best start, but we ended up friends."

That is probably an overstatement. Koch's first book, *Mayor*, published two years after the Housing Partnership was formed, mentions Rockefeller only once, recalling an incident early in the Mayor's first term. Koch had come to a meeting of the Business/Labor Working Group, a group of about thirty business and labor leaders that had formed during the New York City fiscal crisis to focus cooperatively on ways to improve the city's economy and public sector performance. The cochairs of the group were Rockefeller and Harry Van Arsdale, president of the New York City Central Labor Council. This particular meeting of the group was hosted by Rockefeller in the boardroom of the Chase Manhattan Bank. When the Mayor entered the boardroom and was seated between the cochairs, Rockefeller offered Koch a cup of coffee and got him one. (Van Arsdale, as Koch tells it, "ran" to get him a Danish pastry.) Koch found this treatment "extraordinary," so much so that he retells the same story in his 1992 book, *Citizen Koch*. The point Koch extracted from this fleeting courtesy was that Rockefeller was showing deference to the power of the Mayor's office and not to Ed Koch as a man he particularly liked. It seems an odd point to belabor. One would expect a career politician to understand that success and high office usually inspire deference and are a big part of a mayor's package of rewards; to also be *liked* by people who are not your friends is expecting a lot.

Rockefeller and Koch were not friends; and when Koch started writing books — entertaining, gossipy, predictably self-serving ones —

Rockefeller did not enjoy his particular role as a bit player in Koch's triumphant striding around New York's political stage. Yet, despite the unpromising chemistry between the two men, both knew what they wanted and both knew that they needed each other. Gracefully managing the required civilities as leaders of the public and private sectors was no great challenge for either of them. They would set out to become effective partners in housing, but wary ones.

2

POSTWAR NEW YORK: THE RADIANT CITY MEETS JANE JACOBS

David Rockefeller's launching of the New York City Housing Partnership in 1982 represented a fusion of two powerful policy currents in the postwar development of large U.S. cities. The first called for the elimination of large-scale urban "blight" or "slums" and their replacement by the "city of the future": sleek, efficient, aesthetically uplifting, technologically sophisticated, socially and environmentally responsible — a monument to rational, yet visionary, planning by urban elites. The second policy stream, on the other hand, called for adaptive, incremental improvement that largely accepted — and often celebrated — the physical forms and social arrangements inherited from the past. Under this model, the definition of both "blight" — and of "improvement" — would be determined, or at least strongly influenced, by the people who already lived in the city's various neighborhoods.

Following World War II and until about 1960, the first view — call it "urban renewal" — was dominant; it maintained significant force into the mid-1970s and still persists as a way of thinking about the problems of cities. (Problems on a massive scale, it is assumed, require sweeping action of matching scale.) The second approach — call it "community development" — was always a force in the postwar urban policy debate but found its voice in 1961 with the publication of Jane Jacobs's *The Death and Life of Great American Cities*, a spirited and hugely influential assault on the planning orthodoxies driving urban renewal, particularly in New York City. Thereafter, "community" involvement in deciding the fate of urban neighborhoods became a strong policy theme, bolstered by a succession of 1960s federal programs, such as the War on Poverty and Model Cities, that demanded the "maximum feasible participation" of residents of affected neighborhoods. The *process* of planning and decision-making became almost as important as the physical outcome on the ground. In the 1970s and 1980s, large-scale development was further constrained by regulatory activism reflecting environmental, civil rights, historic preservation, disability access, and similar concerns.

Against this backdrop, David Rockefeller, in a 1984 speech at the Citizens Housing and Planning Council, reflected on the "danger of losing our capacity to dream big dreams" and worried about "a pervasive and lingering doubt that anything can work on a large scale." Much on his mind was Westway.

The *New York Times* had said on January 5, 1977, that Westway "probably represents New York's major planning opportunity of the century." Westway was a $1.16 billion mega-project that would have replaced a worn-out road running along the lower Manhattan waterfront with a four-mile segment of the Interstate Highway System. More than a highway project, its proponents argued, Westway's comprehensive plan would create 93 acres of riverfront parkland and 110 acres for housing, commercial, and industrial development. Best of all, the federal government would pay 90 percent of the cost and the state 10 percent; not a penny of city money would be needed. The plan had been in the works since 1971; the federal government gave "final approval" on January 4, 1977. At a press conference announcing the federal action, David Rockefeller joined Secretary of Transportation William Coleman, Governor Hugh Carey, and Mayor Abraham Beame in celebrating what Westway would mean to a city still reeling from fiscal crisis — seven billion dollars in private investment. Rockefeller's cochair of the Business/Labor Working Group, Harry Van Arsdale, president of the Central Labor Council, was also there and spoke of putting unemployed construction workers back to work.

But Westway's opponents did not roll over, despite the *Times'* editorial judgment that their arguments were "so shot with absurdities that it was time to set the record straight and capitalize on the opportunities." Environmental and community groups mounted a series of court challenges that succeeded in stalling the start of construction.

When Rockefeller spoke in 1984, Westway was still alive. Calling it "one of the most imaginative projects in New York's history," he was utterly mystified as to why anyone would fight it. Three mayors, four governors, and four U.S. Presidents and their secretaries of transportation had all supported Westway, along with all the major New York City newspapers. Rockefeller's New York City Partnership had made it the first order of business in 1980 and would "never give up" until it was built. The problem, Rockefeller said, was this:

> Westway represents change and it is big, and both of these attributes are anathema to a very small number of our population. That small number is very vocal, however, as well as skilled in blocking progress and possessing the time to keep up delaying tactics. . . . In the past, moreover, proponents of large and worthy projects often have been beaten down simply because they did not have the time and patience to endure endless litigation and spurious assault. . . .
>
> Westway can, I am convinced, be a turning point where the public interest for once wins out. . . . We will persevere in our support until the myriad benefits of the Westway dream become a magnificent reality for all New Yorkers.

Rockefeller was convinced that "the momentum behind Westway is stronger than ever" and was "optimistic that construction will be underway during the coming fiscal year."

Westway's construction did not get underway, however, and never would. The project was officially laid to rest in 1985, and as late as 1993, Rockefeller characterized its loss as "tragic." Whatever its merits, Westway was a metaphor for the failure of the heaviest of hitters to connect when opponents have such an array of dazzling pitches to throw at them.

Rockefeller could remember when things were different. His 1984 speech referred to "once controversial projects" in the past that had become established and successful — Rockefeller Center, Lincoln Center, and the spectacular revival of the southern tip of Manhattan, which was led by Rockefeller as chairman of the Downtown Lower Manhattan Association, and included Wall Street, the twin towers of the World Trade Center, and the new headquarters of the Chase Manhattan Bank, relocated by Rockefeller from midtown Manhattan. "How many of us would have guessed 25 years ago," he asked with an ironic gesture to one of Westway's environmental impacts, "that we would become experts on the mating habits of striped bass?"

The fate of striped bass was the furthest thing from any New Yorker's mind when thirty-year-old David Rockefeller returned from France after World War II and New York was poised for a quarter-century of development and redevelopment without precedent. For New York and other major cities across America, it was a time to "dream big dreams" of large-scale change, renewal, modernization, and world leadership.

As Joel Schwartz has commented: "The war cast a global perspective on cities that proved impossible to ignore. None of the cities that harbored ambition to be world capitals — Washington, New York, Philadelphia, and San Francisco — could accept the dingy ambience and embarrassing race relations that passed for urbanism as usual. The metropolitan environment demanded modernization. World cities in a global economy needed sleek corporate headquarters, first-class universities and hospitals, modern arterial highways, and convenient, downtown housing. Organized labor, business groups, the medical establishment agreed."

This postwar vision of the city was heavily influenced by the French architect and urbanist Le Corbusier, who called his vision the Radiant City, or "towers in the park." Cities needed to be rid of festering slums — the mess of overcrowded tenements and narrow, sunless streets. In their place, he proposed tall and shining towers surrounded by grass and trees and man-made ponds, places for sport or lolling. The Radiant City would include places for commerce, learning, and cultural enrichment; and the entire urban system would be served by limited-access roadways designed to speed traffic in, out, and around.

Although no city could completely transform itself to Radiant City, New York, more than any other American city, achieved a scale of change in the thirty years following World War II that was stupefying. Six great expressways plowed through New York City's neighborhoods, all built at the same time; hundreds of parks were created; and seven huge bridges, linking the five boroughs, were built. The United Nations complex, Lincoln Center for the Performing Arts, and scores of high-rise office towers went up in Manhattan, and there were major expansions of Long Island and Fordham Universities.

Meanwhile, over a thousand buildings of public housing were built with federal funds by the New York City Housing Authority, for more than half a million tenants; and middle-income housing, built with the help of a variety of public bonding and subsidy schemes, kept pace — usually several thousand units at a crack, culminating in the "megalomaniacal scale" of Co-op City in the Bronx: 15,500 units, thirty-five towers of thirty-five stories each, thrown up in just three years (1968-70).

The man at the center of this astounding transformation was Robert Moses, New York's legendary "power broker." Beginning in the 1930s, Moses wielded huge power over planning and development from the several positions he held (often simultaneously) in city and state government: parks commissioner, head of the Triborough Bridge and Tunnel Authority, city construction coordinator, and head of the Mayor's committee on slum clearance, among others. Before he fell from power in 1968 at the age of 79, Moses was able to enlist vast sums of public funds and orchestrate the political ambitions of a generation of governors and mayors eager to be associated with showy projects. Moses' development plans also were a bonanza for the banks that underwrote his public borrowing schemes and financed private construction, for the construction and real estate industries, and for the building trade unions, whose workers flourished in steady, high-paying jobs. Peter Brennan, head of the construction unions, told Moses biographer Robert Caro: "Look at his record! It's a very good record in the building field. And the relation with our industry is very good. He always thinks big — I mean, everything he does, nothing is done in a small potatoes way." This was "public-private partnership" on a grand scale.

The roots of Moses' power were deep and complex. His big-potato projects needed more than the support of ambitious politicians and voracious moneyed interests; he also responded to the civic impulses of private-sector leaders like David Rockefeller, an "inspired capitalist" who wanted to see the city thrive, and to the altruistic impulses of liberal reformers who wanted better housing, preferably racially integrated, for low-wage working families and for the poor.

Postwar planning orthodoxy further bolstered Moses' schemes. "Professional certitudes seemed easier in the 50s," wrote Dean Macris, reflecting on his planning education in the 1950s at the University of Illinois. Macris, who later served as planning director of San Francisco under three mayors, continued: "We believed — at least many of us did — that federally sponsored redevelopment, or slum clearance as it was then called, would, with time and resources, solve the pressing problem of urban squalor and decay. . . . At the time, as I recall, there was no strong objection to the Corbusier idea of the high-rise in the garden — as it was expressed architecturally at Pruitt-Igoe [St. Louis] and still exists at the Robert Taylor homes along State Street [Chicago]. Modernism in building represented a break with the past, a goal we seemed to favor in the middle 50s. Planners in those days were not particularly constrained by the preservation ethic."

Radiant City could only be built on large expanses of cleared land. People got in the way, when visions of grand scale homed in on long-settled cities. The residents already there, with their dwellings, shops, restaurants, and neighborhood institutions — however "blighted" — cluttered the path to renewal; they had to be moved — "relocated" in planning jargon — willingly if possible, forcibly if necessary, by the use of the ancient royal prerogative of eminent domain. The logic of large-scale solutions as a necessary response to large-scale problems was powerful enough to roll over the objections of the people in the way — people who did not see themselves as slum dwellers, who defended their homes and neighborhoods, and who would have stopped the wrecking ball and the bulldozer if they could.

Whether the postwar pursuit of the Radiant City — when, in David Rockefeller's terms, urban leaders still had the capacity to "dream big dreams" — was ultimately good or bad for New York and other cities is a debate that will not be addressed at any length in these pages. Trying to assess the human and physical cost of what was lost and what was destroyed in the process of "renewal" is only one side of the issue. On the other side of the question is the value of the vision realized — the parks and beaches, the bridges and expressways, the cultural and educational institutions, the medical centers, even the housing.

All the trophies of the Robert Moses era and after — Would New York City be better off without them, and if without some, which ones? To clear the way for his projects, Moses, according to a study cited by Robert Caro, was responsible for uprooting 320,000 people from their homes and neighborhoods in a single ten-year period (1946-56). Was it worth it? Caro, whose 1,162-page book on Moses portrays him as a man of great vision, ruthless ambition, and brutal effectiveness, poses the same question and, perhaps surprisingly, equivocates. Noting that under mayors before and after Moses "the city was utterly unable to meet the needs of its people in areas requiring physical construction," Caro continues:

> The problem of constructing large-scale public works in a crowded urban setting, where such works impinge on the lives of or displace thousands of voters, is one which democracy has not yet solved. . . .
>
> It is impossible to say that New York would have been a better city if Robert Moses had never lived.
>
> It is possible to say only that it would have been a different city.

However one weighs the abuses and achievements of postwar redevelopment, the fact is that the romance with scale began unraveling in the 1960s — not all at once, but piece by piece. In 1961 — ironically the same year that New York City adopted zoning revisions that would foster tower-in-the-park design — Jane Jacobs published her book *The Death and Life of Great American Cities*. Jacobs tore into the Robert Moses-style of city-building with gusto:

> The ruthless, oversimplified, pseudo-city planning and pseudo-city design we get today is a form of "unbuilding" [a Lewis Mumford term]. . . . Routine, ruthless, wasteful, oversimplified solutions for all manner of city physical needs (let alone social and economic needs) *have* to be devised by administrative systems which have lost the power to comprehend, to handle and to value an infinity of vital, unique, intricate and interlocked details.

As an antidote to the planners' sterile and prettified Radiant City, Jacobs celebrated high density — diverse "street neighborhoods" of short blocks where residential and nonresidential uses coexisted messily but symbiotically, where children played on busy sidewalks under the watchful eye of parents and neighbors. Jacobs liked small neighborhood parks but mocked planning orthodoxy's assumption of the virtues of open space, comparing planners to "savages venerating magical fetishes. Ask a houser how his planned neighborhood improves on the old city, and he will cite, as a self-evident virtue, More Open Space. Ask a zoner about the improvements in progressive codes and he will cite, again as a self-evident virtue, their incentives toward leaving More Open Space.

Walk with a planner through a dispirited neighborhood and though it be already scabby with deserted parks and tired landscaping festooned with old Kleenex, he will envision a future of More Open Space.

> More Open Space for what? For muggings? For bleak vacuums between buildings? Or for ordinary people to use and enjoy? But people do not use city open space just because it is there and because city planners and designers wish they would.

To Jacobs, large-scale urban development tore to pieces the delicate fabric of complex and delightfully disordered neighborhood systems — "physical, social, and economic continuities — small scale to be sure, but small scale in the sense that the lengths of fibers making up a rope are small scale." As it happened, the ideal neighborhood Jacobs advocated for was much like her own in the West Greenwich Village section of Manhattan. And when developers backed by the city planning agency targeted her own neighborhood for "improvement" in the early 1960s, she and her neighbors formed the Committee to Save the West Village and fought the plan. The controversy, which dragged on for fifteen years, outlived Jacobs' stay in New York; in 1969 she moved to Toronto.

While Jacobs was leading the assault on planning orthodoxy and its glorification of large-scale urban redevelopment, another movement was taking shape in the 1960s that would more explicitly challenge the political and economic power arrangements driving the remaking of cities. The movement went by various names that contained the notion of "community": community organizing, community action, community development, neighborhood preservation, grassroots planning, and the like. Underpinning the movement was the straightforward notion that city residents should have a voice in what happens to their neighborhoods, particularly when public authorities or outside investors propose to clear them out in order to build a highway, a park, high-rise apartment complex, or an office tower. In addition to insisting on the right to make the case *against* large-scale redevelopment, the movement advocated, on the positive side, smaller-scale preservation and rehabilitation of existing buildings, street improvements, and other measures that would primarily benefit people already living in an area.

Within the planning profession, a counterpart to grassroots activism emerged known as "advocacy planning." Advocacy planners eschewed the impersonal, color-coded maps associated with large-scale master planning and were more likely to be found in storefront meeting rooms and church basements, mapping out legal and procedural strategies for keeping the urban renewal bulldozer at bay.

Other forces conspired against the complete realization of Radiant City. Lyndon B. Johnson's War on Poverty, enacted in 1965, poured millions of dollars into "community action agencies" across the land. One of the premises of the community action program was that "City Hall," backed by powerful "downtown" corporate and real estate interests, was incapable of protecting, much less advancing, the interests of poor people; community action would be a counterforce that challenged entrenched public and private power. Mayors, naturally, fought back. They prevailed politically; community action was discredited as a wasteful failure and its funding dwindled. But on another level, community action was a huge success. It permanently changed the chemistry of urban politics. It created the first network of community development corporations — the base for the burgeoning CDC movement of the 1980s and 1990s. Most important, it was an intensive prep school for a cadre of African-American and Hispanic organizers and program managers who went on to careers in politics, government, and nonprofit development; their influence has been pervasive and incalculable.

Model Cities was another federal program that discouraged large-scale development. Enacted in 1966, it was intended to shift back to City Hall the political balance that had been upset by the community action program. (The two programs actually overlapped in time, causing a confusing jumble of subprograms, funding sources, and political rivalries.) Model Cities would be a "mayor's program," but its array of social service and physical improvement programs had to be targeted to a relatively small "Model Neighborhood" containing no more than 10 percent of a city's population. In addition, the Model Cities administrative structure, although controlled by the mayor, still had to include representation from neighborhood residents and organizations. There was no way that the billions of federal dollars that flowed through the Model Cities program during its brief life — it was folded into the Community Development Block Grant in 1974 — could be effectively channeled to mega-projects.

Other federal actions helped put the brakes on urban expressways and other kinds of headlong development. The Uniform Relocation Act of 1968 made it much more difficult procedurally — and much more expensive — to displace people living in the path of any federally sponsored development than it was in the days of mythical "relocation plans." Federal highway legislation put special procedural restrictions on any highway project that proposed to cut through a park. Environmental regulations piled up. The historic preservation movement gathered momentum. Amendments to the urban renewal program encouraged more rehabilitation and less clearance. (Urban renewal was also folded into the Community Development Block Grant in 1974.) In short, the legal leverage and the money that Robert Moses wielded so forcefully in the postwar period had lost most of their clout twenty-five years later, and the opponents of large-scale development had a whole fistful of tools to work with.

The romance with scale dies hard. Peter Brennan, leader of the construction trades in New York, vented his frustration to Robert Caro:

> Moses always had the opposition — picketing and people lying down in the street and all that garbage — but Moses went ahead and did it. That's the trouble with all these politicians today: They worry about things like that.

> Sometimes people have to be tough with you. How the hell else you gonna get it done? Today they have fights over every park, every road, every playground for kids, but the nuts, the protesters — they're against them. Playgrounds used to be like motherhood, but today they even attack motherhood.

Like it or not, the age of incrementalism had arrived.

3

NEW YORK:
CITY ON THE ROPES

The vision of large-scale urban renewal and the vision of neighborhood-centered community development competed head-to-head in a broader context of sweeping urban change that the proponents of both views could affect only on the margins. They could not control or contain the great migration of the middle class from central city to suburbs and their replacement by migrants from Puerto Rico and abroad. They could do little to stop the economic transformation of the city that by the late 1960s was bleeding tens of thousands of jobs each year from the New York City economy. The question for New York in the mid-1970s was whether the city itself would survive.

George Sternlieb and James W. Hughes recited some of the chilling numbers in their 1975 book on "post-industrial America." Between 1969 and 1974, New York City suffered an *annual* loss of over 80,000 jobs, including 43,000 in manufacturing and 37,500 nonmanufacturing jobs in wholesaling, retailing, insurance, and real estate. These large losses were only slightly offset by annual gains of 2,100 jobs in services and 9,000 in state and local government — a trend that would intensify New York's gathering fiscal crisis.

Coupled with job loss was population decline. New York had appeared to be holding its own compared to other older cities of the Northeast and Midwest: The city lost only 1.4 percent of its population between 1950 and 1960 and then gained it all back in the 1960s with a 1.5 percent increase — while Chicago was losing 5.2 percent, Boston 8.1 percent, and St. Louis 17 percent. But in the period from 1970 to 1973, New York City had "a very abrupt absolute decline of 2.3 percent" — and it would go on to lose a total of 11 percent during the 1970s.

Add to that, beginning in the late 1960s, the actual abandonment and destruction of some neighborhoods, which took the city's leaders completely off guard. This from Nathan Glazer, writing in 1972: "A few years ago, a striking phenomenon — one never before seen in any American city, or perhaps in any other cities, since the decline of the urbanism of the ancient world — appeared in New York: the abandonment of sound housing. The suddenness and scale of this phenomenon left all analysts for a while dumbfounded."

The wreckage of neighborhoods continued as city officials groped for a response. Speaking with great candor in March 1975, Roger Starr, Mayor Abe Beame's housing and development administrator, said at a Rutgers University conference: "I must plead guilty to having a sense of panic and to doing what I think all of us do in city government when we feel the ground slipping away beneath us — we do things which we cannot afford, and we do them more desperately than ever."

"Doing things which we cannot afford," combined with negative and largely uncontrollable economic and demographic trends, propelled New York City toward one of its unhappiest milestones — the fiscal crisis of 1975. Ask any New Yorker when the city's fortunes were at their nadir, and the answer is likely to be 1975. Nineteen seventy-five was the year New York City went broke, when New York's own great banks refused to continue lending the city money to finance its ballooning budget deficit because they doubted the city's ability to pay it back. At the time, Mayor Abe Beame, the diminutive, flinty former city comptroller who had succeeded the dashing John Lindsay in 1973, insisted — as he would always insist — that the fiscal crisis was phony, manufactured by political adversaries who lacked both understanding of and faith in the city's fundamental soundness. But Beame failed to persuade the people he needed to persuade. The city's cash drawer was empty, and the banks' lending windows slammed shut.

The crisis had been long in coming. During the 1960s the city's operating budget tripled, driven largely by increased spending for welfare and social services and by generous wage settlements with the city's powerful municipal unions. During the same period, city revenue from its own sources doubled, helped by a new city income tax passed in 1966. The gap was made up largely by state and federal aid, which increased sixfold; put another way, the city received about twenty cents of every revenue dollar from state and federal aid in 1960 and twice that — forty cents of every dollar — in 1970. But it was not enough.

New Yorkers were not really ready for the 1975 fiscal collapse; after all, fiscal crisis had been part of the political noise between New York City, Albany, and Washington for a long time. A 1972 report, *Profile of a City*, written by economists at the First National City Bank, adopted a jaded tone in discussing New York finances: "New Yorkers are used to hearing each year that their city is in the midst of a fiscal crisis, that their municipal services are about to deteriorate, and that the state and federal government are to blame because they are not providing enough fiscal support."

The report described an annual ritual called "gapmanship" as the city presented its budget. "The script calls for the mayor to proclaim a gap between mandatory increases in the cost of running the city and the revenue expected in the fiscal year — a gap that can be closed only with a sharp increase in state and federal aid beyond that already planned in Albany and Washington. . . . [I]t is particularly tempting to any city administration to declare bankruptcy in order to gain the maximum possible level of new aid." In the early 1970s, as growth in federal and state aid seemed to be slackening somewhat, the city's "concern created an incentive to proclaim 'fiscal crisis' in order to improve the chances for aid-increasing legislation to be passed."

What all this fiscal brinkmanship disguised was that as each "crisis" eased temporarily, New York City was steadily digging itself into a deeper and deeper fiscal hole. It was doing so by writing the textbook on unsound and imprudent budget practices: repeatedly borrowing ever larger amounts to pay for operating expenses; overestimating revenues and underestimating spending; pulling anticipated future revenues into a current fiscal year to artificially "balance" the budget; and postponing current budget obligations to the next fiscal year for the same reason. These practices were well known to anyone who had any interest in New York political affairs, but it was easier to believe that the city's budgetary acrobatics could go on indefinitely, or that new sources of revenue would always miraculously appear, than to apply harsh and painful remedies. Eventually, however, the state's capacity and willingness to bail the city out waned, and the banks that had been willing enough for years to peddle the city's notes and bonds in ever larger amounts began to lose faith in the city's ability to manage its debt. As John E. Zuccotti, New York City Planning Commission chairman and later Abe Beame's Deputy Mayor, said to me on a visit to Chicago in 1974, "Mayors have been saying for years that the wolf is at the door; this time the wolf is *really* at the door."

When New York City's debt became unmarketable in the spring of 1975, Mayor Abe Beame, joined by New York Governor Hugh Carey, journeyed to Washington on May 13 to meet with President Gerald Ford, Vice-President (and former New York Governor) Nelson Rockefeller, Treasury Secretary William Simon, and White House aides. The New York party asked for a little help from the federal government to tide the city over the crisis: specifically, a federal guarantee of one billion dollars of New York City borrowing for a period of ninety days. President Ford thought about it overnight and then sent the Mayor a "Dear Abe" letter. It was clear, Ford wrote, "that the City's basic critical financial condition is not new but has been a long time in the making without being squarely faced. It was also clear that a ninety day Federal guarantee by itself would provide no real solution but would merely postpone, for that period, coming to grips with the problem."

Ford suggested that New York City develop a sound budget plan that would include "curtailment of less essential services and subsidies" and the transfer of other unnamed "activities" to state government. As for the requested federal loan guarantee, Ford told Beame "that the proper place for request for backing and guarantee is the State of New York." In short, the answer from the White House was "No."

New York's leaders were angered by Ford's response; they did not take no for an answer, but continued to press their case for federal assistance directly with Congress. Other big-city mayors in the U.S. Conference of Mayors supported New York's appeal. At the same time, however, the fiscal action did in fact shift back to New York City and Albany. The White House rejection triggered a turbulent period of desperate measures that enabled the city to stagger from payroll to payroll and culminated in the state's assuming effective control over the city's fiscal affairs through an Emergency Financial Control Board appointed by the Governor. To manage New York City's unmarketable debt, the State Legislature established a new corporation, the Municipal Assistance Corporation (popularly known as "Big Mac"), to issue state-backed bonds that converted the city's short-term obligations into long-term debt. Investors were unimpressed: Big Mac's initial offerings got a cool reception in the marketplace and could only be sold with yields well above those in the prevailing municipal bond market. It appeared that the city's fiscal problems would be a millstone pulling down the state as well.

Pressure for a federal rescue intensified as banks feared the consequences of a New York collapse — many banks around the country held large chunks of New York paper in their own portfolios. Key members of Congress began calling for action, and within the Ford administration, Vice-President Rockefeller publicly broke with the President on October 11 to support some form of federal assistance. (In the early days of the crisis, Rockefeller had advised Ford that the state should be able to handle the problem without federal help.) But on October 29, Ford declared, in an uncharacteristically strident speech to the National Press Club, that he would veto "any bill that has its purpose a Federal bail-out of New York City to prevent a default." Ford continued:

> By giving a Federal guarantee, we would be reducing rather than increasing the prospect that the city's budget will ever be balanced. New York City's officials have proved in the past that they will not face up to the city's massive network of pressure groups as long as any other alternative is available. If they can scare the whole country into providing that alternative now, why shouldn't they be confident they can scare us again into providing it again 3 years from now. . . .
>
> Such a step would be a terrible precedent for the rest of the Nation. It would promise immediate rewards and eventual rescue to every other city that follows the tragic example of our largest city. What restraint would be left on the spending of other local and state governments once it becomes clear that there is a Federal rescue squad that will always arrive in the nick of time?
>
> The primary beneficiaries would be the New York officials who would use a bail-out to escape responsibility for their past follies and be further excused from making the hard decisions required now to restore the city's fiscal integrity.

As an alternative to a federal bail-out, Ford proposed special legislation that would allow New York City to file for bankruptcy in order to keep its creditors at bay and place the city's financial affairs under the supervision of a federal judge.

Ford's speech inspired the still vividly remembered headline in the October 30, 1975, *New York Daily News* — FORD TO CITY: DROP DEAD — set off by a large news photo of Ford, his mouth curled in a snarl-like expression. As it turned out, Ford had overreached. His belligerent line-in-the-sand was soon blown away by mounting political pressure from Congressional leaders who rejected the bankruptcy strategy; even hard-liners in the White House, such as Treasury Secretary William Simon, began to have second thoughts about the practicality of a federal judge running a city of eight million people. Ford had promised New Yorkers that the federal government would assure continuation of "essential city services," but he could not say how. Federal Reserve Chairman Arthur Burns, who earlier had pooh-poohed the danger that a New York default would pose to the banking system, became more anxious as the crisis dragged on. Public opinion polls started to shift in New York City's favor.

In the weeks following Ford's Press Club speech, city and state officials cobbled together yet another plan, which included restructuring the city's short-term debt into ten-year bonds that would be purchased with $2.5 billion in municipal union pension funds. Big Mac's debt would also be stretched out. In addition, both the city and the state pledged to raise taxes totaling $900 million, and New York City agreed to balance its budget within three years. The scheme depended, however, on $3.6 billion of federal "seasonal" loans over the three-year period, with New York City required to pay back (with interest) at the end of each fiscal year whatever had been borrowed during that year. Presented with this plan, Ford relented. In Albany, the State Legislature passed its part of the plan and the U.S. Congress soon followed. Less than a month after the Press Club speech, the crisis eased.

The New York City fiscal crisis was about more than budgetary mismanagement and ritual sparring between political leaders in the city, Albany, and Washington. For New Yorkers it was also about humiliation and vulnerability. The government of the proud financial capital of the whole world was put on display as gutless and profligate, forced finally to scratch on Washington's door, tin cup in hand. Where were the bankers, where were the heads of powerful New York-based corporations, where were the civic leaders, when the city was sliding year by year toward financial ruin? They had — overtly or by default — gone along, underestimating the danger until the city's credit rating tanked.

Moreover, the fiscal crisis was seen as the financial manifestation of a much more profound and menacing shift in New York City's fortunes, as documented by Sternlieb and Hughes and other analysts. Not only were the trends running in the wrong direction, but there seemed no ready way to turn them around. Sternlieb and Hughes' prognosis was gloomy: "The future we have sketched is a bleak one; the capacity of the city to deflect the current momentum is questionable."

If 1975 was indeed the low point in New York City's civic morale, not everyone was willing to write the city off. For one thing, the banking and corporate leadership had a huge financial stake in the survival and health of the city. The more footloose could flee to New Jersey, Connecticut, or the Sunbelt; many did. But many could not move because they were tied to multi-billion-dollar investments in real estate and capital facilities; if New York went down the tubes, it would take them down, too. Others would choose not to skip town even if they could and even if it made sense economically to do so. They would stay and fight out of a sense of loyalty and commitment to what Kenneth Lipper calls the "intangible 'New York idea'": "Moscow's circus, Vienna's opera, Paris's Champs-Elysees, Tokyo's stock exchange, Rome's Via Veneto, all pulsating within one vibrant city. Such quality of life is worth a stiff price."

4

After the Crisis: Groping for an Agenda

N ew York City had found some desperately needed fiscal breathing space in late 1975, but that was all. The road to reasonable fiscal stability would still be treacherous. Vast areas of the city, particularly in the South Bronx and Brooklyn, were deserted or in ruins, recalling World War II images of Coventry and Dresden after brutal bombing. City officials had no real grasp of the damage, of how long the devastation would continue, or of what to do about it. The city's business leadership was fragmented among several different organizations and lacked a coherent voice.

In the devastated neighborhoods, official estimates of housing loss varied wildly. Frank Kristof, an official of the state Urban Development Corporation, estimated the loss at 21,000 apartments *annually* since 1970; Roger Starr, the city housing administrator, thought 36,000 was "a pretty good ballpark figure"; an organization of landlords, the Community Housing Improvement Program, put the number at 50,000. Starr could find "no evidence that the rate of abandonment is slowing down."

Another housing official avowed that the city had "absolutely no renovation and rehabilitation plan" for the stricken neighborhoods. The chairman of the City Planning Commission, Victor Marrero, contended that "we have not developed a formula that has had a substantial effect on reducing the rate of abandonment. [We are] still trying to develop a strategy. There is just no easy answer — anyone who says otherwise is either crazy or lying."

Still, New York leaders groped for ways to understand what was happening to their city, ways that might point toward a strategy for eventual recovery. In early 1976, Roger Starr began floating the idea of "planned shrinkage." Starr argued that unplanned "shrinkage" was already happening as a result of depopulation and property destruction in large areas; he proposed to accelerate that shrinkage by offering "inducements" to remaining residents to relocate elsewhere. Once these areas were completely vacated, the city could in effect cordon them off and shut down municipal services such as police, fire, and street repairs, thereby providing some operating budget savings. Also, the city would no longer be committing scarce housing construction or rehabilitation funds to such areas. The vacant land would just sit there indefinitely "until new land uses present themselves," Starr suggested. Although Starr's "planned shrinkage" notion was not presented as a concrete plan, the idea had to be taken seriously on account of Starr's position in the Beame administration and his stature as an urban affairs expert. As *New York Times* newswriter Joseph P. Fried commented, the very fact that Starr was advancing his "approach as a possible alternative for a city in deep trouble is a vivid sign that 'thinking the unthinkable' about the city's future options . . . is no longer limited to academic planning circles."

A variant of Starr's idea popped up a few weeks later in a *Times* front-page story. Felix G. Rohatyn, an investment banker who had been credited with crafting the city's fiscal bailout strategy, called for massive clearance of blighted areas as a step toward industrial rebirth. "Take a 30-block area, clear it, blacktop it, and develop an industrial park with the whole package of tax, employment, financing incentives already in place," Rohatyn proposed. Rohatyn, too, had to be taken seriously: He was chairman of the Municipal Assistance Corporation, the state entity set up in 1975 to issue bonds refinancing the city's overhang of municipal debt. Governor Hugh Carey had also appointed Rohatyn to take the lead in developing proposals for the city's economic recovery. Although Rohatyn acknowledged that he was in an "early 'stream of consciousness'" stage of his new assignment, "he said he was personally convinced that largely abandoned neighborhoods had to be put to use as development land to create jobs and revenue for the city." Roger Starr also spoke of the need for jobs: "If we don't have sufficient jobs, people will leave the city." But he also acknowledged that "we seem to have great difficulty in attracting industry here."

The "planned shrinkage" notions floated by Starr and Rohatyn drew immediate and sharp attack. John Zuccotti, the city's First Deputy Mayor, argued that "it doesn't strike me as practical to close off a large section of the city." Zuccotti, a HUD official during the Lyndon Johnson administration and former head of the City Planning Commission, thought that rebuilding devastated areas such as the South Bronx was feasible. And rather than seeing the remaining population as a forlorn remnant ready for relocation, Zuccotti saw "an active vibrant community who lives there and its continuation is critical to our city." Joining the assault were the two Congressmen — Charles B. Rangel of Harlem and Herman Badillo of the Bronx — whose districts would be most affected if "planned shrinkage" somehow caught on. Badillo, reacting to Rohatyn's clear-and-blacktop idea, was moved "to register the strongest possible protest," accusing him of "following in Roger Starr's footsteps in his callous disregard for human lives." Rangel saw "planned shrinkage" as racially motivated:

> It amounts to an attempt to deport blacks and Puerto Ricans from the regions that are vital to the commerce and transportation of our city. We cannot get away from the fact that if the cities were not inhabited by people of color, the planners would have the ingenious creativity to think of other approaches to our problems.

Starr had denied that he was in favor of "pushing people around" and "forced migration," and he feared that the press would "make me sound like an ogre." But "planned shrinkage" was his catchy phrase, and he was stuck with it. It turned out to be an easy and enduring metaphor for defeatism about the city's prospects, for top-down disregard for neighborhood survivors, and for the readiness of powerful moneyed interests to profit from the city's diminishment.

Although planned shrinkage was a fat target for opponents, there was no abundance of alternative ideas. In the conventional sense, large areas had no market. Yes, a remnant of stubborn survivors seemed to be hanging on, but no one was moving in. Industry certainly was not interested. The customer base was not there for retail stores. And who would put up office buildings in such places?

The only remaining option was housing. Conventional market-rate housing was out of the question: It was too expensive to build, and no one who could afford to rent or buy it would have the slightest interest in living in the bombed-out areas of the South Bronx and Brooklyn. But some people of modest means probably would move into new or rehabilitated housing *if* the government poured in enough public subsidies and protected developers and investors against the risk of failure.

In 1974 Congress had passed a housing subsidy program that could fill the bill: It was called Section 8. Essentially, Section 8 was a rent subsidy program that paid the difference between 25 percent of a tenant's income and the "fair market rent" of an apartment as determined by HUD. For example, a tenant earning $12,000 a year would pay only $250 per month ($3,000 a year) in rent; if the fair market rent was $750, HUD would pay the landlord the balance of $500. This basic subsidy model could be applied to three program variations: new construction, substantial or "gut" rehabilitation, and existing housing. The first two — new construction and rehabilitation — required a private developer or non-profit sponsor to submit specific project proposals to HUD, usually with the blessing of the local government; successful applications also qualified for FHA-insured financing. This meant that if a project went broke, the federal government would pay off the mortgage lender and take back the property.

Section 8 was a very good deal for all concerned: builders, mortgage lenders, and the lucky housing consumers who got quality housing at a bargain rate. All concerned, that is, except the federal government, which bore the cost of deep subsidies — particularly expensive in high-cost areas such as New York — and on top of that, bore almost all the financial risk connected with billions of dollars' worth of projects. (The third Section 8 variant — existing housing — provided a household with a certificate or voucher to shop the private rental market for a suitable apartment or house. This model was far less complex, less expensive in subsidy terms, and did not expose the federal government to financial risk; it eventually became the preferred housing subsidy vehicle for all national administrations after Jimmy Carter.)

In New York City, the Beame administration viewed Section 8 primarily as a vehicle to begin rehabilitating the tens of thousands of vacant and deteriorating apartments that had been abandoned by their owners, thereby putting city government in the unwelcome role of owner and landlord. Ed Logue, the former head of the New York State Urban Development Corporation (UDC), had another idea: Use Section 8 to subsidize massive construction of new rental housing on vacant land owned by the city.

In 1968 Logue had been lured to New York from Boston by then-Governor Nelson A. Rockefeller to run UDC, a powerful financing and development agency created by Rockefeller to implement large-scale housing and other types of development. UDC had the authority to float bonds, condemn land, and override local zoning or other restrictions to get its work done. Logue was ideal for the job; he had been a hard-driving urban renewal commissioner in New Haven and Boston, completing massive clearance and downtown redevelopment schemes in both cities.

Logue showed the same aggressiveness in running UDC, which launched several impressive projects, including a "new town in town" on Roosevelt Island in New York City. But UDC became overextended financially in the early 1970s as the real estate market slumped and UDC bonds were caught in the backwash of the New York City fiscal collapse. Logue had to resign and found sanctuary in an organization called the Commission on Critical Choices for Americans; this was a policy research think tank set up by Nelson Rockefeller in 1973 as a vehicle for Rockefeller to maintain his influence on the national political scene. When President Ford tapped Rockefeller to be Vice-President in mid-1975, the Critical Choices Commission was in a kind of limbo, but the staff toiled on.

Logue was restless. To him, New York City's expanses of vacant land begged for development. Logue had ready access to the White House through the Vice-President; HUD had the housing subsidy vehicle — Section 8 — with the potential for driving new housing construction even in places as desolate as the South Bronx. Mayor Beame would go along with the idea as long as it did not divert the city's regular Section 8 allocation from rehabilitation. Logue had to appeal to Washington for new money to support his scheme.

In February 1976 Logue arranged a meeting in the White House with Vice-President Rockefeller and HUD Secretary Carla Anderson Hills. The proposal he outlined was in some ways a precursor of the New York City Housing Partnership. It focused on high-volume new construction on vacant land; the design would be low-rise town houses; a private sector-backed nonprofit corporation would spearhead mortgage financing and production. But the differences were critical. Logue's proposal was for all rental housing, heavily subsidized by federal Section 8 funds. The long-term cost for a single unit would be on the order of $180,000; what's more, the mortgage financing, although private, would be federally insured, exposing the government to hundreds of millions of dollars in insurance risks if the developments should fail to attract renters.

Logue's idea was to set up a new development entity in New York City that "might be called More Housing for New York, Inc. (MHNY)." The city government would provide vacant land at nominal cost — $500 per dwelling unit. HUD would allocate Section 8 subsidies for 5,000 units of housing annually and would also provide FHA insurance. In addition, Logue wanted HUD to provide "tandem" financing of the mortgage, which was a way of subsidizing the mortgage rate down to 7.75 percent. Local savings banks would make $200 million in mortgage loans available for the first 5,000 units. The city, HUD, and the banks would all need to agree on standardizing and streamlining their processing standards so that high volume could be achieved.

Logue cited city plans establishing that city-owned vacant land was available for over 36,000 units of housing, although he suggested building at lower densities than that figure assumed. The style of housing Logue envisioned would be low-rise row houses, about thirty to forty units per acre.

More Housing for New York, Inc., the entity Logue had in mind to run the program, would be either a nonprofit or limited dividend corporation with a board consisting of bankers, developers, labor officials, and community leaders. MHNY would need about $750,000 to operate during its initial organizing phase, but Logue was confident that foundations and the banks would put up the money.

Logue worked hard to sell his proposal in the waning months of the Ford administration. The Vice-President could ensure that the idea would get a respectful review at HUD, but not much else. In mid-1975 Rockefeller had broken ranks, albeit amicably, with Ford on the issue of federal help to New York City in its fiscal crisis; he was off the re-election ticket for 1976, and he had neither the clout nor the inclination to engage in vigorous special pleading for New York City. This meant that the proposal was essentially at the mercy of Carla Hills' HUD.

Logue probably misunderstood how much HUD and its predecessor agencies had changed since the 1950s and 1960s, when a powerful urban renewal commissioner could put together a plan, fly into Washington, and come away with a several-hundred-million-dollar commitment. In those days, HUD's field offices scattered around the country were there to carry out decisions made in the central office. When the Nixon administration took over in 1969, however, this centralized — and often politicized — management style changed.

Although it seems ironic in retrospect, Nixon's domestic policy managers, led by John Ehrlichman, favored wringing much of the political influence out of the geographical distribution of federal grant dollars. Translated into the policy terms of Nixon's New Federalism theme, this meant advocating general revenue sharing to state and local governments — federal money with no strings attached — and block grants distributed by automatic, need-based formulas with minimum federal oversight. Let it be said, however, that the "politics" Nixon wanted to expunge from federal grant-making was seen by him largely as Democratic Party politics, played by his enemies: big-city mayors, urban renewal hotshots like Logue, Democrats in Congress, and liberal bureaucrats lodged securely in the domestic agencies.

Nixon's HUD secretary, George Romney, who had been Governor of Michigan for six years (and briefly a Nixon opponent for the Republican presidential nomination in 1968), and who had gone through the nation's worst urban riot in Detroit in 1967, did not share Nixon's paranoia, but he did agree that Washington should stay out of imposing specific program decisions at the local level. In putting his own management stamp on HUD, Romney reorganized the department to place almost all authority to commit program funds at the regional — there were ten regional offices — and "area" office level. (Area offices served either a very large metropolitan area or a state.) Housing subsidy dollars were administered by allocating blocks of subsidy to the regions and then pushing the field staff to achieve housing "production" goals. The central office in Washington rarely got involved in project-by-project review; it was up to HUD field managers to deal with local officials and homebuilders, and to make the choices which in their judgment best fulfilled statutory purposes and met program requirements for financial soundness, market feasibility, and quality standards.

When members of Congress lobbied for pet projects, which was frequent — or when the White House leaned on HUD on behalf of a Republican contributor or officeholder, which was also frequent — the central office would routinely refer the issue to regional and area directors for response. If the field staff intended to approve the project in question anyway, that was fine; but if they had reason not to proceed with the project, the central office hardly ever overruled them. This decentralized way of running HUD was still in place when Logue was trying to use his White House contacts to secure approval of his proposal.

HUD's regional administrator in New York at the time was S. William Green, a liberal Republican who was later elected to the Congressional seat in Manhattan once held by former New York City Mayor John Lindsay. Secretary Hills told Logue that Green's support of his proposal would be critical, so Logue did go to see Green on March 10, 1976. Logue left little doubt, however, about where he believed the power lay. As he wrote Hills a few days after the visit, he had "had a long working relationship with Bill Green and it seemed only good manners." But meanwhile, Logue would continue to work his Rockefeller connection.

Green was interested in the Logue proposal, but skeptical. New York City, Green told Hills, had already received an allocation of 15,000 units of Section 8 subsidy; if the city wanted to give 5,000 of those units to Logue's proposed entity, there was nothing to prevent it from doing so. The Mayor, however, was unwilling to divert 5,000 units to Logue; he wanted 5,000 *extra* units.

The city's position was laid out in a May 6th "Dear Bill" letter from Deputy Mayor John E. Zuccotti to Green. Zuccotti wrote that "We are very interested in the proposal that Mr. Logue has developed for the creation of a privately-funded vehicle to build 5,000 units of low-rise Section 8 FHA insured housing on vacant urban renewal sites in New York." Most of New York's regular allocation of Section 8 funds would be used to rehabilitate existing housing, Zuccotti noted, so "we think it is vital that the city receive an additional allocation of 5,000 units for new construction under this proposed program." Roger Starr, the housing and development administrator, and Logue were already assembling a list of sites, Zuccotti noted, and he called on Green to approve the Logue proposal "in principle."

Zuccotti's letter to Green, which Logue may have drafted, set in motion a game of tag with comic overtones. Logue drafted a letter from Green to Zuccotti stating that HUD liked the Logue proposal, and that "after consultation with the Central Office," Green was "prepared to make an allocation of 2,500 [Section 8] units at this time." Logue sent his draft to Rockefeller, who was to send it to Hills, who was to send it to Green, who was to send it to Zuccotti. But by the time Green got word of the Logue draft, he had already sent his own reply to Zuccotti, with a decidedly different import. Green wrote Zuccotti on May 11 to "clarify the situation with respect to the allocation of Section 8 units. . . . I do not foresee," he observed, "an additional allocation of 5,000 units to the New York Area Office for the Logue proposal. Any decision by the City to use the Logue proposal as a funding vehicle for 5,000 units of Section 8 new construction would be as an alternative to other uses to which normal allocations to the New York Area Office for new construction and substantial rehabilitation would be put."

Green went on to suggest that the city wait until the next fiscal year (1977) to incorporate the Logue plan into its regular allocation for that year, "recognizing that the units for the Logue proposal would not be extra. . . ." Secretary Hills sent the Vice-President copies of the Zuccotti-Green exchange, noting vaguely that she was "pleased that the two offices are focusing in on the Logue proposal." It went nowhere.

Although Logue's plan to cover the city's vacant land with subsidized rental housing collapsed, he did not fade away. In 1978 he joined the Koch administration as head of a newly created South Bronx Development Organization (SBDO). President Jimmy Carter had visited the desolated area in 1977 and promised federal help to rebuild it. As head of SBDO, Logue became a vigorous advocate for ownership housing: He wanted to build suburban-style single-family homes on large lots, complete with white picket fences, literally in the shadow of shattered hulks of high-rise buildings. Eventually, Logue secured federal funding for ninety factory-built, three-bedroom homes that were to be installed at a city-owned site on Charlotte Street in 1983. They would be offered for a subsidized price of $47,500 — not including a basement, which was an extra $6,000.

The symbolism of Charlotte Street was heavy, the scale of production, light. Logue called Charlotte Gardens — as the development was named — "the most difficult project I ever undertook." A multitude of procedural problems delayed completion until the summer of 1985 — and by that time Logue had left SBDO for a professorship at the University of Virginia. Still, Charlotte Gardens served a useful purpose as a dramatic photo op demonstrating urban regeneration at a time when the Housing Partnership was getting organized. But what David Rockefeller and the Housing Partnership envisioned was much more ambitious — and risky; they believed that there was a citywide market for thousands of middle-income ownership houses, financed almost entirely by the private banking system, requiring only a modest, one-time subsidy to bring the purchase price within range of working families and no FHA mortgage insurance safety net.

"Planned shrinkage," then, was not inevitable. It was possible, after all, "to dream big dreams," as Rockefeller put it in his 1984 speech to the Citizens Housing and Planning Council of New York. As an example of vision on a large scale, Rockefeller cited the goal of 30,000 units of middle-income housing that he had announced in 1982 as the target for the New York City Housing Partnership. But this was a fundamentally different kind of goal from Westway or a Robert Moses mega-project. It did not call for a grand design, the total clearance of a huge site, the mighty machines of giant construction companies raising up towers of glass and steel. Rather, the Housing Partnership would need to work in small places in every part of the city, building dozens — not thousands — of units at a time, employing mainly homebuilders often using nonunion labor. The achievement of scale would be incremental: an accumulation of small victories.

Unlike a large-scale project — which, once approved, typically goes forward in juggernaut fashion — the Housing Partnership would need to manage dozens of small projects simultaneously, steering each of them through the shoals of city and neighborhood politics, financial risk, innumerable regulations, site preparation and construction, and marketing. As Rockefeller ruefully noted, the Housing Partnership had worked for nearly two years to achieve its first groundbreaking (on December 8, 1983) for seventeen two-family houses at Windsor Terrace in Brooklyn — and at the time of his talk six months later, the city and the Housing Partnership were squabbling over what material to use for the project's curbs. "We would be here for a week," Rockefeller said with little exaggeration, "if I went through all the impediments my associates have identified. I will spare you that agony. . . ."

The postwar vision of the Radiant City had succumbed to the reality of the Regulated City. But the new vision of a city that could still provide decent homes and neighborhoods for its working families — that vision, with all its agonies and messy incrementalism, was still worth the chase.

5

MOVING TOWARD PARTNERSHIP

The 1975 fiscal crisis was the galvanizing force that led eventually to the formation of the New York City Partnership, an organization of the city's most powerful private sector leaders. When the crisis struck, as David Rockefeller later acknowledged, the private sector leadership was "highly fragmented" and in "general disarray" and had "little political clout. . . . Many different business groups, pursuing similar civic goals, tended to represent narrow interests and often competed with each other." The fiscal crisis, he said, "forced the financial community, business, labor, and public officials to work together as never before. This was a painful way to create mutual understanding and joint efforts, but it was certainly effective. Indeed, in retrospect, at least, the best thing that happened to New York may have been the famous 1975 *Daily News* headline, 'Ford to New York: Drop Dead!' That really got our adrenaline going!"

Frank J. Macchiarola, who became the Partnership's first full-time president and CEO in 1983 after serving for five years as chancellor of the New York City public school system, also pointed to the jolting effect of the fiscal crisis:

The financial crisis of 1975 had brought the city to the brink of bankruptcy, and the business leaders understood that they were unprepared for the tasks that were needed to work more effectively with government. Caught unaware of the extent of the city's difficulties and without an organization in place adequately to represent the private sector, they searched for a way to conduct their public affairs.

Macchiarola's reference to a "search" for the right model was apt. It took more than four years from the height of the crisis in 1975 to arrive finally at the "partnership" model that has remained in place.

In referring to the cluttered landscape of business groups at the time of the fiscal crisis, Rockefeller cited two that did not measure up as "strong and comprehensive private-sector organization[s]." The first was the old-line New York Chamber of Commerce and Industry. The Chamber could trace its original charter back to King George III and had been a mighty force at the turn of the century, when banking and corporate titans such as J. Pierpont Morgan and John D. Rockefeller (David's grandfather) were shaping modern New York. On the walls of the Chamber's lavishly appointed headquarters in Manhattan still hung the portraits of two centuries of New York's business elite, but by the 1970s the Chamber had become little more than a haven for Manhattan businessmen to enjoy a reasonably priced lunch in an elegant dining room. "They would have a certain number of speeches," David Rockefeller recalls. "I spoke there a few times. But it really did not represent business in New York City."

A second business-oriented organization, the Economic Development Council of New York City (EDC), was established in 1965, led by such men as Clarence Francis, the head of General Foods, and George Champion, CEO of the Chase Manhattan Bank (and David Rockefeller's predecessor in that position). The EDC, which unlike the Chamber did not engage in direct lobbying, created several task forces in such areas as public education, transit, and city personnel administration, the intent being to supply both policy guidance and expert management assistance through executives loaned to city agencies. The idea driving EDC was that the New York economy could flourish only in a climate of quality, well-administered public services.

Many members of the EDC board of directors also served on the Chamber board, and in the 1970s the two boards decided to form a single board to oversee both organizations, which nevertheless maintained separate identities, board chairmen, and staffs — creating an uneasy and ultimately unworkable amalgam of conflicting roles and personalities.

On another front, as New York's fiscal and economic problems were becoming more ominous in the early 1970s, real estate developer Lewis Rudin took the lead in organizing the Association for a Better New York (ABNY), a group that included "not only real estate but banking, hotel and department store people, business people, and civic and political leaders into a coalition of very concerned citizens who wanted to help the city function better." ABNY aimed to boost the image of New York City in the face of its critics and taunters. "There were too many times when people were giving up," recalled Rudin. "They needed just a voice. There were too many naysayers like Johnny Carson and others that did nothing but make bad jokes about the city. . . . That's the way the media was. So we had to start to do positive things and try to create a positive image about New York." Rudin cited such examples as New York marketing itself as the "Big Apple" and the "I Love New York" campaign. ABNY also organized the New York City Marathon race, which was run for the first time in 1976. ABNY's message to business, according to Rudin, was "Don't move out of the city, don't run to the suburbs; give us a chance in New York to show you that we can make New York run better and that you can do better business in New York than from Stamford, Connecticut, or from North Jersey, or from Dallas or Houston, Texas." In addition to such cheerleading, ABNY and Rudin helped stave off the city's collapse at the height of the fiscal crisis by urging major corporate taxpayers to pay their obligations in advance.

Although the Chamber and the Economic Development Council would later become part of the organizational base of the Partnership, Rockefeller viewed another organization as in many ways "the predecessor really of the Partnership." This was the Business/Labor Working Group, a group that formed at the time of the fiscal crisis but never formally incorporated. The Working Group was cochaired by David Rockefeller and Harry Van Arsdale, head of the New York City Central Labor Council, which represented 550 unions. (Van Arsdale and Rockefeller got on well — Van Arsdale had been a strong supporter of brother Nelson Rockefeller when he was Governor.) Among the Working Group's members were Peter Brennan, head of the construction trade unions; William Ellinghaus from American Telephone and Telegraph; Donald Regan from Merrill Lynch; Richard Shinn from Metropolitan Life; Walter

Wriston from Citicorp; John McGillicuddy from Manufacturers Hanover Bank; and Lewis Rudin, chairman of the Association for a Better New York.

"The Business/Labor Working Group was a wonderful group, it was very effective," Lewis Rudin recalled. Like the Partnership that came later, the group required direct participation by its principals. There were "no staff, no payroll, no assistants," said Rudin. "Either you were there or nobody was there [from your organization]." The group met intensively and produced a report that included such recommendations as a new convention center, the construction of the Westway project in Manhattan, the phasing out of rent control, and various cost-cutting measures aimed at city government. "I think we had a report of forty items and we lobbied for those. Quite a few got through," Rockefeller says. After pushing for its report with some success, the Working Group met intermittently and then disbanded. Rockefeller felt that "there were too many organizations."

Later, three of the most active members of the Working Group — Ellinghaus, Shinn, and Wriston — approached Rockefeller about accepting the chairmanship of both the Chamber of Commerce and the Economic Development Council. Rockefeller said he would consider it because "I felt there needed to be an organization in New York which could speak with a single voice on behalf of the private sector." Rockefeller insisted, however, that the current chairmen of the two organizations — George Champion at the EDC and Oscar Dunn, a senior vice-president for General Electric, at the Chamber of Commerce — would need to resign if he were to take over. This was sticky. The two men "didn't get on; in fact, they hated one another. So all of the meetings [of the joint board of directors] were fights between them and [their] organizations." For some time, neither man was willing to resign until the other did first.

Another Rockefeller condition was that he "would also want to take a look at [the two organizations] to see if they were doing what was needed." Characteristically, Rockefeller wanted a study to review the organizations and "find out what was being done [in] the rest of the country." McKinsey and Company was hired to carry out the study.

The McKinsey consultants called for a "partnership" model that would be more broadly based and inclusive than the Manhattan-dominated "big-business community of male corporate leaders." Rockefeller agreed, and pushed for representation on an expanded board from all five boroughs. Also invited to join were heads of women and minority-owned businesses, presidents of major colleges and universities, and the heads of major nonprofit organizations. The result was "the most broadly inclusive private-sector organization in New York City history," with "an elaborate and complex governance system." It was decided that the Chamber of Commerce and Industry would retain a separate identity as an "affiliate" of the Partnership, "partly because we needed a lobbying arm and the Partnership could not do that and have a tax exemption." The Economic Development Council was gradually absorbed into the larger Partnership structure and went out of existence.

The New York City Partnership traces its "tenuous beginning" — David Rockefeller's term — to October 1979. Organizational housekeeping absorbed the Partnership's attention for much of the next two years: The Chamber's "white elephant building" was put up for sale, committee chairmen and members were lined up, and an entity called "SERVCO" was set up to manage the administrative side of the Partnership, including personnel, fund-raising, public information, and financial management. The Chamber's building "took a long time to sell," but by mid-1981 the Partnership occupied new quarters at 200 Madison Avenue in Manhattan.

In putting together the Partnership, the organizers had to confront a number of delicate issues. One was the role of organized labor. Rockefeller, wanting to build on the success of the Business/Labor Working Group, urged union leaders such as Harry Van Arsdale and Victor Gotbaum (head of municipal workers' unions) to join the Partnership, but they refused because of the continuing role of the Chamber of Commerce and Industry. As a compromise, Rockefeller proposed a business-labor committee of the Partnership, since committees under the Partnership structure had a mix of board members and nonboard members. Van Arsdale and Gotbaum did agree to be listed as committee members, but "we never got them to any meetings," Rockefeller recalls. "That aspect of my original scheme didn't work."

Another issue related to Partnership governance was the role of public sector representatives. Again, the outcome was that government representatives would not sit on the Partnership board but could serve on program committees.

After the Partnership was formally announced in 1980 by David Rockefeller, a special committee was created "to help define the mission of the Partnership. It set the organization's agenda around the theme of economic development: creating jobs, enhancing the business climate, making the city's services more focused on attracting business, and reducing the cost of government." Program-specific committees would be chaired by Partnership board members, but could also include outside people with special knowledge or interest to contribute. Partnership recommendations would draw their credibility from the breadth and prestige of its membership.

Launching the Housing Partnership

To address New York's housing needs, Rockefeller wanted the Partnership to do more than adopt a typical advocacy role; he wanted the Partnership to build housing. It was one thing to document the need for housing, to develop ideas for new programs, and to urge government and the building industry to get on with addressing the need; it was quite another to plunge into the real estate development process itself, with all of its legal complexity, wheeling and dealing, big money at risk, and high political stakes. So the "Partnership" spawned the "Housing Partnership," and it thereby crossed the line between advocacy and implementation in that part of its work.

The business of actually getting housing built in particular places would require an organization within an organization, and that organization, the Housing Partnership, would, for both legal and administrative reasons, need a high degree of autonomy with respect to budget, staff, and operating flexibility. In the beginning, it was not at all clear how the Housing Partnership would operate as a separate corporate entity, yet somehow be under the general policy and administrative direction of the parent Partnership board and president. Very little, in fact, was clear when David Rockefeller told New Yorkers in January 1982 that something called the "Housing Partnership" would undertake to build 30,000 units of housing for middle-income families.

The occasion was the first major public event sponsored by the New York City Partnership. In an effort to make sure that the event would make a big splash, David Rockefeller extended an invitation to President Ronald Reagan, and somewhat to Rockefeller's surprise, Reagan accepted; he would be the featured speaker at a special luncheon on January 14, 1982, in the grand ballroom of the Waldorf-Astoria Hotel. The event attracted a crowd of 1,600 of the city's business leaders and 300 reporters.

"I am still amazed that he came," David Rockefeller recalls. "I was not a particular favorite of Reagan. He and [Rockefeller's brother] Nelson had been opponents in seeking the presidency. I really can't remember how we persuaded him to do it. . . . He made a very positive speech . . . but I have to say that I talked to him before the speech and tried to engage him a little bit in what we were trying to do, and my impression was that his mind was far away."

Rockefeller announced the Partnership's housing initiative at the end of his introduction of the President. Reagan spoke for forty minutes and heaped praise on the Partnership as a national model. Although Reagan probably was indeed not paying much attention to Rockefeller's announcement, it is ironic that his administration, which had vigorously set about dismantling federal urban programs and would continue to do so, would initially also turn out to be the Partnership's primary financial supporter, thanks to strategically placed New Yorkers — starting with Secretary Samuel R. Pierce — in Reagan's Department of Housing and Urban Development.

When unveiled by Rockefeller, the Housing Partnership was a long way from a full-blown plan. He told the Waldorf-Astoria crowd that the Partnership had "spent considerable time in recent weeks looking at what might be done" and had come up with what he called "a concept of unusual promise." Not even the name was clear yet. The concept: "A new not-for-profit corporation perhaps to be called the New York City Housing Partnership, Inc." The charter was broad, and vague: "To bring together the resources of the private sector — together with appropriate resources of and regulatory streamlining by the City, State, and Federal governments — to further the development, ownership and rehabilitation of housing for middle-income residents of New York." "Middle income" meant "families earning between $15,000 and $45,000 a year."

The announcement included a production goal — large enough to be impressive, but far enough into the future to provide a comfort margin. The goal, for the Housing Partnership, "would be the provision of up to 30,000 units over the corporation's first five years [that] could translate into at least $1 billion of direct economic activity and thousands of jobs." How would this come about? "A combination of methods — new construction of three-family homes, possible new technology, rehabilitation of one-to-four-family homes, cooperative conversions of smaller apartment buildings, and moderate rehabilitation of multi-family buildings."

A press release issued by Mayor Koch the same day replayed much of the Rockefeller statement, adding obligatory comments from the Mayor pledging that the city "will make every effort to help this proposal succeed." Koch tossed the ball to Anthony Gliedman, commissioner of his Department of Housing Preservation and Development, asking him "to work closely with Mr. Rockefeller and his associates to make sure that this vision, which can mean so much to so many New Yorkers, will become a reality for our citizens."

Language like "concept of unusual promise" and "vision" was fitting. The Partnership had nothing in place and nothing remotely approaching a plan of implementation. As the *New York Times* reported in its news story: "Many details of the project remain to be worked out, including when it will start, how it will operate, what its sources of funds will be and which institutions and groups will be represented on its board." Details.

6

IN SEARCH OF A
BLUEPRINT

The basis for Rockefeller's January 14th announcement was a brief, three-and-a-half-page "discussion draft" of "A Program to Expand Housing Opportunities for Middle-Income Residents of New York City." The draft — dated December 16, 1981 — was prepared by the Partnership's housing consultant, Edgar Lampert, following a series of meetings with city officials at the Department of Housing Preservation and Development. Although the draft provided few details, it did lay out five "initial approaches," which were "to be tested, implemented and expanded if found successful."

The first approach was the construction of three-family homes on city-owned land. Such housing — costing in the $50,000-to-$60,000-per-unit range — would be cheaper to build than high-rise buildings and would avoid their high operating costs. The role of the Housing Partnership would be to receive city land, negotiate with developers on behalf of the city, and act as a "banker" in securing financing from financial institutions and other sources of capital, such as pension funds. To broaden the base of potential homebuyers, the Housing Partnership would seek to garner subsidies obtained by tax-exempt financing or outright subsidies from the federal or state government.

The second approach to be tested would involve the Housing Partnership in helping the city deal with "a significant number of one-to-four family homes in neighborhoods which could serve middle-income families." Nothing was being done with these homes "because of a number of limitations ranging from [the city's] cumbersome disposition procedures to inadequate financing and lack of rehabilitation skills." The role of the Housing Partnership would be as a "conduit" between the city and potential buyers; it would also arrange financing and oversee renovation.

A third possible program would be to pursue a technological fix for high housing construction costs: namely, manufactured housing, placed on city-owned land, that could chop per-unit costs down to the $40,000-to-$50,000 range. The Housing Partnership would "examine the current state of the art very carefully to determine the feasibility of this approach in New York." The outcome could be the location in New York of a factory to build manufactured housing.

A fourth program activity would involve the Housing Partnership in converting older, smaller rental buildings into cooperative housing for as many current residents as possible. The owners of many such buildings had purchased them using low-interest mortgages with a "balloon" feature that required refinancing — but the very high interest rates of the early 1980s (around 16 percent) made refinancing infeasible. A way out would be for renters to buy their own units, with a payment of say $25,000 to $35,000. The role of the Housing Partnership would be to develop plans that would protect nonpurchasing renters from eviction, but would also modify existing legal restrictions against conversions to cooperative ownership.

With respect to these first four program ideas, there was nothing in place or in sight to implement them. The fifth initiative, however — "the moderate rehabilitation of older, multi-family buildings" — was different. This proposal called for the Housing Partnership to wrap itself around the well-established and thriving Community Preservation Corporation. Although it was not acknowledged in the announcement hoopla, Housing Partnership organizers were counting on CPC to deliver perhaps 25,000 of the 30,000-unit five-year goal.

The Community Preservation Corporation (CPC), which Edgar Lampert had headed in the late 1970s, was organized in 1974 as a non-profit arm of New York City's major commercial banks — the Clearing House banks, so called because of their function of clearing millions of checks daily. CPC pooled capital from the big banks that could be lent to apartment owners and investors for the purpose of "moderate" fix-up and upgrading — usually to the tune of about $15,000 per unit. This low-end type of lending business was of no interest to the big banks individually, but it made sense to pool their resources and set up a small technical staff to handle the business. It was also a way for the banks to deflect criticism that they were "redlining" older neighborhoods by depriving them of investment capital. David Rockefeller, as chairman of the Chase Manhattan Bank, had pushed hard for the creation of CPC, and one of his close associates, Warren Lindquist, was its first chief executive officer.

CPC worked. Under Lindquist and his successors, Edgar Lampert and Michael Lappin, CPC had by 1982 financed the rehabilitation of about 8,000 apartments. Lampert's draft program statement for the Housing Partnership proposed simply that "this successful effort could be expanded and strengthened."

The discussion draft concluded with a short paragraph on "next steps" assuming "the concepts set forth herein are adopted." The next steps would be: "(i) to obtain more detailed data on each of the program elements, (ii) to discuss with City officials specific linkages between the City's housing agencies and HOPE [the name used in the draft for the proposed nonprofit corporation], (iii) to examine with representatives of private institutional lenders how lines of credit or other financing arrangements might be structured, and (iv) to develop budgetary projections for the corporation's operations. These steps, if a concentrated effort were made, could be completed within one month."

As sketchy as the draft was, it was enough to persuade David Rockefeller to launch the Housing Partnership a few weeks later in full view of President Reagan and 1,600 of New York's leading business people. And his commitment to the idea, in turn, was enough to motivate others to buy into its possibilities. If David Rockefeller was for it, there must be something there. The details would come later; they would somehow fall into place.

Two weeks after the January 14th announcement, the Partnership issued its first program statement, which began: "The members of the New York City Partnership are working to establish a not-for-profit corporation to be called the New York City Housing Partnership, Inc. to further the development, financing, ownership and rehabilitation of housing for middle income residents of the five boroughs of New York City." The February 1st program statement was almost identical to the December 16th discussion draft. The name HOPE had been dropped; the time for "next steps" was stretched out from one month to three months. But most important, it was no longer a draft. Those "next steps" had better lead somewhere.

The Housing Partnership — Getting Organized

In the first months following David Rockefeller's January 14th announcement, the organization of the Housing Partnership went forward on two tracks. The first track was to lead to an elaborate design for the housing initiative — its corporate structure, including the Community Preservation Corporation; its panoply of boards, committees, and officers; its program structure; and its financial plan for corporate operations. All of this was the province of Edgar Lampert, who would continue in his consultant role and serve as the interim president and CEO of the Housing Partnership when it achieved corporate status. Lampert would work closely with John B. "Jack" Davies, who was David Rockefeller's aide on Partnership matters.

The second track could be called the production track. This track was to focus specifically on what could be built in what places, by whom, and for what market. Generalities were fine: For example, the city reported that there was an ample supply of vacant land for building sites. But where exactly were these sites, what condition were they in, and how many units would they hold? Construction cost estimates were also helpful, but were there real Joe Homebuilders out there who would agree to build at those costs? And then there was the assumed desperate shortage of middle-income housing. But would New Yorkers necessarily buy whatever the Housing Partnership's product turned out to be? And would New York's contentious neighborhood groups accept the Partnership's incursions?

The production track was the responsibility of Kathryn Wylde. One of a number of loaned executives who worked with Lampert in the organizing phase of the Housing Partnership, Wylde was, in her regular job, assistant to the president and urban affairs officer at the Anchor Savings Bank in Brooklyn. Wylde would later be named by Lampert as executive vice-president of the Housing Partnership Development Corporation and then succeed Lampert as president in 1984, a position she held until 1996.

If David Rockefeller's outlook was shaped importantly by World War II, Kathryn Wylde's was shaped by that period known as "the 60s." As a student at St. Olaf College in Northfield, Minnesota, the Wisconsin native had coedited the college newspaper and been active in Students for a Democratic Society, an anti-Vietnam War protest organization. One of her professors, political scientist Jack Schwandt, remembers Wylde as a student leader with "abundant intellectual energy, a keen sense of campus politics, and an ability to see right through the slickest of snow jobs" attempted by nervous campus administrators. In 1968, the year of her graduation with high honors in political science, Wylde was working at a summer job in the Chicago area and took part in one of the defining events of the 60s — the antiwar protest that drew thousands of twenty-something demonstrators to the scene of the Democratic National Convention. Then she headed to New York City, where she had received a scholarship from New York University for graduate study in political theory. She had an academic career vaguely in mind.

Once in New York, Wylde was offered a full-time job as assistant to the president of the Lutheran Medical Center (LMC), George Adams. LMC was located in the Sunset Park neighborhood of Brooklyn, a once-thriving industrial and residential area where the good-paying jobs had disappeared with the closing of Brooklyn's shipping docks, ship repair yards, and factories like Bethlehem Steel and American Machine and Foundry. Sunset Park's largely Scandinavian residents had bailed out for the suburbs by the tens of thousands, depressing the real estate market and opening the way for rapid ethnic transition as migrants from Puerto Rico streamed into New York City. LMC's Adams was committed to staying in the neighborhood — his predecessor had made plans to move the facility — and making LMC a focal point for organizing the community to fight for its survival. Wylde could not resist the challenge; she shelved plans for graduate school — permanently, as it turned out — and became LMC's point person in the Sunset Park community.

From her base at LMC, Wylde took the lead in organizing Sunset Park's first community development organization, the Sunset Park Redevelopment Committee. SPRC (an acronym pronounced "spark") brought together a coalition of churches, businesses, block associations, and representatives of the emerging Puerto Rican majority in Sunset Park. Wylde was, as former Ford Foundation officer Louis Winnick has written, "to perform a key role in bolstering the fledgling organization with purpose, program, and resources." Wading into the alphabet soup of federal antipoverty and housing programs, Wylde wrote proposals and hustled bureaucrats in a multitude of agencies that controlled pots of federal, state, and city funds. Money flowed in for Head Start, youth employment, health and mental health services, and job training. Ten foundations also kicked in funds, with Ford the leading donor.

The biggest share of Wylde's prodigious energy was devoted to housing. Sunset Park's housing stock of around 30,000 units had been pummeled by a series of blows dealt by a weak economy, rapid ethnic turnover, misguided local zoning regulations, and inept or corrupt federal housing program administration. SPRC set up a nonprofit affiliate, the Sunset Park Housing Corporation, through which Wylde helped to patch together federal housing subsidy funds, city funds, and foundation support in an effort to rehabilitate some of the neighborhood's abandoned houses and sell them to new owners of modest incomes. The corporation also got into the property management business, as local savings banks took back apartment buildings on which they had foreclosed and turned over the management job to nonprofit community groups. In addition, the corporation itself became a developer of subsidized multifamily housing, using the federal Section 8 program as the subsidy vehicle.

In 1979, after more than a decade of community organizing and nonprofit housing development, Wylde made a career move to the Anchor Savings Bank in Brooklyn. This was two years after Congress had passed the Community Reinvestment Act, which required banks to serve the credit needs of their service areas — including those neighborhoods that were a poor risk for banks on the basis of conventional lending criteria. Many banks, uncertain about how to negotiate the treacherous waters of community lending, recruited (as they still do) from the ranks of experienced neighborhood based-organizers and nonprofit developers. For Wylde, it was a chance to attack the challenge of community development from the private sector side. And when David Rockefeller's newly organized New York City Partnership began exploring a major housing initiative, she was eager to take the assignment, from Anchor's president, to go over and help out.

The "Implementation Plan"

On April 12, 1982, Edward Lampert forwarded to David Rockefeller a thirty-five-page "Implementation Plan for the Housing Partnership." In putting together the plan, Lampert had drawn on the advice of a Partnership housing task force consisting of a dozen bankers and insurance executives, supplemented by about seventy-five advisors — representatives of city, state, and federal agencies, real estate interests, unions, banks, insurance companies, and foundations — who had participated in varying degrees in the multitude of meetings leading up to the plan. In listing the people involved, Lampert singled out the "special and continuing assistance" of Jack Davies and Kathy Wylde.

The Lampert plan's opening statement of "general principles" said that the success of the Housing Partnership would depend on "two interrelated factors": broad support by private institutions, including those "whose ordinary course of business lies outside of housing finance and development"; and, on the public side, the commitment of public officials "to transfer initial expressions of program support to the more difficult decisions which affect program priorities and effective implementation by operating agencies."

Another of the "general principles" made clear that bankers would be willing to put more money into housing investment, but only at "basically market rates and terms." This was business, not philanthropy: "Private financial and corporate institutions cannot subsidize projects. . . .To the extent such subsidies are required and desirable, we must rely upon the governmental sectors — the city, state and federal governments."

The plan envisioned "two broad program areas" to start with: "low rise new construction and moderate rehabilitation." Although the plan noted that others might be added later, it was apparent that two of the original list of proposed Housing Partnership activities had already fallen off the table: rehabilitation loans for buyers of one-to-four-unit homes and conversions of older rental buildings to cooperative ownership.

The plan then turned to matters of structure. The first, most obvious question was: What, exactly, is the "Housing Partnership"? The plan called for the parent New York City Partnership to establish a sixteen-to-twenty-two-member committee to be responsible for "program oversight and coordination," for "securing widespread private participation," and for "coordinating governmental initiatives." That committee was to constitute the New York City Housing Partnership, but it would not be a legal entity empowered to enter into contracts, hold property, make financial deals, or act as an agent of a public agency. Such an entity had to be a nonprofit corporation set up under state law, with its own board of directors and staff. The Lampert plan envisioned two such corporations as

"operating companies" under the oversight of the committee: The first
was to be called the Community Development Corporation, which would
be responsible for low-rise new construction; the second was the already
noted Community Preservation Corporation, which was already in existence and was slated to continue operating its multifamily rehabilitation
program, but on an "expanded" basis.

None of the first three components laid out in the plan — the Housing Partnership, the Community Development Corporation, and the
Community Preservation Corporation — had any explicit public sector
representation. This was to be taken care of by yet a fourth component,
to be known as the Housing Partnership Council — a twelve-member
group with six public officials (local, state, and federal) and six Housing
Partnership committee members. The Housing Partnership Council was
"to initiate, oversee, and coordinate public-private programs being implemented by the New York City Housing Partnership." This part of the
proposed structure, however, would never be implemented. Nor, in the
end, would the Community Preservation Corporation see any advantage
to affiliating formally with the Housing Partnership and would maintain
its independence.

Moving on to financial matters, the Lampert plan laid out in general
terms what it would take to make low-rise new construction financially
feasible and marketable for sale to middle-income homebuyers. The city
government would need to provide city-owned building sites at nominal
cost. It would also need to pay for site preparation expenses, since many
sites would be filled with rubble and have other environmental problems.
To bring interest rates down somewhat — they were running at around
16 percent at that time — the city and the state would need to allocate
tax-free bond proceeds to the new construction. Further city assistance
would be in the form of property tax relief — a gradual phasing in of the
property tax levy over twenty years. City and state officials were also to
cooperate in exploring the use of manufactured housing for Partnership
projects, to make concessions on various building code requirements,
and to expedite the city's multiple planning and inspection reviews.

The plan addressed the question as to how the Housing Partnership's operations were to be staffed and financed. The Community Preservation Corporation, which supported itself from fees generated by the
developments it sponsored, was to be the model. The Lampert plan envisioned that the Community Development Corporation would also eventually become self-supporting — but it would need to be financed by

corporate donations and foundation grants for an "initial period" of about two-and-a-half years, from June 1982 through December 1984. Assuming a staff of nine people and the usual operating expenses, the plan estimated that the new corporation would require a total of $1.3 million for the "initial period." In addition, another $1.5 million would need to be raised to finance the construction of about twenty-five "'model homes' in order to establish the market." Although the plan acknowledged that such financing "shall be more speculative than customary construction lending," those institutions putting up the money could expect to get it back after the model homes were sold.

On the revenue side of the corporation's operations, the plan projected annual income from fees of $750,000, based on $1,500 in fees per unit and an annual production rate of five hundred homes, beginning in 1983.

The Lampert plan also included a preliminary list of vacant, city-owned building sites. This part of the plan was the work of Kathy Wylde, who had obtained the site inventory from the city Planning Department and the Department of Housing Preservation and Development. Thirty-eight sites were listed, each with brief, handwritten notations with respect to site condition and neighborhood environment, and each with an estimate of the number of units the site could hold. Sites were distributed throughout the five boroughs — thirteen in Brooklyn, ten in Manhattan, six in the Bronx, five in Queens, and four on Staten Island; site capacity varied from as few as fifteen units (Ackerman Street, Staten Island) to as many as 10,000 (Paedergut Basin, Brooklyn). All told, the thirty-eight sites could hold an estimated 31,634 units. According to the plan, Wylde would serve as "executive director" of an eight-person site review committee "to examine the sites so that we might select the most promising as initial sites for the new construction program."

The plan did not spell out in detail the type of housing envisioned. Although David Rockefeller and the Partnership's initial program statement had referred to a "three-family home" as the likely product, the Lampert implementation plan laid out financing and market assumptions based on a single unit priced at $62,100 and requiring a mortgage of $53,000 after a 15 percent downpayment. Such a home would be affordable to families with incomes ranging from $28,800 to $35,200, depending on the amount of mortgage interest subsidy available from tax-exempt bond financing or other "shallow" interest subsidies. Projected mortgage interest rates ranged from 11 to 15 percent.

The Lampert plan concluded with a brief listing of "next steps": approval of the plan, fund-raising, incorporation of the "Community Development Corporation" and other legal matters, selection and hiring of staff. The city government needed to set up a capital budget line to support the new construction program, agree to contract with the Housing Partnership for site preparation and infrastructure costs, and settle on the first group of specific sites for housing construction.

That was the plan. Later, Frank Macchiarola, who was president of the New York City Partnership from 1983 to 1987 would comment with dry understatement, "From the standpoint of those of us who have tried to make it happen, we know the meaning of the phrase, 'easier said than done.'" The plan exuded an ordered, brisk, and confident tone, but Kathy Wylde recalls a kind of panic engulfing the Partnership staff in the weeks and months immediately following the Rockefeller announcement. David Rockefeller and the corporate giants of New York City had launched a wondrous new housing program, and every person and group who had anything to do with housing — community organizations, builders, realtors, advocacy groups, unions, politicians — all wanted to plug in somehow and get a piece of it. The problem was that "it" did not exist. "There was no there there," Wylde notes, borrowing from Gertrude Stein's comment on Oakland.

Three months after David Rockefeller's January 14th announcement at the Waldorf-Astoria, the Housing Partnership had no permanent staff in place except for Edgar Lampert, no operating budget or office space of its own, and no procedures in place to implement any of the several program concepts that had been floated out. Rhetoric and substance were still far apart.

New Homes for New York: Genesis of a Program

When David Rockefeller announced the Housing Partnership in January 1982, he stressed the "lack of middle-income housing" as one of the city's "most pressing problems." The initial Housing Partnership agenda included a number of program options that would serve this target income group, of which the construction of "three-family homes" for ownership was only one. Although Rockefeller did not single out homeownership as a Housing Partnership goal, it turned out to be the chosen instrument for realizing whatever promise there might be in the collaboration between Ed Koch's city government and David Rockefeller's Partnership.

How did this happen? Partly, it was because of Ed Koch; he *was* committed to homeownership, and had been trying to get a program going since 1978. Partly, too, it was a choice based on pure pragmatism. As Kathy Wylde would later recall:

> Actually, we did not start out by choosing to do homeownership, but homeownership turned out to be the *best* way to do what David Rockefeller wanted to do, which was to mobilize private sector capital to add value to neighborhoods through housing. So that's what we decided to do.

Mayor Koch styled himself as the champion of New York's beleaguered working and middle class; he had run strongly in the outer boroughs, where homeownership rates were relatively high. "Homeownership," he asserted, "is the cornerstone of the City's efforts to rebuild neighborhoods." He saw it as a way "to keep middle class residents in New York" and believed that even "low income residents [should] have the same chance of owning a piece of the Big Apple."

Soon after taking over the Mayor's office on January 1, 1978 — and three years before the Housing Partnership was formed — Koch began pushing the city's housing agency to put together a homeownership production program on vacant city land. As Anthony Gliedman recalls it: "When Mayor Koch came in, he said, 'Why doesn't the [federal] 235 program work here?' Being bureaucrats, the people at HPD [Department of Housing Preservation and Development] told him why it didn't work. He said, 'That's not good enough. You have to make it work.'"

On July 25, 1979, Koch sent a note to his housing commissioner, Nathan Leventhal (soon to be elevated to Deputy Mayor), asking "for concepts designed to spur one and two family private home construction on primarily city-owned land." In his reply a month later, Leventhal agreed that it was a great idea, and then went on to lay out a daunting list of reasons why it would be hard to implement. "Despite the many sound benefits of a home-ownership program," he wrote, "New York City has never been capable or even interested in creating one." One problem was that New York's small homebuilders were a "fragmented and unsophisticated" industry and had never really put any political pressure on city government to act. There were many others.

Leventhal pointed to the city's high construction costs relative to those in the surrounding suburbs. For much of this high cost, he acknowledged, the city had only itself to blame. "Tragically, a good proportion of these costs (estimated as high as 20-25%) are due to the City government's own rules and processing requirements." New York's implacable high costs meant that even free city land would not be enough to bring a new house within marketable range — "a write down [subsidy] over and above nominal land cost is always necessary." Another problem was the "poor condition" of most sites; even on so-called "cleared" sites, "it is almost certain that rubble has been left on the site requiring a great deal of site preparation costs on a unit basis for any low density developments."

Leventhal also posed the fundamental marketing dilemma that confronts any homeownership program in high-risk urban neighborhoods. "No program can work," he said, "without enough individual family decisions that a home and its surrounding neighborhood are worth the substantial investment required to purchase. New York can presently offer few pieces of land where such assurances can be given." The more "questionable" the neighborhood, the deeper the subsidy must be to attract buyer interest. However, at some point, deeply subsidized houses become so cheap that low-income families are induced to "buy" with little or no down payment and no financial reserves. "As time goes by," Leventhal said, "[these buyers] may experience difficulty in meeting rising maintenance expenses which are the same for all income groups and therefore are extremely regressive. Concentrations of low income ownership become dangerous in a neighborhood because they raise the possibility of large scale and physically concentrated defaults or rapid neighborhood deterioration."

Finally, Leventhal warned that low-density construction was "expensive and difficult to administer" for city government, much more so than a big multifamily project that is built on one spot and provides its own self-contained market. A single project, once approved, can trigger hundreds of units without any special regard for the surrounding neighborhood. A low-density homeownership development, however, "is built as the market develops with model homes as the key ingredient. Therefore, construction is a long term commitment and can continue only if the seller can point to well maintained previously sold homes and vacant land which is guaranteed to continue development. Therefore, City commitments must be locked into private progress and cannot be reversed as long as sales continue. This kind of commitment has never been one that New York specializes in. . . . [It] becomes a 'retailing' governmental function rather than a 'wholesaling' one."

Despite this litany of obstacles, Leventhal did not want to tell Koch that his bright idea was simply unworkable, but only that it would be difficult and expensive. Leventhal held out hope that a small-scale home-ownership program could be mounted if all the right pieces could be put in place.

One key piece was the federal government's Section 235 program. This was a homeownership subsidy that provided low-interest mortgages to eligible families wanting to purchase a modestly priced home. Enacted in 1968, the program flourished in the early 1970s, especially in the South and the Midwest, where builders were able to bring out a generally decent product at costs within the ceilings imposed by the law. Qualified buyers could get an FHA-insured mortgage with an interest rate as low as 1 percent, and the federal government paid the difference between that and the market interest rate. In 1973, after President Nixon's landslide re-election in November 1972, Nixon suspended 235 as part of a general moratorium on subsidized housing programs. But his successor, President Ford, at the urging of HUD Secretary Carla Anderson Hills, resurrected the program on a smaller scale and with a shallower federal subsidy: Buyers could get a 4 percent mortgage, not 1 percent. President Jimmy Carter, who was in office during much of Koch's first term, kept the program going; it was killed during the Reagan administration.

In its heyday, Section 235 would not work in New York City because the city's high construction costs far exceeded the federal cost limits. Nationally, more than 400,000 houses were built in the early 70s under the program; New York City had a grand total of 6. Goaded by Koch's interest in homeownership, New York housing officials lobbied for legislative changes and regulatory waivers that would make 235 feasible in the city and put houses within the financial reach of many more families than a market rate program would. Leventhal stated that he believed the changes would be "forthcoming."

Leventhal also reported that he was "exploring the expenditure of [federal] Community Development funds as a means to 'write down' construction or purchase costs." For example, he suggested that such funds could pay for "infrastructure items such as streets, sewers and grading which can account for up to $12,000 of a houses [sic] construction cost." Under normal circumstances, these costs would be folded into overall development cost and be reflected in the price of the houses.

Finally, Leventhal noted that the city would need to proceed with building code changes that could cut building costs, specifically mentioning expensive and unnecessary fire safety requirements for "brick and block" walls instead of cheaper wallboard. "Limiting the changes to specific 'opportunity areas' should satisfy the Fire and Building Departments which have been its traditional opponents," he wrote Koch. The Department of Water Resources was another problem area; it "has maintained an inflexible attitude to small home builders and has established a poor record in terms of the time required to issue approvals."

Leventhal's memorandum went on to list some possible areas where a homeownership program might be tried, such as parts of Coney Island (Brooklyn) and Staten Island. He was dismissive of the South Bronx Development Office, headed by Ed Logue, who had "proposed a widescale application of the Section 235 program. Their ideas, however, do not exhibit a fundamental understanding of 235 and seem mostly superfluous." He was also pessimistic with respect to sites "recently cleared of tenements or other dilapidated abandoned structures where the surrounding neighborhood is not attractive to low income investment"; such areas he saw as "basically unmarketable." "Unfortunately," he told the Mayor, "I think they constitute a large portion of the land you had in mind in your July 25th memorandum."

Still, Leventhal did not want to be a complete wet blanket. His eight-page memorandum concluded that if Koch was willing to commit the land and the subsidies, and if HUD and the city's own agencies really cooperated, an "intelligently coordinated" program "could produce about 400 units a year for 10 years," which he acknowledged was "not a staggering amount."

Soon after delivering his August 23rd, 1979, memorandum to the Mayor, Leventhal was promoted to Deputy Mayor and Anthony Gliedman took over as commissioner of Housing Preservation and Development. Gliedman had been commissioner of Ports and Terminals, but had also worked at HPD for six years (1970-76) during the Lindsay and Beame administrations. As "the first HPD commissioner to live in a house," Gliedman was eager to move forward on Koch's homeownership idea. On December 14, 1979, Gliedman sent Koch a sixteen-page memorandum which he said was a "follow-up" to Leventhal's of August 23.

Gliedman's memo covered some of the same ground as Leventhal's, including the difficulty facing any homebuilding program, but was decidedly more confident and upbeat in tone. "The City's home-ownership program will start with the 235 program. The elements that can make it work are essentially in place," Gliedman wrote. Later, he said, the city would pursue a "long-range approach to make use of other opportunity sites scattered throughout the city." This was "essentially a plan for the future and must await resolution of some significant issues. . . . Our focus, right now, is on the 235 program."

Since taking over HPD, Gliedman and his staff had been busy zeroing in on specific vacant sites and talking to homebuilders who might be interested in developing them. Eight sites — five in Brooklyn, two in the South Bronx, and one in Queens — were identified in the memo as the "most advanced" and described briefly as to condition, readiness, and neighborhood surroundings.

Gliedman stressed the importance of "processing" as "a key element in the program's success. There is no way the program can work without careful planning and coordination between HUD, HPD, and other City agencies . . . including the Department of Environmental Protection, the Department of Highways, the Department of Buildings and the Department of City Planning. . . . I think that the Mayor's Office should take the lead, at least in the beginning, to coordinate the program." As for HUD, Gliedman was confident about its desire to cooperate: "HUD is eager to work with us to make the program a success, and we could have the biggest 235 program in the country."

In February 1980, two months after the Gliedman memorandum, Koch announced that the 235 program was ready to go; private builders were invited to submit proposals for putting about 2,000 houses up on fourteen city-owned sites, most of them in Brooklyn and the South Bronx. HUD's area manager for New York, Alan Wiener, said expansively that the program "could result in several thousand housing units within a couple of years."

Not quite. A year passed before the city finally was able to designate builders for the first projects. As reported in the *New York Times*: "Some builders have expressed dismay over the time the city has taken to get the project going." One builder told the *Times*: "I've been anxious to get in the ground on this thing. . . . It's a good idea, but the city needs a little prodding to get all the bureaucratic pieces to fit together." Joseph Margolis, the president of the New York City Builders Association, feared that procedural delays would mean construction cost increases and house prices higher than the market could stand. "I'm worried the city's numbers won't fly," he said. "A three-bedroom house with a 20-foot lot, by my estimates, is going to end up costing in the neighborhood of $58,000. If people at the Department of Housing Preservation and Development think that's going to sell in Bedford-Stuyvesant, somebody there is smoking something stronger than I do."

The program struggled on. At one point, the entire program was threatened with extinction by the expiration of the national 235 subsidy authorization, but New York's Congressional delegation persuaded Congress to give the city an eighteen-month extension before letting the program die for good.

The second birthday of the Mayor's homeownership program coincided approximately with David Rockefeller's formation of the Housing Partnership in January 1982. Kathryn Wylde, on loan to the Partnership from Anchor Savings Bank, took on as one of her first tasks an analysis of what was happening in the city's 235 program and what lessons could be applied to the Partnership's embryonic housing initiative. Wylde interviewed an assortment of builders, bankers, city officials, and community sponsors involved in 235. She would conclude, in her report submitted to the Partnership's Housing Task Force on February 8: "The 235 experience demonstrates the clear need for a private, professional organization to carry the initiative in implementation of a small homes program directed toward moderate- and middle-income buyers."

Wylde reported that two years into the 235 program, only nine "model homes" on three South Bronx sites were "in various stages of construction." Site preparation and foundation work were underway at a few other sites, but most were still vacant and waiting to start. Based on her talks with builders selected for the program, Wylde wrote: "There is considerable doubt whether many of the builders who responded to the City's RFP [request for proposals] would have done so if they knew then what they know now. . . . Even with the large public subsidies projected for the 235 projects, most developers just hope to emerge whole."

The small homebuilders who were matched up with most sites were "not well suited to the mounds of paperwork and restrictions inevitably associated with City-owned properties and publicly assisted programs. Without the flexibility in design, construction standards and sales price normally available to them, all traditional sources of profit for small builders disappear."

Builders faulted the city's housing agency for letting them "fend for themselves with banks, HUD, community sponsors and technicians." HUD, far from being eager to cooperate, was a major source of delay, with its nitpicking, time-consuming reviews of sites and architectural plans, and resistance to providing appraisals that would support needed mortgage amounts. "Every developer," Wylde noted, "has carried on independent battles with the HUD Area Office with virtually no coordination by the City."

Despite the critical tone of her report, Wylde's purpose was not to bash the city's performance in running the 235 program. She acknowledged that the program was complex and new to everyone involved, that the city housing agency had been trying hard, and that HUD deserved much of the blame for the program's clumsy start and slow progress. Besides, the 235 program was soon to expire anyway; there wasn't much point in beating it to death. The Koch administration would need to find another vehicle to advance its homeownership agenda.

From the city's perspective, it was fortuitous that the Partnership was nosing around for a private sector role in housing at the very time that the city's leading homeownership initiative was floundering. Wylde's analysis was useful in pinpointing where the program was breaking down; it also laid the groundwork for a joint city government/New York City Partnership New Homes program. Her central conclusion was right up front on page one of the report:

> The Partnership could play a vital role in coordinating public and private resources in support of a significant small home/condominium production program. This role would include serving as sponsor for purposes of conveyance of City-owned sites, serving as developer or co-developer of these sites, and serving as a City-wide vehicle for financial packaging, government processing, marketing, management, research and design activities associated with a volume production program.

Within a few weeks after David Rockefeller's announcement, Wylde had a pretty clear idea of what a New Homes program would look like and how it would work. New Homes would be her baby. Over the next two years, other elements of the original Housing Partnership design would flutter, piece by piece, to the ground. Except for New Homes. New Homes would fly. But it would be a long, rough roll down the runway.

7

THE MONEY CHASE

The Housing Partnership needed money to operate. In the first few months following David Rockefeller's announcement, the Housing Partnership functioned administratively as an activity of its parent organization, the New York City Partnership, without its own budget or a staff specifically tied to that budget. Edgar Lampert was on the payroll as a consultant to the Partnership, but all other staff had been donated temporarily by major banks and other members of the Partnership. The Housing Partnership could only tread water until it achieved its own corporate identity and budget.

Business Says No

Lampert's April 12th, 1982, implementation plan had called for a budget of $2.8 million to pay for the first two and a one-half years of operations and the construction of "model homes." But the money had to come from somewhere. Seventeen days after submitting the plan, Lampert proposed a funding plan, scaled back to $2 million, that would carry the Housing Partnership through 1984. In a memorandum sent to David Rockefeller, J. Paul Lyet (president of the Partnership), and E. Virgil Conway (head of the Seamen's Savings Bank), Lampert suggested that the $2 million be raised "from a broad cross-section of New York City's business and banking communities." The private sector would be divided up into nine categories, each with a fund-raising goal and a leader to direct the campaign with support from Partnership staff. On the high end were "corporations," who were to commit $414,000, and the Clearing House (commercial) banks, who would pledge $388,000. On the low end, "utilities" would come up with only $105,000 and "accounting" [firms] with $120,000. Amounts in between were to be coughed up by smaller banks, insurance companies, and real estate developers. "Timing is of the essence," the memo stated, with urgency if not originality. "The funding requirements must be met as soon as possible so that operating staff might be hired and the program's current momentum not be dissipated."

Despite the urgency, the plan fizzled. It was hardly a good time to be raising private money for a shaky venture — even one backed by David Rockefeller. The nation's economy was still in a post-Carter recession, and the big banks, like Citicorp and Chemical, were holding billions of dollars in nonperforming loans from third world countries. Corporate members had already kicked in to support the operations of the parent Partnership and balked at yet another levy for the housing operation. Even for big banks and corporations, $2 million for operations and for speculative "model homes" was a good deal more than coffee money. On June 4, 1982, George Roniger, an aide to Citicorp chairman Walter Wriston, met with Edgar Lampert and expressed concern that the housing program was "moving very fast" and that its projected cost seemed to be going up. Lampert believed that he had "perhaps, eased Roniger's apprehensions," but in the end, neither Citicorp nor the other heavy hitters on the Partnership board were ready to support the fledgling housing program.

One source of money that could be counted on for modest operating support was the Rockefeller Brothers Fund (RBF), a foundation established in 1940 by the five sons of John D. Rockefeller, Jr.: John D. III, Laurance, Nelson, Winthrop, and David. Although dwarfed by the giant Rockefeller Foundation, which could dispense millions of dollars for a single grant, the RBF was capable of being tapped for smaller grants in program areas of interest to one of the brothers. One of David's interests was housing and neighborhood renewal; in the 1950s, for example, RBF provided a key grant to support planning to redevelop Morningside Heights. In 1982, when the Housing Partnership was being formed, David was chairman of the board of RBF. As Kathy Wylde observes, "It was not exactly a tough sell." On October 8, the Partnership sent the RBF a letter asking for $150,000 to help fund "both core staff and consultant services" for the housing program, and the grant was approved at the next RBF board meeting. Also chipping in at the start — after a call by David Rockefeller to his friend, Mrs. Brooke Astor — was the Vincent Astor Foundation, with a grant of $75,000. It was a beginning.

Playing the Pierce Connection

For more serious money, the hunt had moved from New York City to Washington, D.C. David Rockefeller's sponsorship guaranteed that the Housing Partnership would get access and a respectful hearing in Washington's power centers, particularly in Ronald Reagan's White House and at the Department of Housing and Urban Development (HUD) headed by (Reagan appointee) Samuel R. Pierce, Jr., a New Yorker who had had strong political connections to David's brother, Nelson. As Governor of New York, Nelson Rockefeller had twice appointed Pierce to fill judicial vacancies on New York County's (Manhattan's) highest criminal court. (Both times, Pierce ran as a Republican for full fourteen-year terms and, in overwhelmingly Democratic Manhattan, lost.) Later, during the 1960s, Governor Rockefeller appointed him as a member of the New York State Banking Board, which Pierce served on for nine years.

On June 22 and 23, 1982, Edgar Lampert, Kathy Wylde, and housing commissioner Anthony Gliedman made the rounds in Washington, pitching the Housing Partnership to Sam Pierce's executive assistant, Lance Wilson (like Pierce a New Yorker); to Edwin Harper, a White House domestic policy aide; and, on Capitol Hill, to New York Republican Senator Alphonse D'Amato and Congressmen Bill Green, Charles Rangel, and Charles Schumer. The Housing Partnership group focused on a nice round number — $5 million — that would provide "seed money" for the Partnership to get off the ground. No commitments were made, but Lance Wilson at HUD identified several possible program pots where that kind of money might be found, including HUD's research and development program, the Urban Development Action Grant program, and the Secretary's discretionary fund under the Community Development Block Grant program.

On July 7, David Rockefeller followed up on the Washington prospecting trip with a "Dear Sam" letter to Pierce. The letter was cordial and businesslike. He reminded Pierce that President Reagan had addressed the Partnership on January 14. He recalled for Pierce the Partnership's goal of 30,000 units of housing. He listed commitments that the city and

state governments were willing to make, such as land, site improvements, and housing mortgage bonds. Now, "the provision of modest Federal financial support" — $5 million — was "of critical importance to
the new construction aspect of the Partnership effort." The money would
be used "as a vital catalyst" for three vaguely defined purposes: "help
'seed' the initial stages of the new construction effort . . . assist on moving
forward on the manufacturing housing component . . . and serve as the
beginning of a locally-established voucher program for home ownership." Rockefeller assured Pierce that the $5 million would be a "one-
time grant . . . that would clearly demonstrate the creative use of public
funds to stimulate private investment." In fact, the letter claimed with
some hyperbole, a mere $5 million "would help generate $1 billion of
overall investment," a handsome 200 to 1 payoff. Rockefeller wrote that
he looked forward to working with Pierce and his staff "on the details of
further HUD involvement" and concluded that he would like "to meet
with you personally about it in the near future. I will call your office the
next time I go to Washington to see if I could stop in to see you."

If one were to strip the letter of its artful phrasing, the message
being delivered was something like this: "Look, Sam, we've got this
Housing Partnership going with some promising ideas, but we really
need some money to run it for awhile. I care enough about this to give it
a chunk of my personal time to make it work, but I need your help. We're
not asking for the moon — only $5 million. One more thing: I'm going
to keep after you on this, so if you're thinking about turning us down,
you're going to have to do it to my face."

Rockefeller's approach to Pierce was characteristic. According to
Warren Lindquist, Rockefeller's long-time (1951-1977) personal associate and advisor on real estate investments: "When David felt something
was worthwhile, he would pursue it with energy and dogged persistence.
And he was always perfectly prepared to use his name, his position, and
his prestige to lobby public officials to take action on the things he cared
about."

Despite Rockefeller's pitch, Pierce had reasons enough to reject
the request. Vague as it was in the "details," the Housing Partnership
proposal ran counter to Reagan administration housing policy in at least
two respects. First, the program was explicitly intended to help *middle-
income* families, "with incomes in the $15,000-$45,000 range"; but the
Reagan "safety net" approach to all federal subsidies and income sup-
ports was that only the very poor would be protected — all others should

fend for themselves in the private market, without handouts from the government. A second reason for turning down the proposal was that it clearly called for federal subsidy for *new construction* of housing. But Reagan's policy was to *end* subsidized new construction (which, with Congressional assent, his administration had already effectively done), because it was simply too expensive; the preferred way to help poor people with their housing problems was to give them vouchers so that they could shop for decent housing in the open rental market. This is not only a lot cheaper than new construction; vouchers also avoid jamming poor people together in "projects" notorious for high crime and other social pathology. With a voucher, your neighbor paying a market rent need never know that you are paying a heavily subsidized rent.

Since vouchers, in housing program lingo, are always associated with *rental* housing, the reference in Rockefeller's letter to "a locally-established voucher program for home ownership" is puzzling — probably an attempt to invoke a Reagan administration buzzword that would resonate well with Pierce.

But Pierce was hardly looking for reasons to shoot down the Rockefeller request. All he needed was a credible rationale to approve a grant — and Rockefeller's Partnership included all the big names in the New York City business sector, giving the proposal a private sector patina dear to the heart of Reaganites. The city government, too, had locked arms with the Partnership, and Mayor Koch had pledged free land and other assistance. Koch's housing commissioner, Tony Gliedman, had easy access to HUD's tenth floor, where Pierce and aides Lance Wilson and Joseph Strauss, both New Yorkers, had their offices. "They could have said no to a lot of things," Gliedman told the *New York Times*, referring to Wilson and Strauss. "They have been helpful. Part of it is they are New Yorkers. They understand our needs. The other part is we have some creative minds in housing in New York City. We have been useful to them in being a model for innovative programs."

That is the way it works in Washington. To get a federal grant or other benefit, access to decision-makers is 90 percent of the battle — which is why ex-Congressmen and former White House aides can command immediate six-figure salaries as lobbyists (the so-called "revolving door"). Washington also operates on the geographical representation principle — not just in the legislative branch but, informally, in the executive branch as well. Cabinet officers, their aides, and assorted Assistant Secretaries usually come to Washington from somewhere else. They are expected, at a minimum, to be nice to the folks from back home. And if they are able to funnel a little federal money in that direction without breaking the law or bending the rules very much, so much the better. The money needs to be spent somewhere, after all, so why not give some to people they know and who they trust will make good use of it? And if they plan to return home after their stint in high places, they may hope that their generosity will not be forgotten.

No one can say for sure whether the Partnership would have received any help from the federal government if HUD had not been populated with political appointees from New York City. What *is* certain is that it was very fortunate that they were where they were. What is also certain is that without the timeliness and amount of federal assistance that did come through, the Housing Partnership would have limped along ineffectively or failed altogether as a vehicle for housing production. Phrases in the Rockefeller letter such as "vital catalyst" and "critical importance" were no exaggeration.

The Housing Partnership needed two kinds of support: money for staff and other operating expenses, and money for housing subsidies that could bring down the price of whatever was built to within reach of its middle-income target group. With that in mind, the Housing Partnership developed a two-pronged approach to HUD funding that went far beyond the single lump sum of $5 million suggested in the Rockefeller letter. First, the Partnership applied for a smaller amount — $1 million — to pay for operating expenses; the source would be discretionary funds controlled by Secretary Pierce. Second, for housing subsidies, the Partnership went for a big number — $52 million — from the Urban Development Action Grant program, which was not primarily a housing program, but was the only possible source that could be stretched to fit the Partnership's ambitious objectives.

One may ask why the Secretary of Housing and Urban Development has a "discretionary" fund from which he or she can dispense a million dollars at a crack. Actually, the fund in question, the Secretary's discretionary fund of the Community Development Block Grant, is a mere vestige of the days when almost all federal urban grants were under ultimate political control. Enacted in 1974 as part of President Richard Nixon's "New Federalism" thrust, the Community Development Block Grant (CDBG) program converted seven separate urban grants into a single, formula-based grant to all cities of over 50,000 population. With CDBG, HUD secretaries and senior bureaucrats were stripped of their ability to play favorites, cut deals with friendly members of Congress, or stiff their political enemies; this was the intent of the New Federalism — one of many ironies surrounding the Nixon domestic agenda. But the CDBG formula, with a tiny bow to the old ways of federal grantsmanship, set aside just a sliver — 1 percent — of the total block grant pie to be used at the Secretary's discretion to carry out the purposes of the act. One percent is, of course, not pocket change if the total pot is large. In the case of CDBG, annual appropriations were in the $3-to-$4-billion range, giving the Secretary $30 to $40 million for discretionary grants — more than enough to ladle out in million-dollar-chunks here and there.

Still, the Housing Partnership had to make the case for a discretionary grant under the terms of the CDBG law. One of the permitted uses of the discretionary fund was for "technical assistance"; "TA," as it is known, is an elastic term that applies when one organization with expert knowledge helps another organization carry out a program that it could not otherwise carry out in the absence of such help. TA was the rationale chosen in response to the Housing Partnership's application for discretionary funds: The Partnership fulfilled the role of expert organization, while the city government of New York was the organization needing technical assistance. This had to be specifically acknowledged by the city, which housing commissioner Tony Gliedman was happy to do in a letter to Secretary Pierce: "The scope of services to be provided to the City of New York by the Partnership through its non-profit Housing Preservation Development Corporation [*sic*] is essential to allow us to meet the Housing Assistance Plan goals and Community Development Block Grant objectives for the production of new and rehabilitated housing units. In particular, the ability to leverage financial support from private institutions, foundations and other sources through the creation of a trust fund is crucial to the development of affordable housing in New York and is consistent with our Housing Assistance Plan." The one specific in this bureaucratic mush, the "trust fund," would never materialize — though not for lack of trying, as we shall see later. But all the political bases had been duly touched and the verbal rituals observed. On October 23, David Rockefeller told a Women's Forum luncheon that HUD was "hoping to make New York City a kind of pilot project" and had agreed to a $900,000 grant. "I think we will be off to the races very soon on it," he said.

Indeed they were. Soon after, Secretary Pierce approved a grant of $985,000, enough to operate the Housing Partnership for eighteen cru-

cial months — from January 1, 1983, to June 30, 1984. The city's need
for technical assistance would be unremitting: Pierce approved a second
discretionary grant of $870,000 in the spring of 1984, and a third, in
1986, for $687,500. This meant that HUD was paying about three-
fourths of the Housing Partnership's operating costs through the 1980s.
Much of the balance needed was provided by a second grant from the
Rockefeller Brothers Fund in 1984, this time for $100,000.

Going for a UDAG

The other critical funding piece needed was money for housing subsidies. Federal programs for new construction — the traditional source —
had been all but shut down by the Reagan administration and Congress.
And housing subsidies are expensive — a million dollars does not go
very far. For example, a million-dollar homeownership subsidy program
that cuts the price of a new house by $25,000 would cover only forty
houses, and the Housing Partnership was aiming to build housing by the
thousands. The Partnership had to think big.

One hundred million dollars was the initial target settled on for the
Housing Partnership trust fund. It was hoped that most of the money
would come from two sources: HUD's Urban Development Action Grant
program, and the major foundations, led by the Ford Foundation. Once
again, Sam Pierce's HUD came through for New York. The foundations,
on the other hand, said "No."

Landing a "UDAG," as Urban Development Action Grants were
known, was much more complicated than getting a Secretary's discretionary grant. In fact, the very availability of the program was rich with
irony. Enacted in 1977 as the flagship urban initiative of the discredited
Jimmy Carter administration, UDAG was an economic development
program designed to "leverage" the maximum amount of private and
local government investment focused on a particular project so as to generate new jobs. Unlike the formula-driven Community Development
Block Grant, UDAGs were highly competitive; applications were scored
by career civil servants based on such factors as "leverage ratio" — the
ratio of non-UDAG dollars to the UDAG contribution — and the number
and quality of permanent jobs created. Applicants also had to certify to
the so-called "but for" nature of the proposed project: That is, the project
would not be financially feasible "but for" the UDAG, a provision designed to prevent a federal giveaway to projects that would have been

built anyway in response to normal market forces. Never a very large program by federal standards — it amounted to only $675 million annually at its height in 1980 — UDAG was nonetheless immensely popular with mayors because it could be used to attract private investment for high-profile development.

UDAG had its critics. Ridiculing the "but for" provision, frequent attacks on the editorial page of the *Wall Street Journal* labeled the program a wasteful boondoggle that subsidized big downtown hotels and parking ramps that would have been built without UDAG. Other critics charged that the elaborate point system for judging competing UDAG applications was little protection against political manipulation of the actual awards. Whatever the merits of these attacks, for the incoming Reagan administration in 1981 UDAG was a Carter invention that meddled with free market forces — a ripe target for the budget-cutting axe of Budget Director David Stockman, who called UDAG "a statist abomination," and "perhaps the most ideologically offensive and wasteful bit of federal spending on the block." Year after year, Reagan's budget proposed wiping out UDAG, but pleas from mayors and the tacit support of Sam Pierce won a partial reprieve in Congress. By 1988 UDAG had been cut to $216 million, and it finally expired in 1989. It was still there, however, for the Housing Partnership; the challenge was to get it in hand — and that would take years of effort and boundless tenacity.

Although UDAGs for housing were not specifically excluded by law, they were unusual. A UDAG was also a poor match for what the Partnership had in mind — dozens of small projects scattered all over the city instead of a single focused project in one place. Still, UDAG was the only game in town as far as major federal funding was concerned; the Partnership had to go for it. Following the June 22nd, 1982, trip to Washington, Partnership and city staff collaborated on a UDAG application for $52 million to support the New Homes program. The complex application had to be rushed — HUD had decided it would no longer consider any UDAG applications for housing submitted after November 1, 1982. New York's application stressed the amounts of city support and private investment that would be leveraged; it also cited the reclaiming of vacant and blighted neighborhoods that would occur. In late October, the city Board of Estimate blessed the application, just beating the November 1st deadline.

The Ford Foundation Says No

With the Partnership's $52 million UDAG application on its way to a friendly reception in Washington, David Rockefeller next turned to the major foundations, which he hoped would provide $30 million to a "Housing Partnership Trust Fund" over a three-to-five-year period. Of all the foundations, the Ford Foundation was the key, both because it was the biggest and because Ford's prestige as a funder of urban programs would help pull in other foundations. Rockefeller decided that the best approach to Ford would be to enlist Mayor Ed Koch in a joint appeal to Franklin Thomas, president of the Ford Foundation. After a November 11th, 1982, meeting in City Hall between several Partnership board members and the Mayor, Rockefeller took Koch aside and asked him to join in an approach to Ford. Koch agreed.

The meeting with Franklin Thomas took almost three months to schedule. On February 7, 1983, Koch, Rockefeller, and a few aides met Thomas for breakfast at the University Club. As scripted by Rockefeller's aide, Jack Davies, and Housing Partnership president Edgar Lampert, Rockefeller's pitch was that the Partnership represented New York City's response to "the realities of the 1980's" — the private and the public sector must pull together "to provide better housing for New York City's lower, moderate and middle income families." The Partnership goal for a housing trust fund was $100 million, with $30 million to come from foundations. The Ford Foundation should take a "leadership role" in order "to raise the sights" of other funders. As a solid start toward the goal, Rockefeller asked Thomas to commit Ford to a $6 million aid package — an outright grant of $1 million, a "challenge grant" of $2 million contingent on the Partnership's raising $4 million from other donors, and an additional $3 million for "program related investment" — that is, money put in a revolving fund to enable low- or no-interest loans to the trust fund that presumably would be paid back.

Wylde recalls the breakfast meeting with Thomas as "a civilized disaster." The Ford Foundation had long styled itself as a catalyst for community-based program innovation, and Thomas was critical that the Partnership's proposal smacked too much of a "top-down" approach to neighborhood development — this despite the Partnership's intention to enter into agreements with "community sponsors" to help plan and market Housing Partnership projects. The Mayor was no help. Instead of supporting Rockefeller, according to Wylde, "Koch joined Thomas in dumping all over the proposal." The Housing Partnership got nothing from Ford.

From the Mayor's standpoint, the problem with the "trust fund" — a concept promoted by Lampert, but never clearly defined — was one of program and budgetary control. Neither Koch nor his housing commissioner, Tony Gliedman, was really interested in a $100 million pot of money called the "Housing Partnership Trust Fund." Who would decide how and when to spend the trust fund's assets? The prospect of ceding control of that kind of money or even sharing it with a private sector entity was unattractive. The funding model preferred by the city was a grant — such as a UDAG — for a specific amount, intended for a specified number of housing units. Yet the city backed away from striking a fatal blow to the trust fund idea, to which the Mayor had given lip service; the strategy was rather to avoid the issue until the idea would die quietly and unnoticed.

Along the way, there was some awkwardness. David Rockefeller had publicly stated that a housing trust fund would be a key feature of the Partnership's housing initiative. The HUD technical assistance grant to the Housing Partnership had included a provision that a housing trust fund would be created. A similar provision had been written into the Housing Partnership's $150,000 grant from the Rockefeller Brothers Fund, then chaired by David Rockefeller. Thomas W. Wahman, RBF national director, wrote Rockefeller on February 7, 1984 — a year after the Ford Foundation debacle — seeking guidance on the trust fund issue. Wahman noted that fifteen months had passed since the RBF grant to the Housing Partnership; meanwhile, RBF had been getting housing trust fund proposals from several other organizations. Wahman pointed out that he had been referring these organizations to the Housing Partnership as "the organization funded by the RBF to provide leadership for the Housing Trust Fund idea," but that nothing much seemed to be happening. The Wahman memorandum listed about a dozen possible revenue sources, mainly taxes and fees related to real estate transactions, that might be packaged into a trust fund if the State Legislature would go along — not a foregone conclusion. Now, said Wahman, "state officials, housing researchers and planners, foundation representatives, and community group leaders are looking to the NY Housing Partnership for leadership regarding the establishment of a Housing Trust Fund. . . . [T]he response of the NY Housing Partnership leadership has been to

proceed judiciously at best — more accurately stated, to await developments rather than to move forward."

Wahman wanted "DR" to make a "fundamental policy decision"
about the trust fund and offered three options, which he characterized
as (1) "Wait and See"; (2) "Get the Facts and Follow Your Nose"; and
(3) "Out-front Leadership." Wahman's own preference was "somewhere
between Option #2 and Option #3 — that is, to promote the research,
planning and dialogue activities, while determining what leadership
roles the Partnership might play." Rockefeller's choice — whether deliberately or by default I'm not sure — was Option 1.

As Lampert was phasing out of the Housing Partnership, Wylde
persisted in raising the issue with HPD commissioner Gliedman, albeit
with a notable lack of passion. On July 9, 1984, Wylde wrote Gliedman
that under the terms of their HUD technical assistance grant, "we are
supposed to be working with the City on . . . the creation of a Housing
Trust Fund." Wylde acknowledged that this task had been pushed aside
"because of our preoccupation with the predevelopment work to get sites
into construction." In general, she noted, "there is little 'private sector'
support for any of the current proposals for generating additional revenues for a Trust Fund. Our only real activity to date has been generating
revenues from New Homes sites through projected UDAG recapture and
City Land sales (both of which require City confirmation). We might
reactivate the effort to secure philanthropic contributions, along the lines
of a 'United Way' for housing. . . . Any suggestions you may have would
be appreciated." She didn't get any.

A month later, in another memorandum to Gliedman, Wylde included the trust fund among a list of pending "program-wide issues":
"Helping the City establish a Housing Trust Fund is part of our [HUD]
TA [technical assistance] contract. I have sent memos to you on this topic
and would appreciate some direction." Wylde had dutifully pressed the
issue for the record, but that was all; her style was not to plead for "direction." The trust fund idea was allowed to die quietly.

8

THE ELUSIVE UDAG

The Ford Foundation's cold shoulder and the fading of the trust fund idea made the UDAG proposal the last, best hope. By the spring of 1983, the Housing Partnership had labored for over a year without nailing down a solid source of housing subsidy, and the HUD bureaucracy was still massaging the New York application.

Commenting on the UDAG proposal two years later, Stanley Newman, a career HUD official and native New Yorker, twitted the participants at a Housing Partnership conference: "The Housing Partnership was a puzzlement. The Housing Partnership came to us with the brilliant idea of a $50 million grant, given all at once, immediately, on only one condition, and that is that they would spend it on housing. It is a noble cause, but we were a little curious as to exactly how it would work. UDAG really is not a housing program, as such."

Newman's position at HUD in the early 1980s was itself fortuitous. Born in the South Bronx, Newman had worked for the New York City Planning Commission before joining HUD in Washington in the late 1960s to help launch the Model Cities program, LBJ's main urban initiative among the outpouring of federal programs known collectively as the Great Society. Always controversial, Model Cities barely escaped elimination by the incoming Nixon administration in 1969 and was eventually folded into the Community Development Block Grant in 1974. As often happens in large public bureaucracies, however, programs may come and go, but their administrators, shielded by civil service rights, are able to stay on. Newman toiled through the Nixon and Ford administrations in various jobs, and when Carter's appointees at HUD started UDAG, he emerged as a top career official managing the program. Carter's defeat in 1980 sent UDAG's political managers, HUD Assistant Secretary Robert Embry and UDAG director David Cordish, back to their home city of Baltimore. So there was Newman, a Great Society Democrat, in charge of a vestigial Carter program in a conservative Republican administration eager to be rid of it. Newman would surely not be able to deliver the Partnership's UDAG on his own, but he did see himself as a loyal New Yorker, proud of his roots as a graduate of Public School 79 in the Bronx. As he said: "I believe that every dime we spend in New York is a dime worth spending." And as for HUD's expectations of New York's private sector — "The first thing we expect is gratitude, lots of gratitude."

Newman's banter was possible in the warm glow of hindsight. As he acknowledged in his remarks, "In the beginning, the marriage [between the Partnership and HUD] was a little rocky. The first year, as in many marriages, didn't go so well." Newman understated both the time frame and the degree of frustration. Five months elapsed between the application submission date, November 1, 1982, and the first "preliminary" grant award approved on April 1, 1983 — not for $52 million, but for only $4.5 million. The intervening period was taken up with a chain of negotiations over what would constitute a fundable application. A sample project, submitted in December, was rejected as failing to meet HUD criteria.

The prospect of a UDAG and the negotiations with HUD forced the issue of how the construction of New Homes would be financed. The UDAG money — $15,000 per house — would be plugged in only at the end of the construction and marketing process, when a homebuyer was ready to close the deal; but long before a prospective homebuyer was in sight, all of the up-front risk would need to be assumed by a bank willing to advance a construction loan and a builder willing to face heavy losses if the housing failed to attract buyers. HUD insisted that banks make what were called "hell or high water" financial commitments to all planned housing; these were unconditional signed agreements that banks would commit to full financing even if it became clear that the houses were not selling. The New York banks were hardly lining up for the privilege.

The first bank to step forward was Chemical. "It was risky," recalls David Daly, a vice-president in Chemical's real estate lending division. "Instinctively, we felt homeownership was a good idea — that if all we do is build or rehab low income rental housing in some of these neighborhoods, the downward cycle would repeat all over again. But everyone had reservations about whether new construction of for-sale housing would really work." For Chemical (which merged with the Chase Manhattan Bank in 1995), overcoming those reservations required what Daly called a "juggling act" performed by Kathy Wylde. To make the UDAG deal feasible, "Kathy asked each player to concede something. She agreed to find bankable builders who would accept a limited 10 percent profit; the bank agreed not to pound the builders with heavy equity requirements and our toughest underwriting standards; the city agreed to provide free land and some subsidy for site preparation. With everyone giving up something, we were ready to sign a bunch of letters to HUD that committed the bank's participation and would eventually secure the UDAG money."

For the first $4.5 million UDAG, "preliminary" was an apt qualifier. Another thirteen months of wrangling would pass before HUD would release from its grasp the first $510,000 of UDAG money. The milestone was the construction loan closing on May 3, 1984, for the Windsor Terrace project, seventeen two-family town houses to be built in Brooklyn. (A much-publicized "groundbreaking" had been celebrated, as we have seen, five months earlier.) Chemical Bank put up $1.8 million and the city chipped in $170,000.

Getting to the Windsor Terrace closing was no picnic. HUD dithered in preparing the formal grant agreement enabling the release of UDAG funds, so the Housing Partnership drew up a draft and sent it to UDAG staff. After another month of delay, HUD sent back a bunch of revisions that the Partnership could not accept. Meanwhile, the Partnership submitted a second group of sites for UDAG funding and received a second "preliminary" grant award of $330,000 for only twenty-two units.

It soon became clear that as long as the Housing Partnership and HUD were negotiating on a site-by-site basis, the New Homes program would sink into a morass of interminable delays. And so on July 19, 1983, Kathryn Wylde and Anthony Gliedman went to Washington to seek the intervention of Samuel Pierce's office. They were shooting for approval of the idea of a UDAG "master agreement" that would provide a larger pool of subsidies that could be drawn on for any approved site. HUD agreed to the concept, and the Partnership immediately set about drafting an agreement and submitted it in August. When HUD did not respond, the Partnership turned in a grant request for $15 million for 1,000 units pursuant to the draft master, and yet another (the third) site-specific application, for three sites. Thus, by the fall of 1983, the Partnership had peppered HUD with three separate site-specific applications — starting with Windsor Terrace — and a larger, "master" application for $15 million. None was near closure — including Windsor Terrace, which had been given preliminary HUD approval six months earlier.

HUD's UDAG staff pleaded overwork.

Wylde and Gliedman continued to push as numerous drafts and amendments flew back and forth between New York and Washington. When HUD delayed, the Partnership did HUD's legal work for them. Things began to fall into place, piece by piece. The Windsor Terrace closing was on May 8; two weeks later, HUD approved the master grant agreement for $15.1 million, enough to provide $15,000 of federal UDAG subsidy for each of 1,112 housing units. "May [1984] has been a watershed month for the program," Wylde noted in a memorandum to her board recounting the UDAG chronology. "For those who ask 'Where are the houses?'" she commented, "this chronology may be useful. If we could produce affordable homes without federal subsidy, or if the City had asked us to develop market-rate sites, the houses would all be built. But then, the Partnership would not have been necessary."

Even with HUD in politically friendly hands, it had taken well over two years for the Partnership to lock in HUD's firm commitment to hand over the money for real houses on real streets, so that real, flesh-and-blood homeowners could eventually move in. Getting from financing to actual moving in, however, involved a whole additional set of challenges — which we discuss in the next chapter.

The UDAG saga was a kind of prototype of the Housing Partnership's style of operation under Kathy Wylde's executive leadership. A key element of that style was to exploit every possible political advantage — knowing who is connected and obligated to whom in ways that could be orchestrated to gain public agency approval of a particular program or course of action. David Rockefeller's "Dear Sam" relationship with Pierce and Pierce's obligations to the Rockefellers helped smooth the way for HUD's approval of what was in fact a highly competitive grant program. Fellow New Yorkers in the Secretary's office, Lance Wilson and Joseph Strauss, were also eager to pitch in on the Partnership's behalf.

Yet, the UDAG experience also demonstrated emphatically the limits of political influence in a large bureaucracy populated by long-lived cadres of technicians and lawyers. A favorable nod from the Secretary's office may be enough to get the attention of program administrators, but then the decision descends into the ranks of civil servants who are charged with completing the administrative and legal steps leading to implementation. This is a danger zone for many reasons. To give the bureaucracy its due, the tasks at hand may be inherently complex, made more so by a rich growth of regulations and procedures intended to protect against rip-offs of public funds. Then, too, the bureaucratic reflex is to recoil from the novel. The Housing Partnership program was in many ways a marvel of invention and improvisation, an effort to adapt a non-housing program to a housing purpose. But bureaucratic adaptation is an oxymoron; straying from familiar, well-trod pathways produces anxiety, anxiety produces caution, and caution, delay.

Another danger is that political influence can backfire, particularly if the current crop of political appointees is unpopular with the departmental rank and file. This was certainly the case during Samuel Pierce's time at HUD. Compared with previous HUD secretaries of both parties who were vigorous advocates for cities, Pierce was seen as weak and ineffective, a low-profile, obedient soldier in Ronald Reagan's assault on urban programs. His aides were seen as lightweights and opportunists, arrogantly using their positions for political advantage and personal gain. The endorsement of such a crew, even for a meritorious program, was a mixed blessing. Bureaucrats dislike being pushed around by people they do not respect. Although they lack the authority to kill a program decision, they have the means and often the desire to slow down its implementation with roadblocks and detours.

Confronted by HUD's bureaucratic timidity or lethargy, the Housing Partnership style, as applied by Kathy Wylde, was a combination of unremitting pressure and a helping hand. Not political pressure — Wylde understood the limits of political influence and the need to ration carefully the interventions of a David Rockefeller or other powerful allies. The pressure referred to here was the old-fashioned, nuts-and-bolts kind of administrative follow-through. A barrage of telephone calls that went something like this: "About that contract you said would be ready today.

Is it ready? Are there problems? Would you like us to fax you some language you can look at? When do you think we can get this thing wrapped up? OK, I'll fax you something this afternoon and call you next week." And she would. The key was to move a program decision out of the political realm and into the realm where professional administrators work through problems of implementation as peers.

The ultimate goal of this strategy was to transform the novel and the innovative into the familiar and the routine. Getting to that point required more than persuasion, patience, and tenacity; it also required sufficient technical and legal mastery — a willingness to slog through the details — so that the Housing Partnership could engage cautious or resistant bureaucrats on their own ground and even do a good deal of their work for them. Then, when the technical infrastructure was in place, the next application and the ones after would glide along a familiar track — becoming, as Wylde often says, "a cookie-cutter operation: a program, not a project."

The struggle to obtain UDAG funds and then make them work was clearly worth it. UDAG was the indispensable fuel that powered the Housing Partnership through its first successful projects. UDAG made it possible to knock an extra $15,000 off the price of a house — $30,000 off a two-unit dwelling — which, along with the city's $10,000-per-unit subsidy, put Partnership projects in a marketable range. The Partnership went back to the UDAG well time after time, even as the Reagan administration — despite Pierce's objections — was determined to kill the program.

By 1985 the Partnership had racked up $21 million in UDAG grants but needed more — particularly for its biggest and most ambitious project, the 599-unit Frederick Douglass Circle condominium development to be built on a choice site in Harlem on the northwest corner of Central Park. Despite the attractiveness of the site, no developer — either nonprofit or for-profit — had been able to put together a feasible financial plan for at least a decade.

The Frederick Douglass Circle project, also known as "Towers on the Park," was to cover most of two city blocks and consist of two twenty-story towers, two mid-rise wings of nine stories, and a three-story parking garage. Ground-floor spaces would be occupied by commercial tenants. The site, which had once been slated for public housing, presented the Housing Partnership with formidable political and financial obstacles. Because the site straddled the territory of two community boards, one of which (Board 7) favored low-income rental housing while the other (Board 10) supported owner-occupied units, the Partnership had to broker a complex marketing plan that called for setting aside deeper subsidies for a portion of homebuyers who would be lower-income, while more affluent buyers would need to pay full market prices for their units. Development costs would also be unusually high, even by New York City standards, because of extra foundation work required to protect adjacent buildings and a subway station located under the site. The foundation work alone added $6.2 million — about $10,000 per unit — to a total project cost that would finally top $75 million, or $125,000 per unit.

"It was a very speculative deal," says Steven Brown, the Housing Partnership vice-president who had the principal staff responsibility for shepherding the Towers project. "To make it work, we needed a separate UDAG commitment from HUD, and it was tough to get." In January 1985 the Housing Partnership asked HUD for a $6 million UDAG. The application went into the hopper with a slew of others from cities across the nation. HUD bureaucrats scored the proposals, and Towers on the Park came up short. As the UDAG program was nearing extinction, the Partnership resubmitted the proposal for the May 1985 UDAG competition.

This time David Rockefeller weighed in with another "Dear Sam" letter to Secretary Pierce. Noting that he "personally had taken every opportunity to urge the continuation of the UDAG program," Rockefeller wrote that the city government, Chemical Bank, and the project developers had increased their financial commitments, thereby improving the UDAG "leverage ratio" to 8:1. Rockefeller argued further that the project was "the first private investment in new residential construction in the Harlem community in many years," and that it was "ready to go." "We recognize," Rockefeller acknowledged, "that the UDAG award decisions are dictated by competitive criteria, but I did want to call your attention to the special importance of this application." The second time around, Towers on the Park moved up in the UDAG scoring derby and was funded.

Completed in March 1988, the project has been a huge success in both financial and social terms. Deborah Wright, a young investment banker who joined the Partnership staff in 1987 and was put in charge of marketing Towers, recalls the racial tension when the units were first offered for sale. "This was the first private project in three decades. For blacks the issue was how to revive Harlem without giving it up; many believed that Towers was David Rockefeller's beachhead to gentrify Harlem with white buyers who would shut us out. It was completely perverse, but we somehow had to deal with the illogic of the position and the weight of history. I had never done anything like this; it was a harrowing experience, but both racial integration and the income mix turned out to be great." Towers on the Park did indeed attract some white buyers, but they made up only 30 percent of all buyers. The largest group of new owners, 38 percent, were black; 18 percent were Asian, and 12 percent Hispanic. About 10 percent of the units were sold at unsubsidized prices — as high as $240,000 for the best units, with views of Central Park. The average sales price was $98,000, but some lower-income buyers qualified for units at prices as low as about $50,000. UDAG's managers in Washington could hardly have asked for a better outcome.

The Project Fee Issue

Although the Housing Partnership and the city stood shoulder to shoulder in the pursuit of federal UDAG funds, the two partners had to slug out their differences over other money matters.

For example, in October 1983, as the financial documents for Windsor Terrace were being drafted, a dispute arose between Wylde and Charles Reiss, a deputy commissioner at HPD, about whether the Housing Partnership could take out a $25,000 fee (about $735 per unit) to help cover its administrative and marketing expenses.

The issue was critical because it went to the heart of the Housing Partnership's ability to support itself rather than be dependent on uncertain government and foundation grants. Up to that point the Housing Partnership was surviving on special HUD "technical assistance" grants totaling about $2 million dollars, supplemented by grants ($250,000) from the Rockefeller Brothers Fund. Generating income from project fees was the key to its future funding base. The importance of the issue prompted Wylde to lay out the problem in a memorandum to Frank Macchiarola, the president of the parent New York City Partnership, who had overall responsibility for the organization's financial affairs.

Wylde pointed out that until the project fee issue was settled, she would be unable to develop a budget for the Housing Partnership operation. She was also reluctant to pursue foundation money more aggressively "because of the concerns of other nonprofit and community-based housing groups that the Housing Partnership will compete with them for scarce foundation grants." Wylde's conclusion: "If we can neither charge fees nor raise contributions [from foundations] without encountering hostility, I have little hope of securing the level of support necessary for us to function."

According to Wylde, HPD deputy commissioner Reiss "has strongly objected to the Partnership receiving any revenue from project proceeds (including reimbursement for costs)." This was more than Reiss's personal position, according to Wylde: "There has always been a general City attitude that the private sector is giving nothing — i.e., that HUD and the City are contributing, but that the 'fat cats' (who they feel will take the glory) are not putting up cash. Charlie [Reiss] is particularly emphatic (even vindictive) on this matter. . . . I know Charlie has already undermined our intention of charging marketing fees on Bronx projects with the Bronx Borough President. Charlie's comment to me was: 'You're just trying to create a self-perpetuating institution' — which, of course, is true."

Although Wylde stated in her memo that Reiss reflected "a general City attitude" toward the Partnership's "fat cats," she was not sure whether Reiss was speaking for his boss, HPD commissioner Anthony Gliedman, on the specific issue of marketing fees. Part of the purpose of her memo was to suggest to Macchiarola that he intervene with Gliedman to get Reiss to back off.

Wylde's tack was successful, and the marketing fee issue was resolved in the Housing Partnership's favor. But the incident showed how a very important question — the Housing Partnership's very ability to operate — could still be up in the air nineteen months after the city and the Partnership had agreed to a joint effort. The idea of partnership seemed to assume a cooperative, long-term relationship; yet Reiss (at least in Wylde's eyes) seemed to resent the Housing Partnership's attempt to become "a self-perpetuating institution" by taking a token fee for its development services. For all of the partnership happy talk that launched the New Homes collaboration, this incident revealed the fragility of the relationship.

Hitting the State

By 1985, with UDAG's days numbered, the Housing Partnership and the city would need to join forces again to seek a new source of subsidy.

The Partnership's homeownership production program would run aground unless a new pot of money could be found that could fill the $15,000 gap in every housing deal. The city was already contributing $10,000 and could not be expected to do more. The private sector — banks and builders — was already shouldering significant financial risk and was not about to give money away outright. Big foundations weren't interested. The only alternative was the state.

New York State had been an activist state in housing in the 1950s and 1960s, sponsoring tens of thousands of mainly rental units through the Mitchell-Lama program, enacted in 1955, and the Urban Development Corporation, created in 1968. To facilitate homeownership, New York had also established its version of the Federal Housing Administration, the State of New York Mortgage Agency (known as "Sonny Mae" after its acronym SONYMA). SONYMA was authorized both to insure home mortgages and to issue tax-exempt mortgage bonds, the proceeds of which could be allocated to lenders — who in turn would provide qualified homebuyers with mortgages two or three percentage points below the regular market rate. (A qualified buyer would typically be a first-time homeowner earning less than a stated maximum income.) All of these state programs stimulated housing construction, primarily for moderate- and middle-income groups, by means of liberal infusions of development capital at favorable terms, but not with outright subsidies.

State housing programs were not for the poor. Housing for the poor was the federal government's business — big business. Federal money paid the full cost of building public housing operated by the New York City Housing Authority and other housing authorities around the state. And federal money generously subsidized housing built by private developers and nonprofit sponsors for renters whose earnings were a notch above public-housing-tenant income. Subsidies such as those provided by the Section 236 program and, later, the Section 8 program unhinged developments from normal market discipline — the market for new apartments at bargain rents was inexhaustible. Builders would never stop building for risk-free profits until the money ran out, which it pretty well did after Ronald Reagan took over in 1981. Some projects sneaked through for a few years under the nonhousing UDAG program, but that couldn't last either. The "feds" were pulling out; states had to move in if any new housing was to be built at all for people of middle income or below.

New York's Governor Mario Cuomo took a small step in that direction in February 1985 when he submitted his recommended executive budget for fiscal year 1986: $25 million in subsidies for the rehabilitation of low-income housing, with one-third of that amount set aside for the homeless. Nothing for homeownership subsidies, however. Nothing for the Housing Partnership to replace the dwindling UDAG money.

Kathy Wylde cranked up the Partnership lobbying machine. Her aim was to get the Legislature to up the Governor's $25 million to $68 million. The money would come from revenue generated by a mortgage recording tax surcharge enacted in the 1970s to pay off any losses from state-insured mortgages. Since it turned out that that revenue was not needed for that purpose, the money had been dumped into the state's general funds. Cuomo proposed to rededicate $25 million of the surcharge revenue for low-income rental housing; Wylde wanted to rededicate *all* of the revenue for housing assistance and add two additional programs. The first was "a State 'Housing UDAG,' providing up to $15,000 per unit to subsidize new construction and substantial rehabilitation of housing to be privately developed in blighted areas for owner-occupancy by moderate and lower middle income households. This would represent the only State program designed to leverage private efforts to increase the *supply* of moderately priced, owner-occupied housing." Wylde's proposed package also included funds (up to $10,000 per unit) for moderate rehabilitation of older apartment buildings, of the sort carried out by the Community Preservation Corporation.

The Partnership board lined up behind the package, and Wylde orchestrated the lobbying assault on Albany. In mid-March Wylde went to Albany and made the rounds of the Governor's office and the two housing committees of the legislature. Neither the Assembly nor the Senate committees had endorsed Governor Cuomo's $25 million proposal, but they were receptive to the Partnership's three-part plan for $68 million. The key was to get Cuomo and the leaders of the two houses, Assembly Speaker Stanley Fink and Senator Warren Anderson, to agree to the needed increase in the budget. On March 19 Wylde sent an urgent memorandum to the Housing Partnership board, reiterating the threat of imminent federal cutbacks to Partnership programs and calling for a final push on Albany: "After meetings yesterday with the Senate, Assembly and Governor's staff, I can assure you that there is a possibility of securing the proposed Housing commitment, but only if we use all possible means to make a strong case to the Governor, Senator Anderson and Speaker

Fink in the next few days. I would request that you each make an effort to reach out to any or all of these leaders with whom you can be most effective — particularly to explain the importance of this issue to the Partnership and other local public-private housing efforts."

The Democratic-controlled Assembly, with its strong New York City contingent, was ready to support an increased appropriation for housing, but not necessarily the Partnership's middle-income homeownership piece. The key was the Republican-controlled Senate. To most Republicans, housing was a program area best avoided; they associated it with the Urban Development Corporation, which in the 1970s had overreached financially and nearly defaulted on some of its bonds. The Partnership package had a chance, however, if the Senate Majority Leader, Warren Anderson, could be brought around.

Anderson, a veteran legislator from Binghamton, had been a close ally of Governor Nelson Rockefeller in the 1960s, and in 1975 was a key player in the state takeover of New York City's fiscal affairs when they were in chaos. Anderson was approachable, and the right person to approach him was David Rockefeller.

Rockefeller telephoned Anderson on March 20, 1985, to pitch the Partnership plan. Anderson disliked the idea of a dedicated tax for housing but agreed to support an outright appropriation of a similar amount — a total of $65 million. Anderson's legislative aide, Bernie McGarry, remembers Anderson getting off the telephone with Rockefeller and saying urgently — "Get me a bill!" Rockefeller says now that he does "not remember the details of the conversation, but he [Anderson] was certainly very supportive. I don't think there is anyone who compares with Warren. When he believes in something, he goes all out for it."

With Anderson on board, the Partnership plan was in position for approval in the final bargaining stage of the fiscal year 1986 budget between legislative leaders and Governor Cuomo. The Assembly pushed for a total housing appropriation of $50 million, which the Senate would go along with as long as it included $25 million for affordable homeownership. Cuomo was willing to accept both the budget increase and the Senate's condition. The deal fell into place. Shortly thereafter, Cuomo sent a note to William Ellinghaus, head of the New York Stock Exchange and chairman of the Housing Partnership, acknowledging that "your efforts and those of David Rockefeller were essential to the passage of this historic law. . . . Also, let me commend you on the excellence of your

staff, particularly Frank Macchiarola [Partnership president] and Kathy
Wylde."

The state affordable homeownership program, once added to the
budget, became firmly embedded year after year at about the same
amount. Each year during the 1980s, David Rockefeller and a delegation
of Partnership board members and senior staff, including Kathy Wylde,
would journey to Albany, meet with legislative leaders and the Governor,
and throw a reception for the entire Legislature. "I did it eight times,"
Rockefeller recalls. "The fact that we kept coming back every year made
an impression." No doubt about it.

When implemented, the state's $25 million was divided into two
parts: half for New York City and half for home construction in other
parts of the state. Because this was a new program activity for the state,
a new entity, the State Affordable Homeownership Corporation, had to
be set up. In a sense, the implementation challenge was UDAG all over
again. Dipping into the state's coffers and connecting state subsidy dollars to real houses on the street required an intricate network of legal and
procedural steps. Who would be eligible to apply? Who would qualify
for homeownership assistance, for how much, and under what conditions? What types of housing in what kinds of locations would be eligible? What would be the limits on builder profit? At what point in the
development and homebuying transactions would the state's contribution get plugged in? What would happen to the state subsidy if a homeowner wanted to sell the house again? Someone had to draft the
regulations and guidelines, prepare the forms, and touch the required
bases among the banks, politicians, and community groups. For a public
program, these chores rightfully should fall to a public agency. But the
reality is that public bureaucracies are slow to get organized and even
pokier in crafting specific implementing steps.

In the Housing Partnership's dealings with the state housing bureaucracy, the UDAG experience was useful in two respects. First,
UDAG showed the limits of trying to prod an agency into action; rather,
the best way to speed up a process was to do the agency's work for it.
Second, the UDAG program model was in substance similar to the state
program; much of the tedious legal and procedural work done for UDAG
was quite readily transferable. This, of course, was no accident. The
Housing Partnership under Wylde's leadership was, as always, in a big
hurry. An additional advantage was that the state program was explicitly

a housing program, whereas UDAG had to be pulled and stretched to fit a housing purpose.

Between UDAG and the state affordable housing program, the Housing Partnership had managed to tap into wells of subsidy capable of producing a stream just big enough to make their housing marketable, given the willingness of all of the participants — the banks, the community groups, the builders, the politicians, the Partnership itself — to buy into the enterprise despite the real risks involved.

GETTING TO PRODUCTION: CEREMONIES AND REALITIES

A Groundbreaking in Bedford-Stuyvesant

Blue and white police barricades blocked off each end of the 700 block of Quincy Street on a bright June Sunday afternoon in 1993 in the Bedford-Stuyvesant section of Brooklyn. In the middle of the block stood the Mt. Carmel Baptist Church, rebuilt from the ground up after a fire destroyed the original church building in 1986.

Directly across the street from the church was a vacant lot, the site for thirty-nine two-family homes that would bear the church's name, Mt. Carmel Town Houses; the lot was bare except for homebuilder Les Levi's beat-up dump truck. Adjoining the lot was a handsome, boarded-up four-story building with bay windows and decorative cornices at the roof line. Next to that building was a small playground guarded by a high iron fence and locked gate; the play equipment looked sturdy and well-kept. The Reverend V. Simpson Turner, senior minister of Mt. Carmel, explained with a chuckle that the playground harked back to the administration of Mayor John Lindsay in the 1960s, when the city sought to redeem vacant spaces between buildings with "vest-pocket parks." Most were long gone; this one thrived.

The two o'clock scheduled starting time for the groundbreaking ceremony passed. Mayor David Dinkins was expected to speak, but his reputation for punctuality is not great and sometimes he cancels out at the last minute. He is late, and the organizers decide to start the program. There is a festive air that seems almost small-town. Multicolored streamers of little flags flutter over about a hundred parishioners in their Sunday best, sitting on folding chairs in the middle of the street. Another fifty or so people stand in little clumps around the periphery. In front of the gathering, their backs to the building site, is a row of a dozen people who will speak: elected officials, representatives of government agencies, and the Housing Partnership representative, Kathy Wylde. Behind the speakers' chairs is a backdrop of bunting — big half-circles of red, white, and blue crepe paper.

"The Star Spangled Banner" starts the ceremonies, including a seldom-sung fourth verse including the words "Blest with victory and peace, may the Heaven-rescued land/Praise the Power that hath made and preserved us a nation!" A Bible reading from the book of Genesis speaks of land promised and redeemed, of God's ancient promise to Abraham: "'Lift up now thine eyes, and look from the place where thou art, northward and southward and eastward and westward; for all the land that thou seest, to thee will I give it, and to thy seed for ever. . . . Arise, walk through the land in the length of it and in the breadth of it; for unto thee will I give it'" (Genesis 13:14-15, 17). Then another song, "Lift Every Voice and Sing," a hymn known as the Negro National Anthem: "Sing a song full of the faith that the dark past has taught us/Sing a song full of the hope that the present has brought us."

After the anthems comes Dr. Turner's prayer of invocation; he thanks God for the occasion and "for our beleaguered Mayor," who, it is fervently hoped, will show up soon.

The speeches begin. Dr. Turner reminisces about Mayor Lindsay's vest-pocket park and notes that "we've been welcoming political leaders here for twenty-five years." We have been wanting for many years to do something with this site straight across from the church, he says. "Work begins tomorrow," he proclaims, as he shoots an expectant glance at the burly African-American contractor, Les Levi, who nods but looks harried. "We were worried," he continues, "that after groundbreaking, then what? So often we have a groundbreaking and then nothing."

Minister Simpson thanks the assembled dignitaries, beginning with Kathy Wylde, "a very fine lady, aggressive, who gets things done, who is concerned about our community." Then it is the dignitaries' turn — the printed program limits their "greetings" to "1 minute each" and they pretty much stick to it.

As City Councilman Enoch Williams is winding up, there is a bustle at one end of the block; police officers lift aside a barricade and Mayor Dinkins' black limousine eases toward the crowd. Dinkins bounds onto the street, looking casually elegant in an open light blue shirt and black slacks. He is a slight figure, dignified, with the characteristic glow of high officeholders fighting for their political lives. Minister Simpson introduces the Mayor, asserting "without fear of successful contradiction" that he is "the greatest Mayor of the city of New York."

The Mayor feels at home; he speaks reflectively and passionately, without notes or a script. He addresses "my dear good friend, Kathy Wylde, bless you!" He pays tribute to the Mt. Carmel Church, raised from the ashes after the 1986 fire. He praises all who have worked to create "islands of decency, safety, and commitment" in the troubled city. He turns to the drum corps — about twenty kids, trim in their blue shirts: "Stay in school. You can become a mayor. You can do anything you want. But stay away from drugs and fights. If you follow the rule of 'an eye for an eye, and a tooth for a tooth,' all you'll do is end up blind and toothless."

It's shovel time. A dozen new shovels and hardhats are unloaded from the back of Les Levi's truck and handed around to the City Council members, the legislators, the ministers, the city and state bureaucrats, and the builder, and to Kathy Wylde. There is much digging and turning of the stony Brooklyn ground; photographers snap pictures of little groups digging and bigger groups lined up, shovels poised, grinning self-consciously. One imagines some archival researcher in the next century, thumbing through fading snapshots, wondering who these people were and what was the meaning of their ceremonial digging.

The Mayor departs for his next campaign stop. Dr. Turner pronounces a benediction and invites the gathering to the church basement for food and drink: baked chicken, pink punch, and yellow cake with white frosting.

A Ribbon-Cutting in Harlem

A year later, the first phase of St. Charles Landmarks in Harlem was completed and new owners had been moving in. There would be 116 condominiums in all; every one has been sold. It was time to celebrate. By now there was a new Mayor, Rudolph Giuliani, eager to bask in the success and to pledge continued support for homeownership in New York.

The St. Charles site had been sitting vacant for over fifteen years after rotting tenements had been torn down on Frederick Douglass Boulevard in Harlem between 136th and 138th Streets. It is a block from the subway, a short walk to City College, and about a mile from the northern boundary of Central Park. It is also adjacent to Strivers' Row, a group of historic nineteenth-century luxury row houses that had passed from white to black ownership and still maintained their upscale status for over a century. "Location, location, location," intoned Louis P. Jones of Chemical Bank, invoking the real estate cliché at the ribbon-cutting ceremony on July 9, 1994. "It should have been a 'gimme' but it wasn't easy. It took the right partners."

In the late 1970s, Mayor Ed Koch had promised to "bring home-ownership to Harlem," and this same Harlem site was on his original list for building homes under the federal "235" program for subsidized homeownership. A sign went up on the site, and eager buyers offered "binders" — small deposits to hold a unit until construction was completed. Nothing happened. "The project self-destructed," Kathy Wylde says now. HUD couldn't figure out how to appraise the property — one of many glitches that forced the builder to give up. After the "235" fiasco, three subsequent development proposals for the site came to nothing. The Housing Partnership took control of the St. Charles site in 1989, and things began to move along the labyrinthine path toward a ribbon-cutting ceremony under a blazing July sun on a Harlem Saturday.

The occasion was a happening — not on a grand scale, but a happening nonetheless. Local television station minicam crews glided through the crowd of about 150 people milling around the fresh-built platform and the front stoops of the four-story red brick row houses. The *New York Times* real estate reporter, Shawn Kennedy, was there, as were other reporters. Charles Rangel, long-time Congressman from Harlem, arrived well before the scheduled 10:30 starting time, working the crowd, giving interviews, looking expansive. Word came that James Johnson, president of Fannie Mae, was on his way; his flight from Washington had been delayed by fog at La Guardia. (Fannie Mae has been a hugely important financial backer of Housing Partnership deals.)

The Housing Partnership staff began to relax; they had feared an embarrassingly low turnout on a hot Saturday morning and had sent a bunch of last-minute invitations to drum up attendance. The atmosphere had an appropriate charge of excitement, however, and enough people were there for a respectable crowd.

The official starting time passed without much notice. At 10:50 the Mayor's limousine pulled in across the street from the platform. His housing commissioner, Deborah Wright, who had been circulating around the site for over an hour, walked over to meet Mayor Rudolph Giuliani and guided him toward the open door of Doris Bembury's town house behind the platform. He is a slight figure in dark blue blazer and dark gray slacks, with only the faintest "What am I doing here?" look on his smiling face. Giuliani had been Mayor for only six months, and most of Harlem's votes had been cast for David Dinkins, the man he defeated by a handful of votes. This was Giuliani's first Harlem "event" of this sort. As everyone knew, he had played no part in the new housing being celebrated; still, the crowd seems pleased that he is there. As cameras click, he poses amiably with several neighborhood residents, even holding (although not kissing) the obligatory small child placed in his arms.

As the Mayor and other dignitaries emerge from their tour of the Bembury home, Kathy Wylde clears a path to a second-floor front stoop, where a bright red ribbon is stretched between two handrails at the top of the steps. The Mayor grasps a huge three-foot-long ceremonial scissors in his two hands and brings the blades down decisively. The stout ribbon is squeezed but not sundered. Gamely, the Mayor slices at the ribbon again and again as the audience titters. Finally, two people on either side of the Mayor hold the ribbon taut so that the dull blades saw their way through. The applause is louder than it might have been. Somehow the incident seems a metaphor for getting a building through New York's regulatory thickets: One rarely cuts through cleanly, but it is possible to wear down resistance with superior tenacity.

On this occasion the formalities come *after* the ribbon-cutting. Again led by Wylde, the parade of officials take their seats on the speakers' platform. Presiding is Monsignor Wallace Harris, a tall and commanding African-American priest who grew up in Harlem. Harris heads the St. Charles Borromeo Catholic Church, the church that had given the project its name and had also served as its "community sponsor" — the organization that publicizes the homes and holds marketing seminars for prospective homebuyers. In his opening remarks the monsignor invokes familiar lines from the "Negro National Anthem": "God of our weary years, God of our silent tears, Thou who hast brought us this far on our way. . . ."

The sun is hot and the speeches mercifully short — though long enough for each speaker to be generous to the others and still take a piece of credit along the way. After the speeches, Monsignor Harris leads the crowd in a moving moment of celebration and benediction: "Give God the glory! Stand and raise your hands in any direction and bless these houses all around us. 'Except the Lord build the house, they labor in vain that built it' (Psalms 127:1). And we have *not* labored in vain. Amen and amen!"

Groundbreakings and ribbon-cuttings — the Housing Partnership has organized a couple of hundred of them since the first groundbreaking at Windsor Terrace in late 1983. As occasions, they are part social, part political, and part religious; they signify completion, achievement, and more often than not, relief. For a few moments, they bring together the major players — community groups, city and state officials, bankers, builders, the Partnership — in the often contentious process of getting to the ceremonial spade or scissors. They are opportunities to step back and reflect on what the enterprise has been all about: new houses; new homeowners; a neighborhood created, revived, or strengthened. Because they represent the culmination of struggle, they never quite become routine.

High Optimism, Slow Start

By June of 1997 the New York City Housing Partnership had completed 10,092 houses in 118 separate projects. Another 56 projects, with 3,429 houses, were under construction or had financial commitments in place. Partnership projects were distributed in all five boroughs, with the largest production numbers posted in previously desolate areas of the Bronx — 5,151 houses — and Brooklyn — 4,764. Only since the late 1980s, however, has the Housing Partnership achieved consistently high production numbers on the order of 1,000 to 1,500 houses per year.

Although David Rockefeller and Mayor Koch had announced their partnership in January 1982, by mid-1986 the Housing Partnership had completed only six small projects totaling 171 units. Part of the slow progress had to do with managing the logistics of setting up a new organization — hiring staff, securing office space, establishing legal status as a nonprofit organization, and the like. Also in the early years, as recounted in the previous chapter, the Partnership was necessarily engaged in the often frustrating pursuit of money, both to pay for its own operations and to secure the public subsidies that would put its product in an affordable price range. In addition, the Partnership had to begin to line up homebuilders willing to undertake the risks of building and marketing houses in bad neighborhoods, along with "community sponsors" — neighborhood organizations, frequently church-based, that would help pick sites, secure planning board approvals, and assist homebuilders in promoting and marketing projects.

Still, by 1984, it appeared that progress was being made on all these fronts. The technical assistance grant from HUD had enabled Kathy Wylde to hire a small core staff, including Steven Brown, a young Harvard graduate who had previously worked for New York City Council President Carol Bellamy and Congressman Charles Rangel; and Consuela Reese (later Hackett), a real estate finance specialist who crossed over to the Partnership after being on loan from Chase Manhattan Bank.

Wylde had spent months out in the boroughs drumming up interest among small homebuilders for the New Homes program. At first, many builders were skeptical. Harold Bluestone, who with his two brothers, Eli and Norman, is a principal in the Queens-based building firm established by their father in the 1920s, recalls a presentation made by Wylde in 1983 to the Queens County Builders and Contractors Association. "We'd never heard of her before that. She didn't have all the answers, but we were interested enough to have a follow-up meeting with her." Later, the Bluestones were offered the chance to build a project called Springfield Gardens in Queens — thirty-three two-family, semidetached town houses. "We were leery, weren't sure it would work," Harold recalls. "We finally said to each other, 'Are we going to do this, or aren't we?' We decided to get involved. The subsidy gave us the confidence that we could market the houses successfully." The Bluestone organization (which would go on to build many successful Partnership projects) was joined by other interested developers, and by mid-1983 Wylde had put together a list of thirty-three "prequalified" builders.

Drawing on her experience and credibility as a community organizer and nonprofit housing developer, Wylde was also well along in establishing a network of community sponsors for Partnership projects. Wylde understood early and in gritty detail what the Partnership's bankers and corporate CEOs could only dimly grasp: that the Partnership's production goals would never be met without the support of community-based groups acting as advocates, marketers, and homebuyer counselors for individual projects. For many such groups, David Rockefeller might be a remote and vaguely threatening figure, but "Kathy" had proved that she could — in community activist parlance — both "talk the talk" and "walk the walk." With Wylde in the lead, many neighborhood organizations were ready to sign on as community sponsors, welcoming both the neighborhood-stabilizing effects of new homeowners and — not incidentally — the income from fees paid by the Housing Partnership to these always struggling organizations.

The biggest impediment, it would turn out, to achieving a breakthrough in New Homes production was the difficulty of working through the complex relationship between the two main partners in the enterprise: the Housing Partnership and the city government. None of this was evident in December 1983 when a Who's Who of New York's political and civic leadership gathered to break ground for the first Partnership project — seventeen two-family houses in the struggling Brooklyn neighborhood of Windsor Terrace. That had taken fifteen months since the nonprofit development arm of the Housing Partnership was incorporated in September 1982, but the program was on its way. Another two dozen building sites were targeted (optimistically, as it turned out) for construction start in 1984.

May 1984 saw the end of a frustrating, year-long wrangle with HUD over the technical mechanics of Urban Development Action Grant funding. HUD finally signed off on a "master UDAG" agreement that would allow the Housing Partnership to plug UDAG subsidies into a project without excruciating HUD review of every detail. Wylde called May 1984 a "watershed month for the program"; the $15.1 million master UDAG would provide a $15,000 federal subsidy for each of the first 1,112 units in the Housing Partnership pipeline. Having nailed down the master UDAG model, the Housing Partnership could look forward to similar UDAG approvals in the future.

On August 13, 1984, Kathryn Wylde sent HPD commissioner Anthony Gliedman a seven-page "New Homes Status Report" that summarized the status of thirty-eight New Homes sites that could hold more than 4,500 houses. Some of the sites were at an early stage of technical and market analysis; others had suffered delays related to the UDAG logjam or to various procedural and political diversions. Yet the tone of the report was one of confidence and equanimity. Several problems were identified, but they were there to be solved. Wylde's report ended on that note: "After almost two years, I believe we have a most efficient, cost-effective and credible production/financing program in place. I want to go over with you where we ended up, and what snags remain to be ironed out, so that we can 1) be assured the program is serving the objectives you laid out; and 2) get your help in clearing the remaining obstacles that add delays and costs."

The glow of optimism emanating from Wylde's August 13th report carried forward into October, when the Housing Partnership mounted a major conference on the theme "New Homes for New York Neighborhoods." Held at the Hotel Roosevelt on Madison Avenue, the day-long event attracted over 500 people, who paid $35 each to hear speeches from David Rockefeller, Mayor Ed Koch, HUD Secretary Sam Pierce, and Senator Alfonse D'Amato and to participate in panels and workshops on topics such as housing finance, construction, marketing, and neighborhood-based development by nonprofit groups.

The titles of the morning panel discussions, as listed in the draft program sent out with Rockefeller's letter of invitation, were nicely balanced between the themes of opportunity and risk. The panel for bankers would focus on "opportunities, risks and rewards for lenders"; builders and developers would hear about the "new skills required to develop housing for the marketplace with limited subsidies"; and the panel aimed at nonprofit groups would address "the options and limitations for non-profit involvement in at-risk development." The implicit message: The New Homes program is doable, even potentially profitable; just don't expect it to be easy or risk-free.

The October 1984 conference was part celebration, part public relations, part outreach tool to attract new program participants, and part momentum generator. For big-time politicians it was a chance to associate themselves with an apparent success story, and to enjoy the flattering deference of admirers and favor seekers (not easily distinguished); in so doing, of course, they were also lending credibility to an organization and program that was still a long way from completing its first house, and they were incurring some obligation to be helpful in the future.

For people who had backed the Housing Partnership idea from the beginning and played key roles in designing and advancing the New Homes program, the event gave them a platform as speakers and panelists to talk about what they had done and urge others to join in. People like John C. Nelson, a lawyer and real estate advisor to the Rockefeller family, who framed the core legal concepts defining the contractual relationships among the Housing Partnership Development Corporation, the city government, the developer/builder, and the banks; E. Virgil Conway, chairman and CEO of the Seamen's Bank for Savings, an expert on municipal finance who became the first chairman of the Housing Partnership Development Corporation; William Mooney, senior vice-president of Chemical Bank, the bank that stepped forward to risk $20 million in construction loans on early Partnership projects; Alvin Preiss, president of his own marketing firm, who saw in New Homes the "perfect product" for New York's middle-income renters aspiring to own; and R. Randy Lee, a successful lawyer/builder/developer of homes on quasi-suburban Staten Island who saw a kindred spirit in Kathy Wylde and was fascinated by the risk and challenge of building in tough neighborhoods.

Also sprinkled among the panelists and speakers were people who were more skeptical about the Housing Partnership agenda. As a case in point, HPD deputy commissioner Charles Reiss's remarks signaled much of the ambivalence that was to characterize the city's administration of the Housing Partnership's program. Calling the New Homes program "the hardest and most difficult one to get going, and to follow through to construction and occupancy" in all of the city's housing experience, Reiss cautioned that "before we all get too excited about this program, which I believe is one of the most important things that Housing Preservation and Development has been involved in, we ought to understand its limitations and its difficulties." Reiss pointed to how government programs are "hounded by lawyers who revolve around them like broken-up planets. Producing legal documents seems to take longer than the actual construction of the houses. . . . Unfortunately, most are essential." Reiss also cited several kinds of risk: the risk of a weak market in neighborhoods where no construction had taken place for at least a decade; the risk of inducing purchases by families who couldn't really afford homeownership; the risk of financing projects from multiple sources. "In many ways," Reiss said, "the banks have been more cooperative than government, ourselves [the city] included. The actual *delivery* of funds from UDAG, from the [New York City] Board of Estimate, from banks, from SONYMA [State of New York Mortgage Agency], are all separate little rivulets of funding from sources that live in their own worlds and function by their own clocks. Coordination is a death-defying feat. Combine this with uncertain construction schedules, with developers with these type of houses (because few of these houses have been built before) and we have a series of risks that are absolutely enormous. The fact that we have some 1,500 houses built or in construction under our small home programs is really nothing short of a miracle."

Reiss went on to comment on the size and quality of the homes being produced — "not what we would all like to see, not by any means" — and on the importance of community groups in marketing new housing: "The community group has a knowledge, a sense, a feel, an ability to market like no other marketing expert has." There is also, he said, "a political aspect to every site, that manifests itself most directly in terms of how much money is available to a site. . . ."

For all of the misgivings and obstacles, Reiss would wind up on a positive if somewhat paradoxical note. "Government," he said, "has traditionally stayed out of [the development] of one- and two-family homes because it is an inefficient program, given the work required to house one family. What *is* efficient is the product. No program has the capacity to so stabilize, so recreate, and so rebuild neighborhoods as the large scale development of one- and two-family homes for people who could otherwise not afford them."

The October 1984 conference was a great show and served a useful purpose in generating enthusiasm and creating a sense of momentum. Like all such gatherings, this one had its quota of hot air — but it also included considerable hard information, candid commentary, and freewheeling dialogue.

If there was a downside to the conference, it was perhaps that it tended to inflate the actual on-the-ground progress of the New Homes program and declare victory prematurely. For example, the much-celebrated first project, Windsor Terrace, with its star-studded groundbreaking and mediagenic lottery selection of homebuyers in December 1983, had not yet started construction at the time of the conference (October 1984) — and would not until July 1985. Five months later, when construction was 95 percent completed, the city Bureau of Highways refused to approve the project's paving plan, insisting among other things that the curbs be made of expensive bluestone. The dispute dragged on for several months, and the Windsor Terrace homebuyers were unable to move in until September of 1986 — almost two years after the conference.

Whatever else the conference may have accomplished, it did not — as the Windsor Terrace case confirms — signal a bright new era of efficient production for New Homes, nor did it augur a renewed spirit of comity between the Housing Partnership and city government. On the contrary, the relationship deteriorated.

The year 1985 started with a bullish outlook for New Homes production. A January 16th report to the Housing Partnership Development Corporation, prepared by Wylde for the chairman, Virgil Conway, declared: "At present, more than 30 sites that will support construction of almost 5,000 homes are being developed under HPDC. Construction is underway on six sites that will accommodate 800 homes. Our 1985 production goal is 2,000 additional homes — which will double the annual rate of private small home production in the City." As with many narrative reports on Housing Partnership progress, this one did not include a "hard" list of sites and units per site, nor did it explain such terms as "construction underway" and "production." Elusive arithmetic aside, the report appeared to point toward a goal of about 2,800 houses, to be either completed or in some stage of construction by the end of 1985. They would miss that goal by a mile.

The Elusive "Good" Sites

Blocking the way to a New Homes production breakthrough was contention between the "partners" over sites. The issue of where New Homes could, or should, be built had dogged the program from the very beginning and would persist throughout the 1980s.

At the outset of the New Homes program in 1982, the issue seemed elementary: One cannot build housing without a place to build on. The way to meet this need was also obvious, and was never questioned or debated. The city government owned sites, hundreds of them, all over the city — vacant, and unwanted for years by any profit-motivated developer. The Housing Partnership needed vacant city land to develop housing; the city wanted to give the Partnership land to develop housing. The concept was simple; execution was hell.

One issue was site value. A root principle of public policy is that government does not give away its assets for the profit of a private party; if government does not need an item any longer, it sells the asset to the highest bidder. The Housing Partnership's case for seeking city land for development rested on the notion that the land had little or no value in a market sense — that, in fact, it was a public liability in that the city had to maintain it and was not deriving any tax revenue from it. In theory, the city embraced this notion. But applying the theory to specific sites was complicated. A variation of the "Catch 22" problem could quickly come into play. The Partnership wants Site A, claiming it has no value — but wait a minute, if Site A has no value, why does the Partnership want it? Perhaps Site A is worth much more than the token $500 per lot paid the city under the New Homes program. Perhaps another developer is finally ready to step forward to pay real money to the city for the site. What's the rush?

The value of a given site depends on the three traditional criteria of the real estate industry: location, location, and location. Based on these criteria, the original list of thirty-eight sites compiled in 1982 by Kathy Wylde's site review group (which included city HPD staff) was a mixed bag. Some, which came to be known as the "good" or "strong" sites, were located fairly near existing stable neighborhoods and could be considered ripe for development. Others, known as "weak sites" and sometimes as "shit sites," were located in desolate, completely abandoned areas or had daunting topographical and environmental liabilities.

Given the choice, the Housing Partnership clearly preferred the good sites, for two reasons. First and most obviously, the Partnership sought to improve the odds that its homes would sell — hardly a foregone conclusion in the early years. But in addition, the Partnership was hopeful that its most marketable homes on good sites would generate a "profit," which would be deposited in a housing trust fund and then used to subsidize lower-income purchasers — a technique known as "cross-subsidy."

City housing commissioner at the time, Tony Gliedman, now says that he does not recall the cross-subsidy proposal: "I probably would have liked the idea if it had reached me." Still, it's clear that Gliedman took a fairly narrow view of what sites were appropriate for New Homes development. "Why would we do market rate sites with the Partnership?" he asks. Gliedman's idea of a Partnership site was "the least desirable site in the lowest income neighborhood that the banks would still be willing to finance."

From the city's perspective, therefore, the better the site, the less willing it was to turn the site over to the Housing Partnership, because of the likelihood of competing development interests. Put another way, the city's obligation to realize the highest possible return from an asset could conflict with its stated interest in promoting middle-income homeownership in cooperation with the Housing Partnership. This contradiction was the source of intense and continuing tension between the city and the Partnership.

In July 1982 Wylde's site review committee had looked at the city's list of thirty-eight proposed sites for development and had recommended six sites for launching the New Homes program. Three were in Brooklyn (Harbor Village, Atlantic Terminal, East Brooklyn), one in Manhattan (Frederick Douglass Circle), one in Queens (Merrick Boulevard/South Conduit Avenue), and one in Staten Island (Bloomingdale Road). Only three of the sites were eventually made available for development by the Partnership; the Staten Island and Queens sites and Harbor Village in Brooklyn turned out to be too "good" for the Partnership.

In March 1983 Wylde commented, in an internal memorandum, on the city's shifting position: "Theoretically, the Mayor's original commitment to the Partnership and to the concept of supporting middle income housing developments would have been based on consideration of the greater value to the City of housing development on City-owned parcels versus the income from auction sales. If such a determination was ever made, there has been considerable retrenchment." And in April 1983 — more than a year into the program — Wylde told her corporate board: "We have had difficulty in securing sites which had originally been mentioned for the Program. Those sites which have been made available are, with few exceptions, weak ones requiring extraordinary effort and financial assistance to make them 'marketable.'"

Even if agreement could be reached on site value and on the desirability of making a site available for New Homes, issues of *site control* could cause long delays. The term "city-owned land" is actually a shorthand term that masks a much more complicated reality. For a New Homes project to go forward, a site must be legally conveyed to the Housing Partnership by its partner in city government, the Department of Housing Preservation and Development (HPD). But HPD may not have jurisdiction (control) over the site; if so, another city agency must be willing to give up its own control. Initially, one of the most trouble-some agencies was the Department of Real Property, the agency that manages the sale of surplus city property. As Wylde reported in her March memo: "For the past six months, Tony [HPD Commissioner Anthony Gliedman] has been unable to deliver site control on most of the housing sites proposed by HPD for the New Homes initiative. Of 16 sites that HPD recently submitted to City Planning for ULURP/UDAAP [acronyms for land use clearances], HPD has jurisdiction over only 6. DRP [Department of Real Property] controls the balance of sites, and has refused to transfer jurisdiction to HPD." Such standoffs between city agencies should have been resolved by the Mayor's office; but, Wylde observed that "[t]his issue has been before [Deputy Mayor] Nat Leventhal for at least 2 months — apparently without decision."

If neither HPD nor the Department of Real Property controlled the site, any one of several agencies — Transportation, Economic Development, City Planning, Environmental Protection, the Board of Education — might have jurisdiction. And even if an agency *were* willing to give up control, it could take a long time (as agencies do) to decide.

Establishing site control might also encounter unforeseen legal obstacles. For example, a parcel that was assumed to be entirely city-owned might turn out to have a piece that is in fact privately owned. Even though the owner may be long dead and forgotten, the city would need to pursue time-consuming condemnation proceedings to get clear title — what if an heir suddenly appeared and claimed ownership?

Issues of site value and site control were often tied together with what might be called the *politics* of site use. One might think that any development at all of a junk covered site would be welcome. Forget it. More likely, the site has been the focus of multiple visions on the part of a variety of players — community groups, city agencies, investors, and neighbors. The debate is joined when any one development proposal appears to be headed toward implementation and then becomes a target for competing ideas: a park, a school, a commercial strip, higher-density housing. The Housing Partnership and whatever allies it can enlist must engage in a political contest to establish its product as the best possible use of a site.

In New York City, the contest is institutionalized in several levels of bureaucratic and political review, with public hearings at every level. This includes, at the neighborhood level, a community board that must review and advise with regard to every proposal for the sale and re-use of city-owned land. The community board must also hold a public hearing. Until 1989 the Board of Estimate had to follow a similar procedure — a responsibility now performed (with the demise of the Board) by the City Planning Commission. The official review process does not prevent protest meetings, picketing, or other demonstrations — always well covered by the media — on the part of those who may oppose Partnership development of a particular site.

In the game of site politics, the Housing Partnership did have some advantages: Its proposed use was, in fact, often the only feasible use of an otherwise undesirable site. In addition, the Partnership's product often proved to be popular with local politicians and community groups, who saw homeownership as a welcome sign of neighborhood improvement and stability. Even so, site politics could delay and sometimes derail what the Partnership sought to accomplish.

The procedural and political pitfalls of site selection imbued this essential step in the development process with frustrating unpredictability. In theory, at any given time, HPD and the Housing Partnership had an agreed-upon list of sites slated for New Homes development. The reality was much more complicated and contentious; in communications with HPD, Wylde sometimes put the term "list" in quotation marks, signifying the uncertain status of many sites. For example, in May 1985 Wylde prepared a twenty-one-page background report to three HPD staff members who would be working on aspects of the New Homes program. After summarizing the "program model" and discussing "generic" implementation issues, the report commented on the status of forty-eight sites, expressing the "hope that we can 'clean up' this list and restore greater discipline to the process." Thirty of the forty-eight sites were at some stage of the procedural gauntlet, and seemed reasonably certain to go forward eventually.

Wylde's accounting of these thirty sites included both successes and horror stories, rife with confusion and delay. A 210-unit project on Staten Island (Arlington) is cited as a "good illustration of what we can produce when the Builder [Sol Gillman] and Bank [Chase Manhattan] have full confidence in HPD and the Partnership, and we have clear communication with each other. From the time Commissioner Gliedman approved the site and developer, it took less than two months to achieve a full financing commitment and a construction start. . . . The builder will be delivering completed homes within 6 months."

Ironically, even this good example of "what we can produce" hit a snag within days after Wylde's memo. Sol Gillman, the Arlington site developer, had tenant harassment charges pending against him at an unrelated Queens rental development being converted to condominiums. HPD development staff knew about the charges but authorized the Housing Partnership to go ahead with Gillman anyway. At the last moment, the HPD inspector general objected to Gillman, so HPD staff refused to sign closing documents for the construction loan. Eventually, after more delay, Gillman was replaced by another developer, Stephan Jacobs.

The 98-unit Fort Greene project in Brooklyn was another tale of frustration. The site, adjacent to the Carlton Nursing Home, was ready for construction start but could not proceed, because the Housing Partnership lacked clear title to the entire parcel. The city "some years ago" had granted to the nursing home a ten-foot easement that encroached on the building site; the easement was "somehow overlooked" during the land use review process. The nursing home and HPD wrangled for months about trading the easement for a similar swath of property also adjacent to the home. The nursing home threatened litigation. "Unless the City is prepared to intervene immediately, we may end up in litigation that stops the project," Wylde said. Fort Greene had another costly problem when the Metropolitan Transit Authority belatedly got into the act because of the project's proximity to a subway line. The MTA "forced the builder to redesign foundations to their specifications before they would sign off on the release of a Building Permit. This redesign increased costs by about $100,000. . . ."

Wylde's memo cited the Park Slope site in Brooklyn as "the most extreme example of a project that has been totally confused in the identification, assemblage and disposition of the site." Elaborating on this comment, Wylde continued: "Part of the original site had been sold at auction; another part had been mistakenly sold to Fulton Park Development [another developer] . . . but not legally conveyed, so its status was unclear. The original catalyst for the site was a building sold to the Fifth Avenue Committee for rehabilitation. . . . [The building] collapsed, and was [then] intended to be demolished by the City and become a New Homes lot. However, the City has now decided that the cost and liability associated with demolition and new construction is too great, so the parcel is no longer part of the New Homes project. . . . Because of changes in the 'site,' the Developer has had to revise the original plan for three-family homes to condominiums, which has caused some (not much) local 'concern.' Another complication on part of the site was "ten feet of construction debris and rubble [making] it impossible to take borings." Wylde asked for city help in getting rid of the junk.

In addition to the thirty sites Wylde considered to be on a reasonably certain, if rocky, path to New Homes development, another group of eighteen sites reviewed in the Wylde memo had a more ambiguous status. Such a situation could come about in a variety of ways. For example, HPD would sometimes add sites to the list without consulting the Housing Partnership. As Wylde noted: "In the last UDAG quarter, HPD put several very marginal East New York sites on the Partnership 'List' with no prior review by us, the Borough President or City Planning. Is there any particular rationale for the designation of what will be difficult sites?" In other cases, a developer or community group would approach the Partnership directly about a site; if the Partnership considered it a good site, *it* would go on the list. HPD, however, felt free to remove sites from the list, as in two cases cited by Wylde.

The Creston Avenue site in the Bronx was "originally brought to the Partnership by the Northwest Bronx Clergy and HPD's East Tremont Neighborhood Preservation." Later, however, HPD advertised the site's availability to developers outside the Housing Partnership's program. Nothing happened for several months. Wylde wrote: "I have not heard anything since the RFP [request for proposals] was run some months ago, except the Clergy Coalition's continued interest that the site be developed under the Partnership program. . . . We have never had any explanation as to why this site was removed from the program, or whether it was still being considered a potential Partnership site. We had invested some time in it and have a larger 'Partnership' interest in working with the Coalition."

The second case was the Cooper Park site in Brooklyn, which was brought to the Housing Partnership by the St. Nicholas Community Corporation. "After the preliminary review," Wylde said, "we referred it to HPD. In January, we learned HPD had removed the site from the Partnership 'list' without any discussion with us or St. Nicks'. . . . Again, we would appreciate consultation on disposition of proposed sites, particularly when the larger community relations interests of the NYC Partnership may be involved. In addition, if, as with Creston Avenue, HPD is creating Homeownership projects outside the 'New Homes Program,' it is important that we at least know about it, so as to avoid misunderstanding or embarrassment."

Wylde wrapped up her forty-eight-site status report on a note of exasperation: "Well, I hope this is a sufficient update and worth ruining my weekend!"

Big Projections, Big Shortfalls

Wrangling over sites and related program issues meant that the rosy projection of big production numbers in 1985 — some 2,800 units — would fall miserably short. A tally of Housing Partnership production through June 30, *1987*, prepared by Connie Reese for Kathy Wylde, showed only 938 houses completed on thirteen sites and another 1,316 under construction on nine sites — a total of 2,254 units on twenty-two sites. Reese lists only one small 18-unit project, Mariner's Harbor on Staten Island, completed before June 30, 1985, and five others, totaling 153 units completed by June 30, 1986: Windsor Terrace in Brooklyn, Soundview I and Tiffany Fox in the Bronx, Woodhaven in Queens, and Concord I on Staten Island.

Was the Partnership's problem in 1985 an overreaching optimism — a persistent underestimation of the program's inherent complexities — or was it a problem of the city government's wavering political commitment to New Homes, combined with its lumbering, unsympathetic bureaucratic fiefdoms? Wylde's judgment of the matter was conveyed in a twelve-page memorandum to Partnership president Frank Macchiarola on October 1, 1985, whose title revealed her conclusion: "The Need for a Reaffirmation of the City's Commitment to the Housing Partnership and the New Homes Program."

Characteristically for Wylde, the memo contained a good news-bad news message. The good news was that the New Homes program had achieved a measure of success and credibility. "Initial obstacles" had been overcome. A market had been established in places where none had existed for a long time. A standardized "financing/development model" had been put in place. Federal and state subsidies had been secured. Builders, banks, elected officials, and neighborhood groups all supported the program. That was the good news — and most people would have been satisfied with it.

Not Kathy Wylde. "Despite these accomplishments, production is still not moving forward at the pace it should and there is evidence that we have made little progress toward the larger objective of making it easier for the City's private sector, alone or in tandem with government, to efficiently produce moderately priced housing." The problem, in a word, was production.

Wylde had designed a production model, she had seen it work, she saw the possibilities, she wanted more, and she wasn't getting it. "Ironically," she wrote, "just as an efficient public/private development model seemed achievable, we find that the City processes have bogged down." Production was proving to be elusive.

Wylde's report to Macchiarola summarized the obstacles to production under three broad categories. The first was a straightforward problem of managerial coordination: The city has "multiple agencies, authorities and processes that impact on development, and has proved unable to impose an efficient, centralized system on the process." This was a case of the city being at war with its own interests — wanting large-scale development of moderate-income housing, but lacking the ability to harness its multiple and dispersed power centers. The solution should be rational and technical — better management systems, better managers.

The second category of problems Wylde laid out was not managerial but political: "[t]he City's seeming inability to insulate the development process from political factors that interrupt or derail production initiatives making it difficult to sustain a predictable public-private development program." What this meant was that the city's primary goal was not simply "production" in all cases. Other "political" motives might intervene — the desire to reward or curry favor with a well-connected developer, to hold a Housing Partnership project hostage to other related (or unrelated) projects, to play one community group off against another. If these diversions "interrupt[ed] or derail[ed] production," then so be it; "political factors" would take precedence.

Presumably, political factors are generally injected by politicians — chiefly elected and appointed officials. But Wylde also identified a third category of problems endemic to the ranks of city government itself: "[t]he underlying adversarial relationship between the City's public and private sectors, that particularly permeates the municipal bureaucracy, and undermine [sic] good faith 'partnership' efforts." This was not a problem of management in the technical sense, nor of politics — "production" losing out to competing priorities; rather, this was a problem of attitude, or what management theorists might call organizational culture. In this context, Wylde appropriately put "partnership" in quotation marks, recognizing that the notion itself was highly suspect and a little

phony to the typical bureaucrat. After all, the very point of public authority was to prevent or correct irresponsible conduct by "the private sector": to control land use, to protect the environment, to guard against
unsafe buildings, and the like. The mantle of bureaucratic rectitude —
and the shield of civil service protection against getting fired — give the
agency officials the license to say: "We will do things in our own way
and in our own time. We do not snap to attention or jump through hoops,
for David Rockefeller or for anyone else."

All three types of problems, according to Wylde, would yield to
determined leadership and direction from the Mayor and the commissioner of Housing Preservation and Development. She contrasted the
program's situation in late 1985 with the early days: "At the Program's
inception, the highly publicized Mayoral interest in the 'Housing Partnership' [those quotation marks again] seemed to make the wheels of
City bureaucracy move with unusual speed. This was gradually noted
by banks and builders, whose initial cynicism as to the City's ability to
do things differently with the Housing Partnership abated, allowing the
Program to achieve a measure of success." This had changed, Wylde
said. "Despite strong Mayoral and Commissioner-level commitments to
a 'Partnership' program model, the implementation of a successful production program must take place at a staff level across multiple agencies. . . . There is no longer a sense of a 'fast track' for Partnership
projects and agency attitudes generally reflect the view that any concessions or support they give New Homes projects are 'favors' to the private
participants, rather than emanating from a Mayoral commitment to a priority program."

Problems began to pile up, Wylde said, "as the Program became
increasingly visible and moved from conceptualization to production,"
which prompted "growing tension over who 'controls' the Program."
The original program concept was a division of labor between the Housing Partnership and the city along these lines: The Housing Partnership
would screen and select builders, help arrange private financing, oversee
preliminary site planning, determine market feasibility, and contract with
community sponsors for neighborhood support and marketing. The city,
through HPD as lead agency, would select sites and convey them to the
Partnership, review and ratify builder selection, help coordinate and expedite public agency approvals across city government, and make allocations of public funds for site preparation and housing subsidies. In

short, a neat division between "private" and "public" roles, with the parties jointly committed to New Homes production.

It wasn't working out that way, at least not consistently. According to Wylde, a curious reversal of public and private roles had evolved. "As it turns out, our [Housing Partnership] staff is doing most of the legal, technical and inter-agency coordination/advocacy work and HPD's staff is increasingly trying to assume the 'development' and 'financing' decisions." Elaborating on this point, Wylde argued that "HPD staff have sought to greatly expand their original level of involvement in aspects of the Program related to the selection of developers, design of projects, interface with the community, and the specifics of project cost." In other words, Wylde saw the city as meddling in areas it had little aptitude for. The city also did not sufficiently appreciate, she believed, that since almost every Housing Partnership project involved about 80 percent at-risk private financing, it was under an obligation to put such projects on a "fast track." Let the city take its sweet time on 100 percent public subsidy programs, where the private risk is zero, but not on the mostly private Partnership projects, where delay could mean loss or ruin.

The bulk of Wylde's report was taken up with specific examples illustrating her general line of argument. She pointed to the 18-unit Mariner's Harbor development on Staten Island, where the completed houses sat vacant for five months, waiting for water and sewer hookups because of a prolonged wrangle between HPD and the city budget office over the contract for building the water and sewer main. For two projects in East Harlem, the Housing Partnership recommended a single developer from its list of well-qualified builders, but HPD pressured the Partnership to add a second builder — who, it turned out, was in default on an unrelated tax syndication deal; both projects were held up for six months until the syndication problem could be resolved. The Springfield Gardens project in Queens was delayed for almost a year because city planners, in their standard land use review, had overlooked the fact that mapped streets (that were never built) running through the site were not owned by the city. The discovery was made just before the builder was ready to start, but construction had to wait while the city pursued a lengthy condemnation process.

In addition to avoidable glitches on specific projects, Wylde reported every part of the process seemed to be slowing down. It took up to ten weeks for city lawyers to review routine, standardized closing documents, and another two to four weeks just to collect signatures.

"Precertification" of sites — an open-ended environmental review that preceded the time-limited Uniform Land Use Review Process (ULURP) — was stretching out for several months, in contrast to the early days of the New Homes program, when eleven sites were precertified in only six weeks. And HPD staff reviews of builder selection, project design, and community sponsors — which used to take about three months per project — were taking six months to a year.

For Wylde, the usual way of dealing with screwups and maddening delays at the staff level would be to go higher up and appeal to the HPD commissioner to intervene. However, as Wylde complained to Macchiarola, her direct access to Tony Gliedman had been cut off. "Communication is almost entirely limited to junior staff, with occasional contacts with the Assistant Commissioner, and with the Deputy Commissioner for Development, and no direct access to the Commissioner (who refers us back to the Assistant Commissioner on most issues)."

Wylde had "expected 1985 to be a banner year," but it was ending on a note of disappointment and high frustration. As Wylde wrote First Deputy Mayor Stanley Brezenoff, city approval of Housing Partnership projects "came to a halt" in August 1985 due to "policy/jurisdictional issues" among the Board of Estimate and a variety of city agencies. "The Mayor's commitment to affordable housing," she wrote, "must filter down and be reflected at the very 'bottom' of the bureaucracy who exercise wide discretion and control over the approvals processing, scope of work and, ultimately, the cost and pace of development."

For the Housing Partnership, the next couple of years would be better; paradoxically, they would also be worse. They would be better in the sense that the New Homes program would finally break through in production terms. But they would be worse in that the relationship between the Housing Partnership and the city would become still more contentious.

10

THE KOCH HOUSING PLAN: REACHING FOR NEW "PARTNERS"

In November 1985 the voters of New York City made sure of one thing: There would be no new face in the Mayor's office. Ed Koch, at what turned out to be the peak of his popularity, was re-elected for a third term with 75 percent of the vote. He would soon announce plans for housing that were as big as his margin of victory: On Christmas Eve, 1985, Koch challenged thirty-three of New York's largest developers to work with the city to build tens of thousands of middle-income housing units, and in April 1986 he announced a plan to commit $4.2 billion over a ten-year period to build or rehabilitate 252,000 units, mainly for lower-income families. At the Department of Housing Preservation and Development a new team of mayoral appointees would take over to lead the Mayor's housing initiatives. Ironically, Koch would at the same time begin to lose his political grip on the Mayor's office as messy scandals erupted around him; these were largely unrelated to housing programs, but they created a siege mentality affecting how the city managed its housing (and all other) affairs. The combination of these events would impact on the Housing Partnership in complex ways.

By the time of Koch's 1985 re-election, the New York City economy had rebounded smartly, benefiting from the 1980s economic expansion and a boom in the securities, banking, and construction industries. In 1975, Governor Hugh Carey had grimly declared that the "times of plenty, days of wine and roses are over," but by the mid-eighties the wine was flowing and the economy was in bloom. With the city budget in reasonably good shape, Koch resolved to attack housing problems across a broad front. He was under intense pressure to take action against the city's most visible and embarrassing housing problems: the growing homeless population and the huge stock of city-owned *in rem* rental buildings, consisting of both vacant, vandalized shells and occupied older buildings that had been abandoned by their private owners. Homeless families, for lack of an alternative, were often put up at city expense in notorious "welfare hotels," rundown former hotels that had long ago ceased to serve the traditional traveler. Families living in the city's *in rem* buildings were generally a step up in income level compared to the homeless, but were still overwhelmingly low-income and unable to afford market rents. To house these target groups would require 100 percent public funding of the capital cost, mainly for rehabilitation. Since federal programs for subsidized construction had been shut down during the Reagan administration, Koch's only funding alternative was the city budget, with minor participation from the state.

It was clear that Koch needed to concentrate on housing for lower-income families, primarily through various rehabilitation strategies. But he also wanted to greatly expand the city's sponsorship of "middle-income" housing, defined as housing for those with household incomes ranging from $15,000 to $48,000. Middle-income housing would be primarily new construction as opposed to rehabilitation, and would also involve some undefined combination of limited public subsidy and private investment rather than full public funding. This was, of course, programmatic territory already occupied by the Housing Partnership. The obvious course for Koch would have been to crank up the volume on the stalled Housing Partnership program, but he chose instead to go in a different direction.

In December 1985, Koch sent a letter to thirty-three of the city's largest developers, tossing them a challenge: You tell me, he said, what the city needs to do to stimulate large-scale affordable housing production for people in the $15,000-to-$48,000-income range. The challenge went to the developers of skyscrapers and huge luxury apartment buildings and condominiums, not to the small homebuilders from Queens and Staten Island that were being drawn into the New Homes program; and the scale the mayor had in mind was 10,000 units a year, not the several hundred units that were being built annually by the Housing Partnership — which was overlooked on the Mayor's mailing list.

To develop a "unity" response, the recipients of Koch's letter turned to the major organizations representing New York's real estate interests: the Real Estate Board of New York (REBNY), the Owners and Builders Association, and the Rent Stabilization Association. REBNY assumed the leading role in organizing the developers' response. REBNY staff, in turn, approached Kathy Wylde and the Housing Partnership "to supply the component of the response dealing with residential construction costs, building and code reform." Wylde saw the Mayor's gambit as an opportunity to mobilize a powerful real estate constituency behind the cost-cutting administrative and regulatory reforms that she had been advocating from a narrower base at the Housing Partnership. She also saw a possible role for the Housing Partnership in financing and developing projects that might flow from the Mayor's initiative.

In March 1986 the "unity" response from REBNY went back to the Mayor, urging among other things an end to rent control, streamlined processing by city agencies, building code revisions, changes in union work rules, and zoning reforms. As they submitted their wish list, the developers also threw down a surprise challenge of their own to the Mayor: Remove these costly obstacles to development, they said, and we will build 3,000 units of affordable housing without taking any profit, or any public subsidy except land. According to the *New York Times*, the proposal was "hailed by both developers and the city as a breakthrough, a sign of serious commitment by all parties to clear the economic and administrative obstacles that for years have made it virtually impossible to make a profit by building middle income housing on a large scale."

Acting on behalf of the developers, REBNY set about working with the city to identify building sites. The Housing Partnership, according to Wylde, "assisted REBNY with site identification and analysis (raising no objection when the City offered REBNY development rights on some of the best sites that had been committed to the Partnership New Homes Program) and advised REBNY's staff and the City on alternatives for financing their project. We provided most of the documentation, including legal, organizational, and cost models for the REBNY program, as we have for . . . many other affordable housing initiatives."

To deliver on their promise of 3,000 units, the developers would need a nonprofit entity to oversee financing arrangements and production. Wylde argued that "[G]iven the overlapping membership and objectives [of REBNY and the Partnership] it would be counterproductive to mount another private sector middle income housing initiative that could potentially place the Partnership and REBNY in competition for limited sites and funding resources." Initially, Wylde believed she had a deal with RE-BNY and the city. As she wrote Partnership president Frank Macchiarola on April 14: "Another positive event is the decision of the City and the Real Estate industry to use the Housing Partnership as the non-profit vehicle for the production of the 3,000 units that major developers have promised the Mayor they will build on a 'pro bono' basis. . . . We have been working with the Mayor's new Special Assistant for Housing [Abraham Biderman] and the Real Estate Board to flesh out this Program and to negotiate the required reform in City policy. It seems the public relations value of this program has been attractive enough to City Hall to make some real breakthroughs in City policies and to free up some of those large and attractive development sites that have eluded Partnership Homes up to now." Wylde's optimism, however, turned out to be premature.

As the Koch middle-income housing initiative was playing itself out, the Mayor announced on April 30, 1986, a huge new city commitment to housing — $4.2 billion in mainly city capital funds to rehabilitate or build 252,000 units over a ten-year period. The Mayor's "plan" was not tied to specific programs; a decade later, a Housing Partnership report would comment that "New York's . . . housing initiative . . . offered up land, buildings and funding to virtually anyone with a credible and politically attractive proposal for solving some aspect of the urban housing problem." But the Mayor's April 30th announcement did state in broad terms the income groups to be served and the estimated number of units going to each group: Half (125,000) of the units would serve families earning less than $15,000 annually, and most of the other half would go to families in the $15,000-$24,000 range; only about 30,000 units would be for families earning more than $24,000, a category that was to include the Housing Partnership's New Homes program.

Koch's burst of housing activism coincided with changes in key personnel. At the Department of Housing Preservation and Development, a new management team took over. In February Tony Gliedman resigned as commissioner to take a job with New York mega-developer Donald Trump; Koch appointed city finance commissioner Paul A. Crotty to replace Gliedman. Crotty brought in Mark Willis with him from the Finance Department to be deputy HPD commissioner. Within the Mayor's office itself, Koch created a new position, special assistant for housing, and named Abe Biderman to the post. (Two years later, Biderman would succeed Crotty at HPD.)

Before leaving HPD, Gliedman responded to Housing Partnership pressure by establishing an Office of Homeownership Programs, with specific responsibility for New Homes and the vestiges of the federal 235 homeownership program. To head the new office, Gliedman recruited Meredith Kane, a young attorney who took a leave from the blue-chip Manhattan law firm of Paul, Weiss, Rifkind, Wharton and Garrison. Kane worked at HPD for almost two years before returning to her firm. For the Partnership, the new office would fall short as a cure-all, but it was a definitely positive step.

"When I started at HPD, Kathy had been pushing hard for higher production," Kane recalls. "Only a few projects were moving and everything else was stalled. Kathy wanted volume."

"Nobody Trusted Anybody Anywhere"

Kane vividly remembers her first day at HPD because of an event that had nothing directly to do with housing programs or policy, but would dramatically alter the political and management climate surrounding the New Homes program — and make "volume" that much tougher to achieve.

Early on the morning of January 10, 1986, New York police pulled over a car weaving erratically on Grand Central Parkway in Queens near Shea Stadium. The driver was Donald R. Manes, the borough president of Queens and chairman of the Queens Democratic Party organization. Manes was bleeding from slash wounds in his wrist and ankle. Near death from loss of blood, he was rushed to Booth Memorial Medical Center for emergency surgery and treatment. The next morning, Mayor Koch was one of the first people at the bedside of his "good friend."

Three days after the incident, Manes told police a bizarre tale of abduction by two unknown men who had forced him to drive around Queens for hours. The police were skeptical; they believed that Manes had been alone and that his cuts were self-inflicted. A week later, Manes admitted from his hospital bed that they were.

Manes's strange suicide attempt soon lost its mystery. He had known that federal investigators were closing in and would show him to be at the center of a multi-million-dollar bribery and extortion scheme involving city contracts with private firms to collect overdue parking fines. Manes and his friend, Geoffrey G. Lindenauer, deputy director of the city Parking Violations Bureau, routinely demanded tens of thousands of dollars in payoffs from collection firms in return for lucrative city contracts. Manes and Lindenauer also engineered a $22.3 million city contract with a company called Citisource, Inc., to develop a portable hand-held computer for use by parking enforcement agents. Citisource had no obvious qualifications for the task except that Manes was a concealed part-owner of the company. The Citisource deal also drew in Stanley M. Friedman, Democratic Party leader in the Bronx, who received $750,000 in Citisource stock for helping grease city approval of the contract. As details of the scandal piled up, Manes resigned (on February 11) as borough president and Democratic chairman. A month later, Lindenauer pleaded guilty to extortion and mail fraud and agreed to give evidence against Manes and other city officials. On March 13, three days after Lindenauer's guilty plea, Manes took his own life with a kitchen knife in his Queens home.

The pathetic self-execution of Donald Manes punctuated what was to become a chain of scandalous revelations reaching into numerous city agencies and touching dozens of elected and appointed officials. The brazenness and extent of the corruption shook the Koch administration to its foundations as details of the scandals filled the media for months. Koch himself was never implicated in any wrongdoing, but many of his political allies, friends, and appointees were in it up to their necks. As Koch frantically sought to control the damage, his usually endearing cockiness turned to self-criticism, penitence, and a resolve to clean up the mess. "I am embarrassed, I am chagrined, I am absolutely mortified that this kind of corruption could have existed and that I did not know of it," Koch said. He acknowledged that he had become "too close" to some of his political allies in the Democratic organization and that he had permitted them to wield "undue influence" on city contracts and on patronage appointments to key government jobs. He pledged to rid the city of the "cancer" of corruption.

Koch's response to scandal was to follow a fairly well-defined road map for well-intentioned political leaders who discover or inherit a pattern of abuses of public trust. It is not enough to replace crooks with honest people. Typically, an entire system for making decisions, particularly decisions involving public money, is discredited as too vulnerable to venal influence. Political damage control, therefore, demands additional checkpoints and layers of review that cannot be tampered with, that are above suspicion. This usually means centralizing many operating decisions that previously were delegated to lower levels of administration. Ultimately, if you are a Mayor, the only way to be absolutely sure a decision is uncorrupted is to make it yourself — or, failing that, to entrust it to people you know to be incorruptible. Koch decided, among other things, to set up a special five-member screening committee to recommend the most qualified candidates for city boards and commissions; he personally would make the final selection, without the usual input from party bosses. He also created a contract review committee, headed by a deputy mayor, that would be responsible for reviewing and approving all city contracts obligating the city to pay more than $10,000 — an exceedingly low threshold for a multi-billion dollar operation like the City of New York.

The impacts of the Mayor's procedural safeguards followed a predictable path. Initially, the new machinery itself and the atmosphere of fear and defensiveness that permeated agency bureaucracies had the effect of slowing decisions to a crawl. The system choked up; actions were delayed; very little was getting done.

Eventually, Koch's safeguards were to suffer the fate of all such attempts to centralize a multitude of discrete decisions. As any Management 101 text will explain, the volume of pending actions sooner or later overwhelms the capacity of the central control point to respond. To avoid a near-paralysis in the flow of decisions, there are not many options. One is to turn the control point into a rubber stamp; this speeds up the process, but also undermines the very purpose for imposing an extra level of review in the first place. For example, the *New York Times* reported in August 1986 that the Mayor's contract review committee was "catching up" on its backlog of thousands of decisions that had built up since its creation in January. After being "badly stalled earlier in the year," the committee was whittling down the backlog by "often [deciding] on more than 600 issues in one session." This is "review"? The other management choice is to redelegate most decision-making authority back to the operating agencies and try to make sure that the people there are honest. Competence also helps.

In post-scandal politics, the inexorable logic of decentralized management eventually overcomes the initial centralizing reflex. But the transition process can take quite a long time and is likely to be bumpy, as paranoia subsides and administrative and political arrangements gradually sort themselves out into a more normal pattern.

For the Housing Partnership, the scandals of 1986 and their aftermath superimposed an additional layer of complexity on a program that had already been struggling to break through administrative and regulatory gridlock. In the New Homes program, the Housing Partnership had largely dominated the process of selecting builders who would benefit from city subsidies and would build on city-owned land. Suddenly, the city approvals required to move ahead on specific projects were lumped in with all other city contracts and had to be scrutinized for the slightest possible taint. The Mayor also created a special land disposition review committee chaired by a deputy mayor, Robert Esnard. The Partnership had to compile a mountain of documentation to support the transfer of every proposed site. And after the committee signed off, the process was repeated by the Board of Estimate. "They were very tough. Everything was being examined," recalls Meredith Kane. "Nobody trusted anybody anywhere."

Problems at HPD were compounded by the turnover in the commissioner's post. Although Housing Partnership president Kathy Wylde had often complained about Tony Gliedman's mixed support of the New Homes program, they had also fought side by side to get vitally needed subsidy funds from HUD and the state. At bottom, they got on quite well and respected each other. Not so with respect to Gliedman's successor, Paul Crotty. Crotty and Wylde tangled in what Kane called "a fight for control" of the New Homes program.

"Crotty did not trust Wylde," recalls Kane. Wylde always believed that she knew who the "good builders" were, based on their track record of delivering a quality product without big cost overruns or other problems. But "nobody knew where the Housing Partnership builders came from," says Kane. "Given the political climate at the time, Crotty felt he could not simply say to the deputy mayor that a builder was the Housing Partnership's choice. Each builder designation required an exhaustive, elaborate justification. There had to be an absolutely clean procedure."

Quite apart from post-scandal slowdowns, Wylde continued her criticism of New York City's costly and convoluted approval process for housing. Some of these criticisms got into the newspapers — which further undermined her relationship with Crotty. Wylde says she never sought out reporters in order to attack HPD publicly. "What am I supposed to do?" Wylde shrugs. "Reporters call me and ask me questions. All I do is answer them factually."

In May of 1986, Mayor Koch established an Office of Housing Coordination that reported directly to deputy mayor Robert Esnard. Jody Kass, who went to work in the new office and later joined the Housing Partnership staff, recalls that "many people, including me, think the office was set up because of Kathy." The housing coordination office was intended to prod city agencies into acting more quickly and to resolve interagency disagreements. This set up an interesting tension. Responding to scandals, the Mayor had set up one piece of machinery to give extra scrutiny to pending actions, which meant slowing things down. A few months later, the Mayor — responding to criticism of a laggard bureaucracy — created the housing coordination office to speed things up. It was all part of what the Mayor would refer to as "a delicate balance." Referring to the post-scandal mood in city agencies, Koch said, "It's both good and bad. . . . It's good because you can never be too cautious. The bad part is if commissioners, as a result of the environment, are too cautious and slow things down." The Office of Housing Coordination was a sign that Koch wanted to pick up the pace of housing production, as well as stave off criticism from the Housing Partnership and other nonprofit groups that the city was stifling housing development.

The new housing office and the Housing Partnership got off to a testy start. At a May 23rd, 1986, meeting in the Mayor's office, David Rockefeller told Koch that the "complex and lengthy regulatory process that encumbers residential construction in New York City adds as much as 30% to the price of new housing." The Mayor's people countered that the city's high construction costs were mostly driven by higher than average prices for land, materials, and labor — factors pretty much beyond the control of the city government. Wylde commented on the issue four days later in a follow-up memo requested by Partnership president Frank Macchiarola. Macchiarola forwarded Wylde's three-page memo to the Mayor with a cordial "Dear Ed" cover note; the Mayor handed it off to his deputy mayor for physical development, Robert Esnard, and to the housing coordinator, Susan Wagner. About three weeks later (on June

24), Esnard sent Macchiarola a note and an attached three-page rejoinder to Wylde, prepared by Wagner and by Stuart Klein of the Office of Housing Coordination. The Wagner/Klein memo was a defensive yelp that referred to Wylde's memo with such phrases as "glaring . . . inaccuracies," "unclear, at best," and "unreasonable and unfair."

Wylde's memo was the sort she could write in her sleep; over the years she had written many versions of essentially the same memo making essentially the same point: that the city needed to get its bureaucratic house in order if it really wanted to stimulate affordable housing production at lower cost to developers and consumers. Even before joining the Housing Partnership, for example, Wylde had drafted a position paper for the New York Building Congress noting that the city had "created literally dozens of authorities and kibitzers, with often contradictory notions of design, environmental factors, financial considerations and public interest." Her May 1986 memo to Macchiarola had a less contentious tone and was adapted to address the specific cost issue suggested by David Rockefeller.

The easiest way to demonstrate New York's 30 percent cost difference, Wylde wrote Macchiarola, was to compare the price of two identical three-bedroom modular houses built in a Pennsylvania factory, with one to be installed in New Jersey and the other in New York City. The manufacturer can produce such a house for about $40,000. "The New Jersey house is completed and delivered to a homebuyer in six months at a price of $70,000; the New York house is completed and delivered in 15 months at a price of $93,000 (both exclusive of land cost)." This comparison, Wylde said, "supports the conclusion that the City's extraordinary housing costs are less a factor of labor, materials or land costs than of time and bureaucracy." The memo then shifted away from the modular housing case and elaborated on the "time and bureaucracy" themes, with a recital of "[k]ey factors in the extraordinary costs of new housing in New York City."

Wylde divided these key factors into two categories: the *predevelopment* process (the period from site identification)" and the *"construction* period (from Building permit to Certificate of Occupancy)." Predevelopment, according to Wylde, took an average of two years, depending on the number of separate approvals required for a specific project. In the meantime, a builder would need to absorb the high cost of "architectural, engineering, legal and expeditor fees to prepare, negotiate, and redesign special submissions for each agency with jurisdiction over development." ("Expeditors" are people paid to stand in line in city agencies to get needed approvals for projects.) Once a development is ready to break ground, the construction period "typically ranges from 14 to 30 months," again depending on the specific project, the number of agencies that get into the act, and the time they take to decide. Wylde's memo gave a sampling of agency jurisdictions during the construction period: "the Departments of Sanitation (fill and dump permits), Transportation (sidewalks, curbs, paving, street construction), Environmental Protection (sewers, drainage, water meters), Parks (tree removal), Bureaus of Electrical Supply and Plumbing (hookups, code compliance), Fire (access, hydrants, code compliance), City Planning (compliance with restrictive declarations), the MTA [Metropolitan Transit Authority] (approval in 'area of influence' of subways), Finance (tax assessments, abatements and tax lot subdivisions), Buildings (controlled inspections, code compliance)."

Because of "this maze of multiple approvals and discretionary authorities," builders must pad their construction budgets to allow for unpredictable delays, according to Wylde. The long construction period increases the cost of borrowing, the cost of securing the building site against vandalism, and the cost of labor. All of this is then factored into higher housing prices with "a profit margin sufficient to justify excessive risk and time associated with a development project."

Wylde's memo to Macchiarola was more a description of the general climate for housing production in New York than a catalog of gripes about how the Housing Partnership was being hassled by the city; the Housing Partnership in fact was not even mentioned until the very last paragraph, and then it was to make the point that the Partnership was having some success in bringing costs down and getting builders to accept less profit by absorbing "pro bono" much of the predevelopment and construction period expenses. "This effort," Wylde said, "suggests that it is possible for the City to significantly enhance its competitive position in residential construction with a focused effort to streamline and manage both its predevelopment and construction approval process."

At City Hall, Wylde's memo was taken as a broadside attack rather than as an appeal to the new housing coordination office to seize the chance to "streamline and manage" the city's development process better. So the Mayor's housing people struck back; they made the case that New York's high costs were mainly the result of higher prices for land, materials, and labor. Citing comparative data on these cost factors, the Wagner/Klein memo concluded: "Accordingly, it is the consensus of most leading experts that cost differentials cannot be solely attributed to processing delays and, in fact, were very much a function of labor, materials and site development." This was, of course, not an argument Wylde had advanced, since her memo focused entirely on the *additional* costs imposed by the regulatory maze — over and above any other cost differentials that might apply to New York. Wagner and Klein called "unreasonable and unfair" Wylde's example of a 33 percent price difference between the same modular house delivered from a Pennsylvania factory to New York City and New Jersey. They suggested that Wylde may have been comparing "a suburban environment" with a more complex urban environment — Wylde's memo had not specified the location in New Jersey. Then came the classic defense of bureaucracy at bay: "The density, infrastructure needs, fire dangers, traffic congestion, etc. are part of the urban environment and city procedures to mitigate the impact of construction are not 'bureaucratic' obstacles, but necessary services that the government must provide its citizens." To be sure, Wagner and Klein did acknowledge that "some unnecessary delays exist which tend to increase the cost of housing construction in New York City," but these were not the main problem, and besides, the housing coordination office was set up to deal with them: "[T]he work needed to improve the system and promote the construction of affordable housing has already begun."

Wylde chose not to return fire in this skirmish by memo but did send Macchiarola a few comments, noting with some irony: "Susan [Wagner] and Stuart [Klein] present a well-researched discussion of cost issues not raised in my memo. I focused on those areas of cost that the City might be able to do something about. It would have been useful if the rejoinder had seriously evaluated the issues I raised, relating to factors *other* than labor, materials and land. . . ." Wylde also called "the defensive tone of Susan and Stuart's memo really disheartening. The Partnership has, for the past four years, struggled without much overt encouragement to get some housing built." The housing coordination office, which Wylde had viewed "as a long-awaited and very positive response by City Hall," was not turning out to be the aggressive bureaucracy-shaker she had hoped for.

David Rockefeller draws the name of the winning buyer of the first home in the Housing Partnership's inaugural project in Windsor Terrace, Brooklyn, in December 1983. New York City Partnership President Frank Macchiarola (in hat), Governor Mario Cuomo, and U.S. Senator Alfonse D'Amato look on.

The Windsor Terrace project, consisting of seventeen two-family homes financed by Chemical (now Chase) Bank, were completed and sold in 1984 for $115,000. Their value a decade later exceeds $250,000.

E. Virgil Conway, David Rockefeller, and Kathryn Wylde at the 1984 citywide housing conference organized by the Housing Partnership. Conway, then CEO of Seaman's Bank for Savings, was recruited by Rockefeller to chair the board of the nonprofit development corporation established to carry out the New Homes program.

Mayor Ed Koch opens 1983 Housing Partnership Conference. Seated from left, E. Virgil Conway, David Rockefeller, and Alvin Preiss, a marketing executive who helped design the New Homes marketing strategy.

Mayor Ed Koch, HPD Commissioner Abraham Biderman and Staten Island Borough President Ralph Lamberti at opening of new homes in the Stapleton section of Staten Island in 1989.

The Partnership's first two-family homes in the South Bronx were built on an urban renewal site in Hunts Point, cleared 15 years earlier after fires swept the area and blocks of tenements were condemned and leveled.

Rev. Congressman Floyd Flake, the pastor of Allen AME Church and founder of redevelopment efforts in South East Queens, Borough President Claire Shulman, and Deborah McCaffity, Executive Director of Allen Community Development Corp., lead the dedication of Partnership homes in South Jamaica.

Preston Robert Tisch, Chairman of the New York City Partnership from 1988-92, joins homebuilder Michael Dubb, Kathryn Wylde, and City Councilman Victor Robles at the opening ceremony for Partnership new homes in East Williamsburg, Brooklyn, in 1988.

Herman Bernstein Assoc.

Before and After: Urban renewal site at the northwest corner of Central Park at the gateway to Harlem that lay vacant for 20 years. Towers on the Park, the Housing Partnership's only high rise development with 600 condominium apartments, opened in 1987.

Harvey Wang

Heron Pond condominium apartments, built on the North Shore of Staten Island, a project that included reclamation of a protected wetland.

Deborah Wright (left), a former investment banker who joined the Housing Partnership in 1987, at a Neighborhood Builder project developed by Marge and Raleigh Hall (center) with "veteran builder" Eli Bluestone, who served as a mentor for the Halls on their first Partnership project.

Les Levi, Neighborhood Builder, congratulates new homeowners at Mt. Pisgah Partnership Homes in Bedford-Stuyvesant as Tom Osterman, Kathy Wylde, HPD officials, Assemblyman Al Vann and others look on.

New homeowners celebrate dedication of the Mt. Pisgah Partnership homes.

Community celebrations at the completion of a Housing Partnership project showcase the pride of homeownership.

Before and After: The cleared tract that became the site for one of dozens of Partnership developments that reintroduced homeownership in the South Bronx. Composite photos of 109 two-family homes built by R. Randy Lee in the West Farms section of the South Bronx between 1991 and 1994.

Harvey Wang

Manufactured modular housing produced by Deluxe Homes of Berwick, Pennsylvania, is erected on Vyse Avenue in the South Bronx in 1990.

L. Racioppo / NYC-HPD

Completion of Partnership homes are typically a neighborhood celebration. The school choir dedicated Rivercourt Partnership Homes, 33 two-family homes on Vyse Avenue in the South Bronx (1992).

Joan Vitale Strong

In 1990, Edmund T. Pratt (second from left), former Chairman and CEO of Pfizer Inc., who led that company's efforts to revitalize the Brooklyn community surrounding their original plant, was joined by Mayor David Dinkins (center), E. Virgil Conway (left), Kathryn Wylde, and other officials at the groundbreaking for a New Homes development.

L. Racioppo / NYC-HPD

Lloyd Price, 50s rock 'n' roll singer, was a co-developer of new homes in the Bronx which, appropriately, were dedicated with a musical event.

Before and After: Thurston Plaza II Partnership Homes, 49 two-family homes in the Crotona Park section of the South Bronx, were completed in October 1992. A South Bronx-based developer, the Procida Organization, built the housing with financing from Chase Bank.

Longwood Avenue Partnership Homes, 50 two-family homes adjacent to the Longwood Historic District in the South Bronx. Developed under the Neighborhood Builder Program by Desmond Emanuel, whose family immigrated to the Bronx from Antigua. Completed August 1994.

Mayor David Dinkins cuts the ribbon to 44 new homes in the South Bronx built by the Velez Organization under the Partnership's Neighborhood Builder Program (1992).

Before and After: In Bedford-Stuyvesant, Brooklyn, development of 50 two-family homes was completed by Full Spectrum, an African-American-owned company that became a homebuilder through the Partnership's Neighborhood Builder Program.

Governor Mario Cuomo joins Kathryn Wylde and John Mascotte (left of center), Chairman of the Housing Partnership from 1988-94, and representatives of international banks to announce a new $75 million public-private financing initiative for the Housing Partnership New Homes Program known as GRAND.

Fannie Mae Chairman James Johnson joins Mayor Rudolph Giuliani, who continued the commitment to homeownership and the Housing Partnership. Deborah Wright, Giuliani's first Housing Commissioner, joins in the announcement of a new homeownership funding initiative.

In 1995, Mayor Rudolph Giuliani led the ribbon-cutting ceremony for New Homes in Bushwick, Brooklyn, where he was joined by local elected officials and neighborhood residents.

New homeowners at their completed two-family homes in Bushwick.

REBNY Strikes Out

The squabbling and finger-pointing between the Mayor's office and the Housing Partnership carried over into the middle-income housing initiative Koch had launched with the city's big developers, who had promised to deliver 3,000 units on a nonprofit basis in exchange for city concessions on rent control and regulatory streamlining. The developers were dealing with the city through the Real Estate Board of New York (REBNY), but the Housing Partnership was cooperating by feeding REBNY analyses of regulatory roadblocks and recommendations for reform. The Partnership also expected to be the nonprofit development vehicle that was needed to carry out the initial 3,000-unit demonstration; this would show what scale in housing production could be achieved when the city and major developers joined hands — and thousands more dwelling units would surely follow.

It didn't work out that way. REBNY staff began holding separate meetings with city staff without Wylde's knowledge. Eventually, the word filtered back to her "that REBNY staff felt they had negotiated a 'better deal' with the City and did not want us [the Partnership] involved with their program in any substantive way." For a mixture of reasons and motives, the Housing Partnership had been dealt out.

Part of the problem was a fundamental difference between REBNY and the Partnership about how financial risk should be distributed and shared. The Housing Partnership program model called for the builder/developer to personally guarantee a construction loan and the cost of project construction; the builder must perform as promised or pay the price. The REBNY people, in contrast, wanted the city and the banks to provide construction loans without having developers share financial responsibility if something went wrong. Under the REBNY model, the builders would receive a fixed fee for completing projects at an agreed-upon price, whether that price was actually achieved or not. In that sense, REBNY did offer a "better deal" to its big developers, but the deal also exposed the city and any banks involved to the real danger of cost overruns.

Still, the city was willing to throw in with REBNY. The Mayor had made a grandstand play for fast, large-scale action on middle-income housing, and the big developers had responded with a grandstand play of · their own. At HPD, the new commissioner, Paul Crotty, saw the Housing Partnership, with its clientele of small homebuilders and its scattered projects, as a "boutique" operation incapable of playing in the big leagues. Crotty's deputy, Mark Willis, who came over with Crotty from the Finance Department, recalls that they felt that HPD was in danger of becoming too dependent on the Housing Partnership for middle-income housing production and needed to reach out to other sponsors in order to get the high volume the Mayor wanted.

The new REBNY-city partnership moved forward. REBNY said it would create its own nonprofit development entity, and the city agreed to donate a large site in the Kingsbridge section of the Bronx, not far from the affluent Riverdale neighborhood. Because the city was unwilling to abolish rent regulations as demanded by the developers, the project was planned as a condominium development that would still be within reach of the middle-income target population. It would make a suitably big splash — 1,015 units, to be known as Tibbett Gardens. It would be a credible first installment on the promised 3,000-unit demonstration of what streamlined production could achieve.

Tibbett Gardens turned out, however, to be a flop — a never-built, embarrassing fiasco. Nothing went as planned. Despite the appointment of a "blue-ribbon" mayoral panel, the city was unwilling to make the regulatory changes sought by the industry. Meanwhile, REBNY's cost estimates for Tibbett Gardens soared far above the reach of the middle-income family. In order to save the project, the city's response to the cost problem was to offer subsidies — something the developers had said in the beginning they would not need. But even with the city kicking in $25,000 per unit — a total of over $25 million for the project — the cheapest two-bedroom condo would carry a price tag of $107,000, too expensive except for the very top of the middle-income range (about $50,000).

Tibbett Gardens had other problems. The community board serving the Kingsbridge area opposed the project. So did the Bronx borough president, Fernando Ferrer. But the city and REBNY continued to negotiate back and forth until the late 1980s over cost issues and environmental and other regulatory matters. At one point they agreed to reduce the scale of the project to 750 units.

As Tibbett Gardens was floundering, the REBNY staff turned to the Housing Partnership for advice and assistance, even complaining to the recently installed new president of the Partnership — Ron Shelp, who had succeeded Frank Macchiarola — that Wylde was being uncooperative. Wylde retorted in a memorandum to Shelp that the Housing Partnership "has consistently been cooperative and enthusiastic in support of an expanded constituency for affordable housing" and had only recently spent a morning with REBNY staff showing them the Housing Partnership's marketing procedures. "In fact," she concluded, "if there is an injured party in the historic context it is certainly we who were summarily dumped from a process in which we had a significant interest and to which we had contributed a great deal."

Abe Biderman, the mayoral assistant who took over HPD in 1988 after Crotty, later summed up the Tibbett Gardens debacle in a few terse sentences: "We worked with REBNY for three years. Nothing ever happened. The Housing Partnership said it wouldn't work. The Partnership was right. The site is still there, still vacant."

The REBNY-city initiative was indeed a demonstration — although not the one intended. Tibbett Gardens demonstrated the pitfalls rather than the advantages of large-scale projects — the costly consumption of time, the greater cost of construction, intensified political controversy at the community level, more extensive environmental impacts, a more complex regulatory gauntlet. It also demonstrated how resistant the city was to serious internal reform of its development process, preferring to pay through the nose with costly subsidies in an ultimately unsuccessful attempt to salvage something from the original pledge by powerful allies to make a big housing production splash. "A terrible admission of defeat by the real estate industry," housing expert George Sternlieb called Tibbett Gardens.

11

PRODUCTION
BREAKTHROUGH

The scandals of 1986 added extra steps to the already daunting development approval process; but the Housing Partnership kept pushing and prodding to get its pipeline of sites into production. Although projects moved fitfully, they did move. For any given project there would, finally, be an end to the agency reviews, the sign-offs, the political stroking and base-touching, the cajoling, the community meetings, the financial packaging. Rubbish on the site would be carted off. And the building would begin.

By the end of 1986, the pace of production was picking up. "The Partnership's process for selecting builders became fully accepted and institutionalized by early 1987," recalls Meredith Kane. It was Kathy Wylde, according to Kane, who "really designed the New Homes production system. She is a visionary, a tremendous producer with the tenacity of a bulldog."

The process was based on the issuance of an open "Request for Qualifications" (RFQ) that invited any homebuilder interested in Partnership projects to submit documentation on completed projects, financial status and backers, ability to borrow, and any performance problems

in the past. The key question was simple: Can this builder be counted on
to do a good job, on time and on budget? And the corollary question: Is
this builder willing to personally guarantee a construction loan so that
failure to perform would cost dearly? It was very important, Kane says,
that once a builder was "qualified" under the process, there were "no
distractions," particularly with respect to design questions. That was the
builder's responsibility. "We were able to get a lot of very good projects
through, despite the inherent tensions in public-private deals," Kane
says.

The breakthrough in New Homes production did not mean that
city-Partnership relations became bathed in sweetness and light. Wylde
never let up on the pressure to speed up production and was quick to
needle agencies and specific individuals she saw as laggards. For a city
official or bureaucrat, it was no fun being on the receiving end of a Wylde
barb. Some believe that Wylde created an unnecessarily high level of
friction and animosity. Meetings between Housing Partnership and HPD
staff often became shouting matches about who was responsible for projects stuck at some stage of the approval process.

"There was a history of finger-pointing," says Jerry Salama, who
took over HPD's homeownership program office in early 1988, after
Meredith Kane returned to her law firm. "Kathy was out there making
commitments to builders, to community groups, to borough presidents,
but she really wasn't into the details of the city's process. If things didn't
go her way, it was always the city's fault." Salama, a Harvard Law graduate who headed the city's homeownership programs until 1991 and later
returned to HPD in 1994 as a deputy commissioner in the Giuliani administration, calls himself "a *good* bureaucrat." He says Wylde sometimes "made promises she couldn't deliver on," and blaming the
"bureaucracy" was an all-purpose excuse. The challenge, according to
Salama, was "to routinize who was doing what," to shorten the twenty-
two-month process from builder designation to construction start, and to
"fill a pipeline with 'real' projects." Getting there was "a painful process," Salama acknowledges. After each monthly meeting of the HPD and
Housing Partnership staff, Salama would produce a status report on each
pending project, detailing what had been agreed upon. Still, there was
"constant debate," Salama recalls, with one side saying, "We're waiting
for you," and the other saying, "No, we're waiting for *you*." Karen Sunnarborg, who joined the Housing Partnership in 1986 and participated in
many of these meetings, notes simply, "There was not a lot of trust."

Despite the squabbling and personality conflicts, New Homes production continued to gather momentum. By the fall of 1988, sites for 2,000 homes were ready to go, and behind them were sites for 2,000 more. Earlier in the year, at the HPD commissioner post, Abe Biderman, a Koch insider, had replaced Paul Crotty, who had been skeptical about New Homes and had sometimes clashed with Wylde. "We were very positive on the Housing Partnership," Biderman now says. "One of the Mayor's priorities was middle-income homeownership. We achieved our production goals and never had trouble selling Partnership homes. The incredible thing about the Housing Partnership is that they built homes people would buy in the city of New York, even with some terrible areas nearby. In the early 1980s, nobody thought that was possible. The city could never have done it. It took the aura of the public-private partnership to make it happen — David Rockefeller's leadership and clout, Kathy Wylde's skills and knowledge."

As for city government, "It is not a monolith," Biderman says. "Other agencies [outside of HPD] have their own agendas, their own turf to protect. Given the bureaucracy, our responsiveness was relatively high." But, he adds after a pause, "not fast enough for Kathy."

Ed Koch would need more than one program's success, however, to keep him in the job he had wanted to hold "for life." The 1986 scandals had left him vulnerable to challenge from within his own party, and he was increasingly seen as a divisive force in a city where racial tensions were always simmering. Koch fought hard and spent millions in campaign funds to regain lost political ground, but he fell short. In a four-way Democratic primary on September 12, 1989, Koch got 42 percent of the vote; David Dinkins, the African-American Manhattan borough president whom the *Times* described as "placid, contained, conciliatory," won with 51 percent. He would win the same share of the vote in the November general election in narrowly defeating Republican challenger Rudolph Giuliani.

After Dinkins won, Kathy Wylde emerged as a candidate for HPD commissioner. But the new Mayor followed a less venturesome course in naming Felice Machetti, a veteran HPD official who had risen through the ranks to become Abe Biderman's deputy. While Biderman had been Koch's highly respected "brilliant tactician" in the housing field, Machetti had been the inside manager, who had been more directly exposed to the conflicts between the Housing Partnership and the HPD bureaucracy. The strained relationship between Wylde and Machetti —

who declined to be interviewed for this book — did not improve after Machetti became commissioner. The skirmishing between the public and private partners would continue, even as production sailed up.

Dinkins endorsed and pledged to continue Koch's massive budget commitment to housing production and rehabilitation, first announced by Koch in April 1986 as a $4.2 billion ten-year plan and then increased, two years later, to a $5.1 billion plan extended to 1998. A $500 million commitment to "constructing new affordable homeownership units" nestled securely in the much larger total program, which necessarily directed most money toward rehabilitation for lower-income groups and the homeless. In New Homes, Dinkins inherited a program that was well established, well regarded, and running quite smoothly. Like Koch, Dinkins also embraced middle-income homeownership as an essential component of sound neighborhood development strategy. Politically, it was a program with literally no downside.

In the early 1990s, as New York's fiscal position deteriorated and fear of crime was pervasive, Dinkins' fragile coalition of African-American and liberal white voters eroded just enough to cause his defeat in his 1993 rematch with Republican Rudolph Giuliani, who won with 50.7 of the vote. Giuliani's hard-edged message of budget-cutting, social conservatism, and tougher law enforcement on the streets has not prevented him from sticking with the activist housing posture assumed by his two predecessors, although the scale of his commitment has been cut back under fiscal pressure. He, too, has embraced the New Homes program.

Similarly, at the state level, Republican Governor George Pataki, who defeated three-term Governor Mario Cuomo in 1994 with promises of tax cuts and smaller government, has found room in his budget for continuing the state's $25 million commitment to affordable homeownership production. (Half flows to the New York City Housing Partnership.) New Homes, it seems, has become a program for all political seasons.

"Whose Program *Is* New Homes?"

The Housing Partnership's ability to weather political transition testifies to the fundamentally nonideological character of the New Homes program. At bottom, the Partnership's "political" agenda was production. In mid-1984, thirty months after David Rockefeller's announcement, it all came down to the question that was being thrown at Kathy Wylde: "Where are the houses?"

"Production" is what Rockefeller, Wylde, and the Housing Partnership wanted, and that could happen only with a "program" in place, a program whereby all the partners had a more or less clear understanding of their respective roles and responsibilities: a program rather than a "project" — or chain of projects — for which a different deal must be cut each time around. It took about five years for the Housing Partnership and the city to, finally, embrace that principle — longer probably than was expected when the Partnership was launched in January 1982 under Ronald Reagan's benign gaze, but not very long, really, when one considers the complexity of the enterprise.

Both the Housing Partnership and the city, of course, wanted production. But the Housing Partnership had the signal advantage of being a small, flexible organization that was single-mindedly fixed on a well-defined objective — the production of new homes for middle-income homebuyers; it operated in a political context by necessity, but its production goal was never linked to any particular political leader or ideology. Mayors, commissioners, and bureaucrats could come and go (sometimes to jail) without fundamentally changing the program structure; all that was needed was a willingness to continue producing new homes using a proven program model.

On the city side, getting to the point of a durable program model was so hard because many things got in the way of production. The sleekness of the Housing Partnership operation and its highly focused objective contrasted starkly with the city's multiple political power centers and the lubberly agencies of city government. Kathy Wylde, with the backing of David Rockefeller and a powerful board of private sector leaders, relentlessly documented what the Partnership viewed as bureaucratic clumsiness and delay, regulatory excesses and inanities, and political maneuvering that obstructed production.

The Partnership's one-track aggressiveness was a strength, but that same quality sometimes made the Partnership seem overbearing and hectoring to the people and agencies that were the targets of its prodding. From city officials' perspective, the Housing Partnership was often insensitive to the fact that all of city government did not revolve around the New Homes program and that many competing problems and programs clamored for their attention. Says one former HPD official in the Dinkins administration: "We [HPD] had a tremendous 'in rem' problem [more

than 5,000 apartment buildings owned by the city because of tax delin-
quency]. Thousands of people were living in rat traps and on the street.
To many in HPD, these problems were much more urgent than middle-
income people wanting to buy houses at subsidized prices. But the Partnership took the position that no one in HPD knew anything about
housing. With Kathy, it was either her way or no way, and you got the
feeling she could hurt you, that she would not only get mad but get even.
She didn't seem able to accept that public money meant public control."

The city's maligned bureaucracies did have their legitimate roles to
play — someone had to pay attention, after all, to soil contamination,
sewers, curbs, pavement, electrical hookups, and trees. The Housing
Partnership, for its part, never questioned the appropriateness of these
roles — only the city's lumbering pace in executing them. Because of the
contrast in structure and style between the two "partners," a measure of
tension and conflict was built into the relationship — exacerbated at
those times when the people involved did not like or trust each other. A
sense of joint program ownership proved elusive, even as production
took off in 1987 and 1988.

"Whose program *is* the New Homes program?" asks former HPD
deputy commissioner Mark Willis, who later joined Chase Manhattan's
community development finance arm. "Is it the city's or is it the Housing
Partnership's?" Karen Sunnarborg, who joined the Housing Partnership
in 1986, recalls that the "city and the Partnership had a constant problem
of defining roles." To HPD it appeared that "the Partnership had all the
sexy parts of the program, and the city's role was largely paperwork and
expediting." Or, as another former HPD official put it, "It sometimes
seemed that the city did all the work and the Housing Partnership got all
the glory." Issues relating to the uneven distribution of "work" and
"glory" would tend to flare up in connection with media coverage of New
Homes groundbreakings, ribbon-cuttings, and other events; the "partners" were (and are) sensitive about who got quoted in the *Times* or who
made it on to the evening news. With Koch on the ropes politically because of the scandals, his administration craved positive news stories
showing accomplishment and happy New Yorkers. For the Mayor's people, it wasn't easy to see David Rockefeller and Kathy Wylde at center
stage; at other times, it was the Partnership's turn to be ignored in the
coverage of a program success. Persistent issues of "control and credit,"
as Wylde called them, would never quite get sorted out, but were part of

the everyday challenge of managing an ambitious program in a highly charged political environment.

To the Housing Partnership, the question of program "ownership" was less important than establishing a system for efficient housing production at the lowest possible cost — a characteristic private sector goal. Ironically, the Partnership gained significant leverage in the push for production by conceding — even asserting — that New Homes was, in fact, the city's program. A policy decision to spend taxpayers' money on middle-income ownership housing could be made only by government; there could be no New Homes program unless the Mayor and other elected officials determined that it was in the public's interest and their own political interest to support such a program.

Wylde called attention to the city's initiative and control in an April 1986 letter to the editorial board of the *New York Daily News*: "In 1982, the City asked the Housing Partnership to help generate private sector financial support, expertise and cooperation in generating a moderate to middle income homeownership production program." (The letter was in response to a Jimmy Breslin column four days earlier that stated, erroneously, that the Housing Partnership was backing a high-rise apartment development in Brooklyn despite neighborhood objections.) Wylde stressed that in the New Homes program the Housing Partnership "helps" the city to review sites, pick developers, and find project financing. But the final decisions are all the city's.

Advancing the city as lead partner and program "owner" gave the Housing Partnership leverage in the many disputes that arose over site selection and control, property disposition, regulatory review, and a myriad of other procedural and political matters. The Partnership's leverage lay in being able to say: "Look, this is *your* program, but you need us to make it work. We are trying to drive the process so that you, the city, can achieve the production you say you want. Why, then, can't you get your act together?"

The Housing Partnership knew perfectly well that it was not so simple for the city to shape up and pursue housing production with the same single-minded ferocity exhibited by their private sector partner. Nor was it easy for city officials to be on the receiving end of tough and embarrassing criticism. But the partners' joint interest in a successful program ultimately prevailed. Both partners embraced middle-income homeownership as good public policy; despite much delay and conflict, both hung in and made it work.

The New Homeowners

The production of new homes would be an empty effort without willing buyers ready to invest a big chunk of their personal resources and to commit themselves to building secure and thriving neighborhoods. As we have seen, the conventional wisdom around 1980 in New York City (and other cities) was that such prospective buyers were rare; the path of upward mobility and the American dream of homeownership, it was felt, invariably led to the suburbs. The surprising market demand for the Housing Partnership's New Homes proved this conventional wisdom wrong. Who were these buyers, and where did they come from? Each one has a story; here are a few of them.

Mary Boswell owns a neat, two-unit town house on 166th Street in the South Jamaica section of Queens. In 1964, at the age of eighteen, Ms. Boswell moved with a baby daughter from Alabama to New York City, "just trying to survive," she says. She studied for her GED, went to secretary's school, and landed a job at Consolidated Edison, where she is still employed. For seventeen years she lived in a cramped, fifth-floor apartment in the Queensbridge project of the New York City Housing Authority. In 1984, she heard about Housing Partnership homes being built in Queens and got herself on a list of prospective buyers. She would wait six years for the call from the Allen AME church — a Partnership community sponsor — telling her about the last unit available in the Partnership's Guy Brewer development, being built by the Bluestone Organization. She "jumped at the chance," paying $155,000 for a home with a market value of about $255,000. Now Ms. Boswell "loves working in my garden" and regularly attends meetings of her block association. "It feels like a neighborhood," she remarks; "each looks out for the next one."

Elsa and George Ortiz own a two-family house on the Reverend James Polite Avenue in the Bronx. The Ortizes moved to New York City from Puerto Rico and lived for sixteen years on the seventeenth floor of an East Harlem public housing project plagued by vandalism and frequent elevator breakdowns. George, who works at the Coach leatherware firm, started putting money aside for a down payment on a house. One day, driving through the South Bronx, the Ortizes spotted the Housing Partnership development known as Thurston Plaza, then under construction. They contacted the builder, the Procida Organization, and asked for an application. "We were lucky," Elsa Ortiz says. A house priced at

$157,000 was still available in phase two of the development. In early 1992, the Ortizes moved in with their two young sons; Elsa's parents occupy the downstairs unit. Thurston Plaza's homes form a perimeter around a spacious common courtyard, where children play and adults socialize. "It's very quiet and safe," Elsa says, "like one family — neighbors look out for each other. From here, we're not going anywhere."

In the Coney Island section of Brooklyn, Maryanne Manousakis lives in a two-bedroom town house she bought in 1991 for $79,900. Ms. Manousakis grew up in Brooklyn's Bay Ridge neighborhood, married, and was widowed many years ago with a small daughter to raise; she now works as a public school custodian in a Brooklyn elementary school. "This place has changed my life 100 percent," says Ms. Manousakis, who had been renting an apartment on Staten Island. "I'm a gardener who needs to be rooted somewhere. I was meant to be a homeowner, but couldn't possibly have done it without Partnership Housing. Now I have no reason ever to move." Ms. Manousakis speaks warmly of her neighbors, who are "from everywhere" — Barbados, Jamaica, Poland, Italy, China, and elsewhere. She worries about the Chinese, who are "so cloistered. They get on a bus in the morning and go somewhere to sew all day. They never see anyone except other Chinese. We've got to do something about that."

On Valentine's Day, 1994, Doris Bembury dug through a pile of snow and moved into her new brick, two-bedroom row house on Frederick Douglass Boulevard in Harlem. Ms. Bembury is a native New Yorkers, who is employed in a foster care agency. She had been renting a small apartment in Manhattan when she spotted an item in the *Amsterdam News* about the planned construction of the Housing Partnership's St. Charles Landmarks homes. After attending a homebuying seminar at the St. Charles Borremeo Church, the community sponsor, she filled out an application and eventually became one of the 116 fortunate buyers of the sold-out development. "This is a very good area," Doris observes, "close to transportation. I have always wanted a house and had been saving for awhile. I'm very pleased."

The ordinariness of these brief stories is striking: Working people, heretofore all renters, aspire to homeownership and the economic, social, and psychological rewards that American culture associates with the attainment of homeownership status. What is not ordinary are the places where new homes have been successfully marketed to realize these ownership aspirations, and the scale of production achieved by the Housing

Partnership. As of June 1997, 174 separate Housing Partnership projects accounted for 13,521 units of housing. Although New Homes have been built in all five boroughs, most — about three quarters — are located in the two boroughs — Brooklyn and the Bronx — that suffered the most profound blight in the 60s and 70s.

Also extraordinary about these buyer profiles is *who* they are: mainly blacks and Hispanics, both native- and foreign-born — groups that have been dramatically underrepresented among the ranks of United States homeowners. According to data compiled by the Housing Partnership, only 10 percent of its homebuyers are white, 47 percent are black, 30 percent are Hispanic, 11 percent are Asian, and 2 percent are "other." As I will discuss further in chapter 14, the Housing Partnership's success in selling New Homes to these groups points to an urban homeownership market that is largely untapped — one of many hopeful signs of urban rebirth in major cities across the U.S.

Yet, the transformation of these desolate areas has received surprisingly little attention. A March 12th, 1995, *New York Times* editorial, referring to the South Bronx as "the nation's most infamous symbol of urban blight" and "a synonym for hopelessness and decay," urged its readers: "Take a Sunday drive and you will be surprised to see that the burned-out Bronx is largely gone. . . . The Bronx has clawed its way back and is rapidly becoming a borough of middle-class homeowners. . . . Neighborhoods once made up entirely of the poor are being economically integrated. With ownership comes pride in community — and vigilance against crime and disorder. While small patches of desolation remain, the vast empty stretches have all been renewed. Neatly kept town houses have cropped up where the eyesores used to be. Markets and retail stores are cautiously returning to the neighborhoods. . . . [T]he signs of promise spring abundant."

The *Times*'s exultant editorial writer dished out credit for the "Bronx Miracle" to city government, to neighborhood-based community development corporations ("the heroes of this story"), and to courageous first-time homebuyers and their "huge leap of faith." Inexplicably the editorial neglected to mention the New York City Housing Partnership, the organization that not only had championed the idea of urban homeownership but, more importantly, had figured out ways to make it happen under a multitude of different circumstances in the nation's toughest political environment.

The Nehemiah Plan:
A Competing Implementation Model

In early 1982, as David Rockefeller, Edgar Lampert, and Kathy Wylde were getting the New York City Housing Partnership off the ground, a very different group was hatching a new homeownership program — the Nehemiah Plan, named for the Hebrew prophet in the fifth century B.C. who led the exiled people of Israel in rebuilding the walls of Jerusalem. The group was East Brooklyn Churches — thirty-six churches whose leaders had organized to confront the physical and social devastation of some of Brooklyn's worst slums. Moving among the leadership was the spirit of Saul Alinsky, the famed Chicago-based theorist and tactician of the community organizing movement who organized the Industrial Areas Foundation in 1940. For the Nehemiah Plan, the bearer of the Alinsky legacy was Michael Gecan, an Industrial Areas Foundation organizer invited to Brooklyn to help shape the churches' agenda and guide their strategy. High on the list of objectives was housing — ownership housing that the mainly black, working-class church members could afford.

Like the Partnership's New Homes program, Nehemiah Plan Homes would prove to be a success — albeit on a lesser scale — and for some of the same reasons. The market for ownership housing was unexpectedly strong, and the Nehemiah Plan offered a product that people were eager to buy, at a subsidized, below-market price. Nehemiah's sponsors also secured free land owned by the city as building sites, and they were able to extract regulatory concessions from city bureaucracies. But there were important differences, too, between the Housing Partnership and Nehemiah. These differences ranged from the type of housing brought to market to more fundamental divergencies in political stance, neighborhood planning philosophy, and methods of financing and building houses. Exploring their differences may suggest which model has greater potential for staying power and for replication in other places.

Both programs, of course, have had to function in the context of city politics. Neither the Housing Partnership nor the Nehemiah sponsors can make a move without city government cooperation in the form of land, subsidies, and regulatory relief. But the two groups approach city government in very different ways. The Housing Partnership is careful to nurture the "public-private partnership" idea with the city and in fact portrays itself as an implementer of city policy. The relationship is hardly a cozy one; the tensions between the public and private players can become raw. Yet, disagreements have generally been kept out of public view, and there has been an underlying commitment to work things out.

The Alinsky-Industrial Areas Foundation model embraced by the Nehemiah Plan's sponsors is fundamentally adversarial — the opposite of a "partnership." This model calls for awakening the latent power of the "people" in order to confront political and corporate power on equal terms, and then wresting concessions by means of "actions" that intimidate or embarrass opponents. In pushing for Nehemiah's first project in Brooklyn, leaders of East Brooklyn Churches and their developer, retired builder I. D. Robbins, secured a meeting with Mayor Koch to present their plan and ask for city-owned vacant land, property tax concessions, and $10 million in city subsidies for the first 1,000 houses. EBC claimed to have raised $12 million from the churches for a construction loan pool, although only $2.5 million had actually been committed. Koch seemed receptive but made no firm commitments. Three weeks later, EBC called a press conference and "announced plans to build 5,000 single-family town houses" in the next five years. Koch was boxed in. He agreed to support the program but wanted to start small, with a hundred units. At a subsequent meeting with Koch, an EBC delegation threatened to walk out unless he agreed to at least 1,000 houses. Koch gave in.

Since the Nehemiah Plan delivered its first house in 1984, the program has produced about 3,000 houses. Most of these — about 2,300 — were built in Brooklyn in the 1980s on large tracts of city-owned land covering several square blocks; the remainder are being built in the 1990s on sites in the South Bronx. Although the units sell quickly, as architecture they are not much to look at: identical, block-long rows of houses, each eighteen feet wide, with small windows and brick facades. *New York Times* reporter Alan S. Oser has commented: "That unvaried product, running up and down all sides of the street, has created a dreary physical landscape." Another critic, architectural historian Richard Plunz, called the Nehemiah design "primitive," "horizontal barracks," and "reminiscent of nineteenth century mill housing." What Nehemiah homes lack in elegance and spaciousness, however, they make up for in extraordinary low cost and price: The Brooklyn units cost about $60,000 to build and sold for about $50,000, including a $10,000 city subsidy which must be repaid upon resale.

In contrast, the Housing Partnership's production of about 12,000 houses far outstrips the Nehemiah Plan. Each Partnership project has a different design, as determined by the individual homebuilder's architect, and there are well over one hundred separate Partnership developments compared with Nehemiah's few mega-projects. Because the Partnership favors a two-family design (the owner's unit plus a rental unit), direct cost comparisons are difficult, but there is no question that the Partnership is not able to produce as cheaply as Nehemiah. A detailed cost analysis done for the Partnership in 1988 by an independent architectural firm showed per-unit costs ranging from $57,000 to $137,000 for a sample of ten Partnership projects. (The high-end figure was for a project which suffered extraordinary construction delays because of site conditions, builder financing problems, and special historic district design requirements.)

How does Nehemiah do it? Part of the reason for the Nehemiah Plan's low cost lies in the efficiency of its production process. Nehemiah will not build unless it can "create a critical mass — 500 to 1,000 units in an area, not a few here and there, not a pilot project." Obviously, it's cheaper to build an identical product in high-volume, assembly-line fashion than it is to build "a few here and there" — which the Partnership frequently and deliberately does. In addition to Nehemiah's sheer production efficiency, the plan wrings out more cost savings by radically departing from the conventional system for financing housing. The Alinsky-inspired East Brooklyn Churches believed that it "must have money power to complement its people power," and so with heroic effort, EBC eventually raised $8 million from churches and religious organizations to form a construction loan pool. Nehemiah's single developer, I. D. Robbins, drew down interest-free loans from the pool to finance construction costs and repaid the loans as houses were sold. Robbins, a maverick retired builder with a point to prove — he had been claiming for years in newspaper columns that he could build a very low-cost house if the city would give him land — charged Nehemiah a token fee of only $1,000 per completed house — another significant saving. The unusual combination of high-volume construction, churches that acted like banks, and a builder that was not interested in making much money guaranteed Nehemiah's rock-bottom costs.

The Housing Partnership's somewhat higher costs are tied directly to a different set of assumptions about the way its housing should fit physically into a neighborhood setting, and about its role as a contributor to the economy of neighborhoods. The Housing Partnership rejects the notion of "critical mass" as a criterion for development. Early on, the Partnership confounded skeptics by successfully marketing houses built on so-called "shit sites" of varying size. If a large site is available, the Partnership will not shy away from building one or two hundred houses. But such sites are the exception: More than three-fourths of its projects are less than one hundred units, and many of these are packages of small infill sites grouped together to make up a project. Building on infill sites is especially popular with the Partnership's community sponsors because it gets rid of ugly "granny tooth" gaps in an otherwise sound block. From a builder's perspective, however, infill development is riskier, more costly, and less efficient than building a block-long row of identical houses.

Still, the Partnership believes that the trade-off between cost-cutting efficiency and mending a neighborhood's delicate fabric is worth it. As Kathy Wylde told the *New York Times*: "'Experience has shown that in the long run, the economic considerations of low-income communities are better served by infill and rehabilitation than by slum clearance." Nehemiah's combative developer, I. D. Robbins, who once talked of building as many as 200,000 Nehemiah homes in New York City, dismisses Wylde's thesis as "the legacy of the soft muddle-headed Jane Jacobs cult of the '60s." It was better, the *Times* reported him as believing, "to begin anew and do it on a scale that will create an entire neighborhood."

The Nehemiah Plan's insistence on "critical mass" — at least 500 and preferably 1,000 units at a crack — has dramatically slowed its momentum since the highly successful East Brooklyn project was completed. Because the first Nehemiah project — with its evocative name, appealing bootstrap image, and anti-establishment tone — was also a public relations triumph, New York City officials have been careful to praise the program and pledge continued support. But despite the city's vast inventory of vacant land, it has been hard for Nehemiah's sponsors and the city to agree on specific sites that can accommodate the Plan's demands for scale.

The sticking point in most cases has been the need to clear out existing homes and businesses to make way for I. D. Robbins' efficient builders. To Robbins the issue is simple: "We're doing God's work. Nobody can argue with that." A grocery store owner in East Brooklyn, however, had a different view: "The Nehiamiah [*sic*] plan started off by saying, we want to build on empty lots. Now they went from building on empty lots to . . . taking — acquiring this man's furniture store, acquiring our grocery store. Where will we have the shops? Where will we go?

Where will my father go? He has finished paying for his house, now they want him to pay for another mortgage. Now we have reverends coming in, dressed up in cloth and giving us prayer while they're taking our homes and telling us we have to go."

As Nehemiah has sought to expand into new sites in the 1990s, conflict over scale has continued. In October 1992, the *New York Times* reported on contention between Nehemiah sponsor East Brooklyn Congregations and other nonprofit groups who wanted Nehemiah "to integrate its townhouses with viable existing buildings and reconstructed apartments. But the group [EBC] has resisted, arguing that it needs a critical mass — at least 800 to 1,000 in East New York — if its new communities are to be stable."

It is an old and persistent dilemma in urban planning since World War II: Is it better to clear away yesterday's and today's messes and rebuild afresh — or to preserve, improve, and replace? The disagreement between the Housing Partnership and the Industrial Areas Foundation on this issue holds a peculiar irony: The Housing Partnership people, who in a sense are the agents of corporate money and power, have taken a gentler, more pragmatic approach to reviving neighborhoods; while the disciples of Alinsky, clothed in religious garb, have seemed more ready to call in the bulldozers.

In 1984, in the first rush of enthusiasm about the Nehemiah Plan, New York Congressman Charles E. Schumer pronounced it "just a fabulous undertaking" and submitted a bill called the "National Nehemiah Housing Opportunity Act." Schumer's bill was modeled roughly on the New York City program, including a provision that local projects should have at least 100 units located on contiguous parcels of land. In responding to Schumer's request for comments on the bill, Kathy Wylde applauded Nehemiah's East Brooklyn project as "excellent," but cautioned that it would be "very difficult to translate that experience into a national program that will work in other situations." Schumer continued to push his Nehemiah bill and succeeded in getting it incorporated into the 1987 housing act — but the program never caught on. In 1989 the first 1,321 units were approved for federal funding (none of them in New York City, which found the national program unworkable); when Congress rewrote housing legislation in 1990, Nehemiah was quietly "zeroed out." Meanwhile, several of the nonprofit sponsors who had received Nehemiah grants in 1989 "found it difficult to organize and implement the program planned"; by August 1993 only 392 units had been completed nation-wide.

In the New York City context, the Housing Partnership has created less excitement than Nehemiah but gets more done. One reason is that the Housing Partnership sets no artificial thresholds for its building projects; it goes in and builds to whatever scale the neighborhood can absorb. Many small projects, 174 of them by mid-1997, eventually add up to big production numbers. Nehemiah's projects make a larger splash, but its demand for scale has turned out to be self-limiting. The political stance of the two programs also makes a difference. Essentially, the Housing Partnership accepts as legitimate the politicians' aspirations for power and the private sector's desire for profits; the Partnership is, after all, their creature, brought to life — somewhat paradoxically — for the very purpose of disciplining and channeling those impulses to produce a social good. And when talented and politically savvy implementers on both the public and private sides are able to work out the requisite (and complex) administrative arrangements, a program such as New Homes can achieve consistent production volume. In contrast, Nehemiah's sponsor, the Industrial Areas Foundation, "welcome[s] new challenges and confrontation" in an unending struggle against "government control" and "corporate greed." This model has also produced some impressive results, but they are seen as victories over hostile political and corporate adversaries. The public and the press enjoy seeing politicians and fat cats getting beat up — and the truth is, they often deserve it. The danger, however, is that the "God is on our side" rhetoric can wear thin — as it sometimes has in New York, where there has been conflict between Nehemiah and other nonprofit groups with competing visions of a neighborhood's future, and where city officials have resisted Nehemiah's insistence on large scale, including total clearance and rebuilding from the ground up. So its victories have been sweet, but relatively few.

12

BEYOND NEW HOMES: EXPANDING THE PARTNERSHIP AGENDA

I t had taken the Housing Partnership and the city government five years to thrash out their respective roles to the point where New Homes production could take off and sustain momentum. By the late 1980s, New Homes had achieved a level of political acceptance and administrative predictability that would assure annual production of 1,000 to 1,500 units for many years into the future.

"The affordable housing community has pretty well figured out how to produce housing quite efficiently," Kathy Wylde says. New Homes was creating what Mayor Dinkins had called "islands of decency, safety, and commitment," but what was to be done about the surrounding, menacing seas of indecency, terror, and despair? The Housing Partnership and its parent organization, the New York City Partnership, were in no position to take on the whole battle against bad schools, the drug culture, crime, welfare, and joblessness — the dreary litany of so-called underclass problems. Yet, they were also unwilling merely to sit on their success with New Homes. They would instead reach out for new challenges, embarking on a still more daunting and risky agenda for the rest of the century and beyond. They would, in short, seek to move from building houses to building neighborhoods.

The Housing Partnership's expanded agenda includes the Neighborhood Builder program — a concerted and systematic effort, begun in the late 1980s, to bring struggling, minority-owned building contractors into the mainstream of New York City's white-dominated construction industry. In 1994, the Housing Partnership launched the Neighborhood Entrepreneurs Program (NEP), which targets New York City's most intractable housing problem — the thousands of city-owned, mostly dilapidated, apartment buildings that have fallen into the city's hands since the 70s because of property tax delinquency. NEP uses the Neighborhood Builder model to develop a for-profit, neighborhood-based property management and ownership industry.

Finally, the parent New York City Partnership is raising money for a new $100 million Investment Fund intended to serve not as a profit-making venture, but as "a recirculating source of 'seed money' for the development of high-impact public and public/private ventures, chosen for their potential to create jobs . . . that will benefit low- and moderate-income residents of the city's five boroughs." Kathy Wylde, who was ready for a fresh challenge, became the New York City Investment Fund's first president and CEO in 1996.

The Neighborhood Builder Program

Raleigh Hall and his wife, Marge, started a home improvement business in Queens in the 1960s. They both worked together at the post office in the early years to support the family until the business got established. Leslie Levi, Jr., set up shop as a plumbing contractor in the early 1950s in Brooklyn; in the 1960s and 1970s, one steady source of jobs was sealing off the open pipes of burned-out buildings in Bedford-Stuyvesant. Gerson Nieves moved to New York with his family from Puerto Rico when he was 13; after serving in the Air Force as an airplane mechanic, he set up a real estate brokerage office in the Bronx and then branched out into buying and rehabbing small apartment buildings. Desmond Emanuel, a native of Antigua, earned degrees in architecture and urban design in the 1970s and worked himself up to project manager at the giant construction company of William O. Crowe. Ambitious and confident, in 1982 Emanuel set up his own company, Santa Fe Construction: He liked the big, bold railroad image, but Santa Fe barely eked out a profit for years. Andrew Velez had been a carpenter until an injury forced him to give up heavy labor. In the early 1970s he started a small general contracting company in Manhattan. Velez supervised jobs in the field while Elizabeth, the oldest of his seven daughters, took over the business side of the company.

The Halls, Levi, Nieves, Emanuel, and Velez had three things in common. They all ran small, minority-owned firms that operated precariously on the edges of the huge New York City construction industry. None of them was "bankable"; that is, none of them could walk into a New York bank and borrow on their own signature. And the third thing they had in common was that they were selected in May 1989 in the first round of the New York City Housing Partnership's Neighborhood Builder Program.

Up to that point, the Housing Partnership had been haunted by a profound embarrassment: Out of the dozens of homebuilding firms that had won contracts to build New Homes — mainly in black and Hispanic neighborhoods — not a single one was minority-owned. This was a problem that would not solve itself or go away; something had to be done. The Neighborhood Builder Program was the response.

Minority firms were out there — and from the beginning, the Housing Partnership had actively recruited them. The problem was that no bank would lend a million dollars or more to companies that lacked both a conventional track record and the personal connections necessary to cement a deal. It was "the classic 'Catch 22' scenario: they can't qualify for credit without a track record, but they can't establish that track record without credit." Only two minority contractors had managed to meet the New Homes program threshold qualifications, and neither one could get a construction loan. It became clear that the financing impasse would not be broken without a direct attack. As with other challenges the Housing Partnership undertook, meeting this one would be neither quick, cheap, or easy.

On June 27, 1984, Kathy Wylde sent Partnership president Frank Macchiarola and other key staff a nine-page draft proposal and budget "for a minority business demonstration for the Partnership New Homes program." The Wylde proposal recounted the frustration of trying to recruit specific minority firms for New Homes. Various public and private agencies had "lists" of "approved" minority contractors, but Wylde argued that the lists were "of dubious quality and provide no meaningful evaluation of the firms identified." In addition, those few minority contractors who had done business in federal housing subsidy programs were "finding it difficult to make a transition to conventional development, where access to financing, purchasing prowess, and the discipline of the marketplace require a significantly different combination of skills and resources." The federal programs had minority "set-asides" and were larded with subsidy; when they disappeared in the Reagan years, minority contractors who benefited under them had trouble competing in the harsher, market-driven climate. "[I]t has become clear," Wylde said, "that there are no shortcuts to achieving a significant level of minority business participation in the program."

Wylde's proposal was essentially to hire a new staff person who would be specifically responsible for implementing a minority business demonstration. That person would intensify the search for promising minority firms, especially those that had a good track record as subcontractors, and steer those firms into the regular competitive process by which New Homes builder/developers were selected. Then the staff person would "assist these firms in securing whatever technical assistance and financing they may require to carry out a particular job." It was hoped that with a little extra help, minority firms would be able to break into the circle of qualified New Homes builders. Wylde concluded, somewhat vaguely, "The first year trial experience of a Partnership-sponsored contract referral, evaluation and technical assistance effort tied to New Homes projects will provide the basis for a larger initiative in the second year."

The budget Wylde proposed for the two-year program was $167,000, enough to cover a program director, a half-time secretary, miscellaneous expenses, and overhead. Wylde believed that the program was a "fundable activity from sources that would not otherwise give to the Partnership" — a pointed reference to the Ford Foundation, which in the previous year had turned down flat a personal appeal from David Rockefeller for major support of the Housing Partnership. Rockefeller's daughter, Peggy Dulany, a vice-president of the parent New York City Partnership who worked on education issues, had talked with Ford Foundation president Franklin Thomas about funding the minority initiative, and Wylde had sounded out Louis Winnick, a Ford program officer. They seemed interested.

Despite the urgent tone of the draft proposal, the idea of a specially staffed minority business program faded to the back burner. At the time Wylde prepared the draft — mid-1984 — she was confident that the Housing Partnership would be "sponsoring construction of 5,000 new homes in more than 30 neighborhoods throughout the City over the next three years." But New Homes took much longer than that to gain real momentum; in three years, less than a thousand houses had been completed. Wylde and her small staff were fully absorbed in the immediate tasks associated with getting New Homes off the ground. The effort to recruit minority builders continued, but on an ad hoc basis and with the same disappointing results, although minority subcontractors did pick up an increasing amount of business from New Homes builder/developers.

It was not until 1987 that Wylde concluded that a new corporate entity would be needed to crack through the wall of obstacles keeping minority contractors from full participation in New Homes. In September 1987, a Wylde memorandum to Partnership board member Ellen Sulzberger Straus floated the idea that the Partnership would sponsor "the creation and spin-off of a non-profit, professional development entity that is specifically dedicated to, and led and staffed by the City's Black (other minority?) community." Wylde told Straus that the core professional leadership of such an entity was already on board and had successfully executed the Housing Partnership's largest and most complex project — the 599-unit "Towers on the Park" in Harlem. Here Wylde was referring to Steven Brown — who had first joined the Partnership staff in 1983 as a liaison with neighborhood groups and later extended his activities into project development — and to Deborah Wright, a former investment banker who had come on board in 1986 and supervised the marketing of Towers on the Park. Given Partnership support for two years, Wylde said, "our current staff (8 professionals) could be forged into the Black community's first City-wide professional development and finance corporation." The Housing Partnership would help the new corporation get established and carry out demonstration projects; it "could then be spun off, maintaining on-going liaison with 'the larger business and civic community' via the Partnership."

The idea of a separate corporate entity would survive, but there would be no "spin-off." In December 1987 Wylde proposed the creation of a "Community Partnership Development Corporation." The proposal was a somewhat vague one-pager suggesting that the corporation would have two functions. One was to serve "as an intermediary between the 'haves' (banks, business, government, and the real estate industry) and the 'have-nots' (low and moderate income households, their neighborhoods, and the non-profit organizations that serve them)." The other function — reflecting the influence of Partnership board member Donna Shalala, then president of Hunter College — would be to train minority graduate students "in all aspects of housing finance, development, and management." Only one feature of this proposal, however, would eventually be adopted — the name "Community Partnership Development Corporation."

A Non-"Minority" Minority Program

In 1988 the Housing Partnership again began to focus more narrowly on the issue of the absence of minority builders. As New York approached the 1989 mayoral election year, political pressure for action was building. Bronx borough president Fernando Ferrer and Manhattan borough president David Dinkins stepped up their attacks on Mayor Koch for the lack of black and Hispanic contractors in the Mayor's multi-billion-dollar housing initiative, announced in 1986. Koch was in a tight spot. The 1986 scandals had torpedoed his public approval ratings, and he was seen as highly vulnerable to a Democratic mayoral primary challenge from several candidates, including Dinkins. He was also being blamed for worsening racial tensions in the city; it didn't help that he had consistently opposed any sort of affirmative action or minority set-asides with respect to city contracts. Koch was swayed, however, when James D. Robinson III, the CEO of American Express, who had succeeded David Rockefeller as chairman of the New York City Partnership, personally urged the Mayor to get behind the minority builder initiative.

Wylde pushed ahead on negotiations with the Mayor's office. The city would need to agree to designate specific sites on which builder competition would be limited to minority contractors who would not otherwise be strong enough to qualify if the competition were open. Koch finally agreed, but with an Orwellian condition: This minority business initiative could not use the forbidden word "minority." Playing along, the Housing Partnership submitted a detailed proposal to the city in August 1988, describing the program as aimed at "locally-based enterprises," or LBEs. (Initially, the program was known as the Small Builder Assistance Program — a name objected to by the first participating firms, who did not want to be thought of as "small." Wylde then settled on another ethnically neutral name, Neighborhood Builder, which had all the right echoes and which everyone liked.)

The Mayor's willingness to cooperate was an essential step toward implementation, but it was up to the Housing Partnership to structure the program and make it work. In April 1988 the executive committee of the parent organization, the New York City Partnership, had approved the creation of a separate nonprofit entity to be called the Community Partnership Development Corporation (CPDC). CPDC would have its own board of directors and would serve as a vehicle for receiving grant funds from foundations and other sources wanting to target their support to the Housing Partnership's work with minority businesses and community-based nonprofit groups. This time, the Ford Foundation did come through with a little help — a $100,000 grant to get the new entity off the ground. Other private funders also chipped in: the dependable Rockefeller Brothers Fund, the J. C. Penney Foundation, the New York Community Trust, the Taconic Foundation, the Uris Brothers Foundation, and others.

The selection of the right chairman for the new corporation was crucial. Wylde recommended Fred Wilpon to James Robinson. Wilpon, the CEO of real estate giant Sterling Equities and co-owner of the New York Mets, speaks of himself as "a kid from Brooklyn who grew up in a neighborhood of strivers." A passionate believer in homeownership as a way to leverage neighborhood change, Wilpon would put his prestige and energy — and his money — on the line to make Neighborhood Builder succeed. He also brought in Tom Osterman, a junior partner at Sterling Equities, who played a key role in bringing the program from concept to implementation.

To direct the Neighborhood Builder program, Wylde turned to Deborah Wright. Wright, the soft-spoken, deceptively low-key daughter of a Baptist minister in Bedford-Stuyvesant, had earned a combination law and MBA degree from Harvard and started a career in 1984 as an investment banker at First Boston with a six-figure salary. "I hated it," she says. "It was not me." After three years at First Boston, she took three months off for "personal soul-searching." A meeting with Peggy Dulany, Ellen Straus, and Kathy Wylde about the Housing Partnership turned out to be "love at first sight. It was a way to keep a foot in both the private and the public camps, a way to put my energy into solving problems I care about

— a perfect fit." Wright took a job at the Housing Partnership at a salary of $35,000 — a pay cut of an even $100,000.

"Entrepreneurship, ultimately, is the only answer," says Wright. "People hire their own people. Sure, the housing is great, but the builders are white, the bankers are white. Billions are poured into poor neighborhoods, and the unemployment rate still sits at 50 percent. It's ridiculous. The question is, how can we become producers and not just consumers?"

In the fall of 1988 the Housing Partnership and the city Department of Housing Preservation and Development issued a "request for qualifications" (RFQ) for minority builders to develop housing on five city-owned sites — two in the Bronx and one each in Queens, Brooklyn, and Manhattan. Thirty responses to the RFQ were filed; twelve were selected as finalists.

Deborah Wright went into the field to interview all the finalists. "Kathy was angry that I was out all the time, but it was absolutely necessary," Wright says. "We were getting political pressure from the Mayor's office to pick some of the applicants who seemed to be the weakest. But actually, they were *all* weak. None of them had any money." After checking them all out, Wright recommended five firms: R. W. Hall General Contractors, Livel Mechanical Corporation, Nidus Realty, Santa Fe Construction, and the Velez Organization. Each was matched up with a site; project size ranged from fourteen two-family homes in Queens to fifty two-family homes in the Bronx. Total development cost for the five sites was $9.6 million dollars. Each builder was also paired with a "veteran builder," an experienced New Homes developer willing to provide informal advice and guidance as needed, in a mentoring role. The veteran builder also had to agree to complete a project if the Neighborhood Builder failed.

Banks, even public-spirited ones, were still unwilling to lend millions of dollars to the likes of the Neighborhood Builders. Under the regular New Homes program, builders had to personally guarantee payback of their construction loans and show that they had the assets to do so — bringing to mind the familiar banking adage that the only way to get a loan is to prove you don't need one. The Neighborhood Builders really did need the money, and they lacked collateral.

To reassure the lenders, Wilpon and three other large developers — Martin Raynes, Bruce Eichner, and Lawrence Silverstein — agreed to set up a $500,000 loan guarantee pool to "backstop" the Neighborhood Builder construction loans against possible cost overruns. But when the time approached to commit the funds, the three backed out. Raynes and Eichner had suffered ruinous losses in the late-1980s real estate slump; Silverstein changed his mind about the whole idea, declaring that "minorities should follow the same 'bootstrap' path as majority companies." That left Wilpon by himself. But instead of folding, Wilpon said that Sterling Equities would put up the entire $500,000. "It took tremendous guts," says Wylde. Wilpon himself is more matter-of-fact: "It was delicate," he says, "very delicate. But we thought we could manage the risk."

As it turned out, Wilpon's backstop guarantee was not needed after all. The solution came from Albany — from the State of New York Mortgage Agency (SONYMA). Wylde had approached SONYMA about doing something the agency had never done before: providing a state guarantee of private construction loans. SONYMA was initially reluctant, but was reassured by the assignment of veteran New Homes builders to each of the minority builders. In addition, E. Virgil Conway, then CEO of the Seamen's Bank and the first chairman of the Housing Partnership Development Corporation, helped make the case to the SONYMA Board. The president of SONYMA, Carmen Culpeper (from New York City's Puerto Rican community), was finally persuaded that the risk was reasonable; SONYMA would guarantee 75 percent of a Neighborhood Builder's construction loan. That was good enough. According to a 1994 evaluation of Neighborhood Builders sponsored by the Housing Partnership, all of the commercial lenders involved in the program said that "SONYMA insurance has been the most significant factor in permitting them to finance small minority builders who could not otherwise have received credit approval under bank and regulatory standards defining reasonable commercial risk."

Bank financing was only one of the hurdles that faced the Neighborhood Builders, however. They needed help with pre-development costs for such things as site analysis and the professional fees of architects and engineers. Again, the Housing Partnership scoured the landscape for low-interest "seed" loans. The city, with HUD's concurrence, was willing to make available about a million dollars in loan repayments from previous New Homes projects that had received UDAG assistance. Brooklyn Union Gas Company came through with seed loans for the two projects in their service area. The Housing Partnership also negotiated for over a year with the state Urban Development Corporation, which had a "Minority Revolving Loan Program." The UDC program, however, was so snarled in procedural red tape that it proved almost useless

— only one builder managed to get a loan approved, long after he needed it.

No Shortcuts

The first round of the Neighborhood Builder Program was clearly a struggle. "Each builder was idiosyncratic; it was not as easy as I thought it would be," recalls Wright, with obvious understatement. Interlaced with all the financial and technical complexity were the personality quirks, the sensitive egos, the pulls of old loyalties. All five were "like family," says Wright, and it was she who played multiple roles — sometimes as correcting parent and other times as big sister. "These five guys, with all their flaws — believe me, it was worth it."

The first round was a success, in that four out of the five builders completed their projects on time and on budget; the fifth project, slated for a site in Harlem, was derailed by litigation unrelated to Neighborhood Builders. (The city offered a substitute site in the Bronx, which was successfully completed by Desmond Emanuel's Santa Fe Construction.) Marketing of the houses also went well; all of the developments sold out quickly.

The first round fell short, however, as far as fulfilling what the Housing Partnership calls the "central principle of the program, [which] is to enable each builder to secure and repay a private loan, thereby establishing a banking relationship and credit history upon which to build future business." One project was not enough. When the awards were made for round two of the Neighborhood Builder competition in May 1991, three of the five builders from round one also applied and were among the seven selected: Livel Mechanical, the Velez Organization, and R. W. Hall. Subsequent competitions have also resulted in a mix of new firms and previous winners. Only one firm, Gerson Nieves' Nidus Realty, "graduated" into the main New Homes program after a single Neighborhood Builder project.

After three rounds of Neighborhood Builders, a 1994 evaluation toted up the results: 807 units of housing completed or under construction by twelve different minority firms, financed by a combination of private loans and public subsidies totaling $92.4 million. Over a five-year period (1989-93), the twelve firms had, on average, increased their annual gross business revenue from $1.6 million to $4.5 million, their construction contract value from $1.0 to $8.9 million, and their annual payroll from $325,000 to $1.4 million. And, as Deborah Wright had anticipated, the minority builders did indeed hire "their own people." About three-fourths of all subcontractors were minority-owned firms — who themselves employed minority workers, from architects and lawyers to plumbers and laborers. Many already lived in the neighborhood where the housing was going up, and in at least one case, a tradesman hired by a Neighborhood Builder bought one of the houses in the development, "thanks to the stable employment he acquired through the Program."

Not all Neighborhood Builders were success stories. Four firms that were selected for the program had to withdraw for financial reasons, and a fifth had to be replaced by a veteran builder during construction.

Then there was Les Levi of Livel Mechanical and Equipment Corporation, who exemplifies how tough and precarious the nurturing of a minority contractor can be. Levi, an amiable and earthy man in his sixties with deep roots in his Bedford-Stuyvesant neighborhood, had scratched out a living since the 1950s as a hand-to-mouth contractor doing small renovation jobs, sewer construction, and plumbing work. "Everybody likes Les," remarks Deborah Wright; "he has street sense and knows construction. But he can't map out a schedule and he can't meet with bankers."

When Levi came into the Neighborhood Builder program, Wright teamed him up with Felipe Ventegeat, who had an MBA from the Massachusetts Institute of Technology and became a partner in Livel Mechanical. The project they took on was the Mt. Pisgah development — nineteen two-family homes in Bedford-Stuyvesant. Livel would do all the site preparation and foundation work, but the actual houses would be modular units manufactured off-site by DeLuxe Homes, a Pennsylvania company that had supplied other Housing Partnership projects. Although Mt. Pisgah was completed and successfully marketed, there were problems — and cost overruns — along the way, the main one being that the foundations and the modular units didn't fit together well. "I'll never do another modular," Levi now says, ruefully. Levi claims that whatever profit was generated by Mt. Pisgah all went to pay DeLuxe Homes; Livel, he says, made nothing. Wright's careful pairing of Levi and Ventegeat also failed to take hold. "I love both those guys, but Les had trouble dealing with Felipe as a real partner," she says. After Mt. Pisgah, they parted ways.

Levi was back in 1991 for round two of Neighborhood Builders, this time to build thirty-nine two-family homes on a site across the street from the Mt. Carmel Baptist Church in Bedford-Stuyvesant, Brooklyn — only a few blocks from Levi's own town house on a handsomely restored block of Macon Street. Construction was to start in 1992, but by the spring of 1993, Levi had still not secured the sewer and other city permits he needed before he could start. Mt. Carmel Church, the community sponsor for the project, was becoming impatient as church leaders saw other, nearby Housing Partnership projects going up. Their parishioners were eager to buy.

On May 19, 1993, Wylde called Levi into the Partnership offices to meet with the father-and-son team of ministers at Mt. Carmel, the Reverends V. Simpson Turner, Sr. and Jr. Responding to gentle prodding from the Turners and the Housing Partnership staff, Levi insisted that pre-construction arrangements were falling into place and that he would be able to start building before long. To step up the pressure on Levi, the Turners called for a public event that would show movement, and it was agreed that Mt. Carmel would hold a groundbreaking ceremony at the site in late June. Mayor Dinkins, Governor Cuomo, and other dignitaries would be invited. Levi had better be ready.

The groundbreaking took place on June 27 on a festive Sunday afternoon. Within days, Levi's crew went to work on the site. But two weeks after the groundbreaking and just before the formal closing on a $5.3 million construction loan, a stunned Housing Partnership staff learned that Levi's business and personal finances were in much worse shape than they were aware. His business premises were in foreclosure. He had fallen behind on a $90,000 minority business loan and on his own home mortgage. He owed taxes to the federal government and to New York City. All told, Levi's liabilities ran to over a million dollars.

The Housing Partnership and the construction lender — in this case the Community Preservation Corporation — were obligated to inform the state housing agency (SONYMA) about Levi's troubles because SONYMA was being counted on to guarantee 75 percent of the construction loan. SONYMA could have withheld its guarantee, which would have sunk the construction loan — and put Livel Mechanical out of business. But SONYMA officials advised that they were willing to stick with their guarantee if the Housing Partnership could arrange a rescue.

Kathy Wylde and her staff were unhappy that Levi had failed to fully disclose the extent of his financial problems, as he should have. But they decided to try to save him anyway. Levi was probably the most visible of the Neighborhood Builders; his picture had been in several newspapers, and the *New York Times* had done a long feature on him in November 1992 under the headline "A Minority Contractor Builds Upon His Dream." Public relations aside, the Housing Partnership saw Levi as an extraordinarily hard worker who turned out a quality product. They liked him. They did not want to see him go under. They would give him one more chance.

Wylde dipped into Housing Partnership funds for a $150,000 loan to Levi and prevailed on Brooklyn Union Gas to put up another $150,000. This would enable Levi to pay off his taxes and buy enough building supplies to keep the Mt. Carmel project going. Then Levi had to agree to sign over all of his profits from Mt. Carmel and apply them to his debts. "We put all our ducks on Mt. Carmel," Levi says, "or we wouldn't be around the next year." Completed in 1994, the project was a big success. "Every house could have had three buyers. I'd sit on my front stoop and eight people would come up to me wanting those houses," says Levi.

After completing the Mt. Carmel houses, Levi began picking up contracts other than Housing Partnership jobs. In early 1995, he needed surgery to remove a nonmalignant brain tumor, but he recovered well. He acquired a new partner to shore up the business side of the operation, and Livel climbed out of debt. "I don't know," says Steve Brown with some caution, "but it looks like this story may have a happy ending after all."

The Neighborhood Builder program had begun in late 1988 as a two-year demonstration, was first extended to five years, and now has become a regular activity of the Housing Partnership. Costs are covered by project fees, supplemented by foundation grants. In October 1993, Citibank extended to the Housing Partnership a million-dollar line of credit to make loans for working capital needed by minority contractors and subcontractors. A fourth round of Neighborhood Builder selections was made in late 1994, and the Partnership plans to add at least five minority builders to its roster annually for the foreseeable future. Not all will succeed, but many will. Tens of millions of dollars will cycle through minority businesses, their employees, and their neighborhoods and community institutions — money that formerly would fly away into the established networks of white-owned construction companies. Getting to this point had taken unremitting effort and a willingness to take risks on the part of all parties. More of the same would be called for. There are, as Kathy Wylde says, no shortcuts.

Rebuilding Neighborhood Economies

"Economic development has not kept pace with the residential rebuilding programs," wrote Kathy Wylde in a March 1996 paper prepared for the New York University School of Law. "As a result, New York finds itself without the strategy for job creation and economic development required to mitigate the impact of federal and state cutbacks in Welfare, Medicaid and housing that will disproportionately impact low income communities. The challenge ahead is to adapt the resources of the community development movement and the network of public-private partnerships to the task of building a new urban economy that is less dependent on public funding."

The New York City Partnership has taken up that challenge in the 1990s with two high-risk initiatives: the Neighborhood Entrepreneurs Program, which is modeled on the Housing Partnership's Neighborhood Builder program; and the New York City Investment Fund, a program of the parent Partnership.

Neighborhood Entrepreneurs

The numbers are big and stark. When the Giuliani administration took over in January 1994, the city government of New York was the unhappy owner of 5,600 apartment buildings — about 50,000 rental units. Three thousand buildings were occupied by about 30,000 renter households; the others were vacant. Median tenant income was declining as the city used its buildings to house homeless families. Renters paid an average rent of $261 per month, but it cost the city about $400 per month to manage a unit; the city's annual cost was about $300 million. The problem was getting worse: Another 13,000 properties were seriously behind in their property tax payments and could end up in the city's lap.

In New York, these properties are known as "*in rem*" housing, and constitute a problem unique to that city. "*In rem*" is a Latin term meaning "against the thing," and refers to a legal action whereby the city takes title to a property if the owner fails to pay taxes owed. Prior to the 1975 fiscal crisis, a court would grant title to the city only after an owner had been in arrears for four years. It was thought at the time that owners were deliberately holding back on payments to gain a short-term financial advantage, while in the process depriving the city of desperately needed revenue. The grace period was shortened first to three years and, in a 1977 law, to only one year.

The city's "fast foreclosure" threat worked on some owners, but in general, it was a failure. Landlords were caught in a declining real estate market as wealthier tenants departed for the suburbs and were replaced by much poorer ones. They extracted what money they could by cutting back on maintenance until the tax collector closed in; then they handed over the keys and walked away. The city's inventory of *in rem* buildings quickly ran up to more than 13,000, concentrated in the older parts of Manhattan (such as Harlem), Central Brooklyn, and the South Bronx, where the city became the owner (and landlord) of up to two-thirds of the buildings in some neighborhoods.

In 1979 the Department of Housing Preservation and Development (HPD) took over responsibility for the *in rem* problem and thereby evolved into a "second-tier public housing authority" — a bureaucracy of several thousand persons that oversees the management of about 30,000 units. (The "first tier" is the New York City Public Housing Authority, which has about 180,000 units under its management.) In the 1980s, with the city under court order to provide for its growing homeless population, the vacant *in rem* stock — after being rehabilitated at huge expense — became the main source of housing for this group. At the same time, HPD also pursued a variety of disposition strategies in order to get as many occupied properties as possible off its hands and into the hands of new private owners, nonprofit organizations, or the tenants themselves. Disposition, however, failed to keep up with intake, so that by 1994 HPD was shedding about 3,000 units annually while taking in about 4,000.

Since the onset of the *in rem* problem in the 1970s, the *least* successful disposition technique has been what might be called a pure "privatization" approach — which was simply to auction off properties, as is, to the highest bidder and let market forces determine the fate of the stock. But in the early 1980s, when the Koch administration did an analysis of buildings that had been auctioned off in previous years, "we found," as Ed Koch's HPD commissioner Tony Gliedman put it, that "nothing good happened." The typical pattern was that buildings suffered further deterioration or complete destruction and then were back in city hands within a few years.

Later, Koch took another stab at privatizing some of the *in rem* stock with a program called "POMP" — Private Ownership and Management Program. POMP was able to unload 250 buildings between 1986 and 1992, but the program had many problems. HPD, which was to provide funds and arrange for repairs and rehabilitation for buildings that needed them, managed this aspect of the program badly, "leaving many violations uncorrected and encouraging owners to look for short-run profits rather than longer range appreciation of the property." Other POMP owners, whose buildings were in good shape, sometimes "drove out low income working tenants in favor of those with higher incomes or more secure welfare rent subsidies," according to a City University of New York study. After David Dinkins was elected Mayor in 1989, POMP was phased out.

In his attempt to deal with the *in rem* problem, Dinkins put increasing emphasis on disposition to community-based nonprofit organizations through a program called Neighborhood Ownership Works (NOW). NOW had two parts: In one, the city, through HPD, directly contracted for rehabilitation and then gave the property to a nonprofit; in the other the city gave the nonprofit the unimproved building plus a flat $30,000 per unit and then let the nonprofit oversee contracting and rehab. This second approach had the advantage of circumventing the city's own bureaucratic and time-consuming procurement process, which heavily favored large, established construction firms; this approach also lodged the cost and quality control incentives with the nonprofit, which was to be the eventual owner.

Dinkins' defeat in 1993 passed the *in rem* albatross on to Mayor Rudolph Giuliani. Giuliani's general approach to governing is driven by the reality of New York's always stressful fiscal situation and by his philosophical commitment to trimming New York's traditionally expansive public sector role in the life of the city. As applied to the *in rem* stock, this called for a renewed emphasis on transferring as many buildings as possible to private entrepreneurs. The challenge was how to do this without repeating the mistakes and rip-offs of the past.

As a former U.S. district attorney, Giuliani had no experience with running housing programs, but he tapped as HPD commissioner someone who did: Deborah Wright. The first director of the Neighborhood Builder program, Wright had left her position at the Housing Partnership in 1990 when Mayor Dinkins appointed her to the New York City Planning Commission. Later, Dinkins appointed Wright to the board of the New York City Housing Authority, and at the time of her appointment by Giuliani, she was serving as the acting general manager of the Housing

Authority. "The authority has spent a billion dollars on capital improvements and modernization," she observed then. "None of it stays in the community. That has got to change." Her appointment by Giuliani would give her a new, high-leverage opportunity to put her convictions about minority entrepreneurship into action.

As HPD commissioner, Wright teamed up with her good friend Kathy Wylde to put together a fresh attempt to transfer a significant fraction of *in rem* properties to private, for-profit ownership. Patterning it in some ways after the Neighborhood Builder program, they call it the Neighborhood Entrepreneurs Program. According to a Housing Partnership funding proposal submitted to foundations in May 1994, previous private ownership initiatives by HPD had "ignored the aspirations of local residents and business proprietors seeking to build their own economic base and to secure jobs or contracting opportunities. Absentee owners selected by HPD have had difficulty with community and tenant relations, often resulting in rent strikes, lockouts of contractors and other problems that jeopardize efforts to stabilize the properties." Neighborhood Entrepreneurs would be rooted in their communities; the entrepreneurs' rehab contractors, their building managers, and their tenants would be their neighbors. If they performed well, they would make money; otherwise, they would fail.

Neighborhood Entrepreneurs was structured to increase the odds of success. The Housing Partnership would once again play the role of "honest broker" — a citywide, nonprofit intermediary with the power and credibility to tap corporate leadership, financial institutions, and foundations. By marshaling these resources along with the political and administrative commitment of City Hall, the Housing Partnership was also able to enlist community-based organizations in a systematic attack on selected target areas — "neighborhoods where the city's control of residential property has destroyed [local real estate markets and property values]." Instead of the usual building-by-building methods of dealing with the *in rem* stock, Neighborhood Entrepreneurs would go "block-by-block," targeting "clusters" of city-owned buildings, both vacant and occupied, for rehabilitation. For each cluster of up to 200 units in a several-square-block area, a neighborhood task force of local people would guide the process of selecting the Neighborhood Entrepreneur and provide oversight during the rehabilitation and tenant selection phase. Meanwhile, as part of a broader program called "Building Blocks," the Giuliani administration would step up building code enforcement and beef up police patrols in the areas where Neighborhood Entrepreneurs are active.

This is no quick fix. Neighborhood Entrepreneurs calls for a transitional period of up to three years, during which the Housing Partnership holds title to the property while the new "owner/manager in training" demonstrates the competence to become a responsible owner. Also, the Housing Partnership is entering into contracts with community-based organizations to work with and provide services to the tenants living in the buildings being taken over. As spelled out in the Partnership's July 1995 interim report, these nonprofit groups are needed "to serve as agents of the Partnership in orientation of the tenants, to carry out tenant assessments required to qualify them for rent subsidies and apartment assignments, to provide referral and support services as needed and to assist and monitor the relationships between tenants and the Entrepreneur." A political purpose is also served by the contracts: By buying services from groups known for tenant advocacy, the Partnership also buys credibility with wary tenants and helps to neutralize opposition from those who believe for-profit ownership of low-income housing to be unworkable, evil, or both.

With the Neighborhood Entrepreneurs Program, the Housing Partnership has chosen to wrestle with the city's most intractable housing problem. The odds for success were seen as not very good. As Susan Saegert of the City University of New York told the *New York Times*: "The easiest stuff to rehabilitate has really been done. What remains is really tough. It will be much harder to do in every way. The buildings are in worse shape, they are occupied, and it will cost more to renovate them. . . . The comprehensive block-by-block strategy is an improvement. But the city is always inventing expensive new programs, churning out one after another, spending time and talent on this instead of trying to find permanent solutions." Others, such as Harold DeRienzo, chairman of the Task Force on City-Owned Property, a coalition of tenant advocacy groups, worry that the new private owners will push out poor renters in favor of market-rent payers once the owners are free of the city's oversight. "What happens when the city is out of the picture?" he asks. "It is not feasible for for-profit owners to operate housing where tenants earn, on average, less than $7,000 a year."

All the hopes and fears about Neighborhood Entrepreneurs are being put to the only test that matters: implementation. Within the Housing Partnership operation, Neighborhood Entrepreneurs is being managed by Gale Kaufman, the Partnership's vice-president for policy and administration, who first joined the staff in 1988 after earning her MBA at Columbia. After Mayor Giuliani announced the program on September 14, 1994, Wylde, Kaufman, and Wright's HPD staff led by her deputy, Jerry Salama, drove it forward along several fronts simultaneously: screening and selection of entrepreneurs, identification of *in rem* building clusters, contracting with community-based nonprofit groups, meeting with tenants in targeted buildings, lining up banks for construction financing, drawing up lists of contractors with experience in building rehabilitation.

"What the Housing Partnership brings to the task is tremendous energy," says George Calvert, a twenty-five-year veteran of neighborhood-based housing development in Harlem. "You just can't get that out of the bureaucrats at HPD." Calvert, the former director of Hope Community, Inc., was brought on as a consultant to the Housing Partnership to assist in implementing Neighborhood Entrepreneurs. According to Calvert, the property management staff at HPD "did insane things" in trying to fix up *in rem* buildings and had "absolutely no sense of how to get things done in logical order." They would, for example, replace an entire kitchen and leave rotting steps nearby untouched; soon after, everything would need to be done all over again. But this time, according to Calvert, with the Partnership teaming up with the prospective owner to put buildings in shape, the job should get done right.

On June 5, 1995, a key milestone was passed — on schedule. The city transferred management control of the first 106 buildings (1,157 units) to eleven Neighborhood Entrepreneurs who were selected from among ninety-six applicants. The eleven targeted building clusters, which include both vacant and occupied buildings, are located in Harlem, Brooklyn, and the Bronx; by mid-1996, rehabilitation work in ten of the eleven clusters was underway and by mid-1997, forty-eight buildings were already completed and another 185 buildings were under rehabilitation or had bank commitments in place — for a total of 2,417 units in the program so far. The winning entrepreneurs are locally based property management and real estate firms — almost all minority-owned — with experience in managing other people's property for a fee. The promise of Neighborhood Entrepreneurs is that these managers can be transformed into successful developers and owners of what they manage.

The idea of treating occupied and vacant buildings as a neighborhood cluster has never been tried before by the city and is a critical element in the program's neighborhood-building strategy. Newly rehabbed buildings, it is hoped, will attract wealthier tenants able to pay market rents. This would, of course, shore up the cluster financially, perhaps easing the pressure for scarce rent subsidies; but the larger and more important objective is to create mixed-income neighborhoods with prospects for long-term stability and a sense of community.

If such is to be achieved, the unemployed poor must also have a decent shot at getting a job. The Housing Partnership, in a program linked to Neighborhood Entrepreneurs, is taking on this challenge, too. It's called, simply, the Employment Pilot, a welfare-to-work initiative funded by the Rockefeller Foundation that is intended to plug poor renters into jobs directly tied to the rehabilitation and management of properties being transferred to Neighborhood Entrepreneurs. A goal to place 100 people into both skilled and unskilled jobs was reached in early 1997. An independent evaluation, also funded by Rockefeller, will assess the program with a view to possible replication in other cities.

The New York City Investment Fund

A *New York Times* editorial in August 1994 called the idea "smart and simple": One hundred civic-minded wealthy persons and corporations would each put $1 million into an investment pool that would be used to create new business and job opportunities throughout New York City. The "pot of gold," to be called the New York City Investment Fund, would be a subsidiary of the New York City Partnership and would be chaired by Henry R. Kravis, known for his prowess in financing leveraged buyouts as a principal in the Wall Street firm of Kohlberg Kravis Roberts and Company. Fifteen million dollars was already in hand, including contributions from Partnership stalwarts Kravis, David Rockefeller, Jerry Speyer, and the major banks.

According to an Investment Fund brochure issued in February 1995, the fund would "address the twin crises of a shortage of jobs and a shortage of confidence"; it would be a "'can-do' fund" that will "*get things done*." Making money would not be the object of the fund, which "will not seek any significant return on its investments; rather, it will seek a return of capital which will allow the recycling of funds into additional worthwhile undertakings. Indeed, the success of the fund . . . will be measured by the successful completion of selected projects and, ultimately, by their contributions to the enhancement of life in New York City." By mid-1996, the Investment Fund had amassed $50 million; yet, despite the "can-do" tone of its publicity, not a single deal had been closed. The idea that the *Times* called "smart and simple" two years before was stumbling over a familiar problem: the complexity of implementation. And so the fund's leading sponsors successfully recruited the Partnership's best implementer, Kathy Wylde, to move over from her Housing Partnership position and take over as president and CEO of the Investment Fund.

The first investments of the fund are likely to be in a project called "Partnership Plaza," a demonstration program announced in 1995 and intended to plant "at least 250,000 square feet of retail space on vacant City-owned land along targeted commercial corridors."

The idea of Partnership Plaza — which, despite its name, is not a single project, but many — is to attract retailers to neighborhoods where new housing has created a customer base, but commercial and retail facilities have not followed. According to mayoral advisor Richard J. Schwartz, who along with Deborah Wright and Kathy Wylde designed the program, "in the past, planners and others assumed that the private market would respond to housing development by opening retail stores to new residents. Unfortunately, in many communities this never happened. . . . Assistance is needed to stimulate the private market."

Partnership Plaza as a program model is in many ways the retail counterpart to the New Homes program. Vacant, city-owned sites, designated for "economic development," have sat idle for at least ten years — often twenty — as one scheme after another is floated and then sinks. Leaders of the New York City Partnership are eager to put the business community behind a program that has many elements of risk but also promises high-visibility payoffs for New York City. At the same time, as with New Homes, political leadership must step forward with pledges of land, money, and support from agency bureaucracies.

In Partnership Plaza, the various pieces are in place. Development sites located near New Homes in Harlem, Brooklyn, and the Bronx have been designated for the program. The Mayor's office has also transferred control of these sites from the city's economic development agencies to HPD. "They have had twenty years to do something with this land. That's long enough," notes Kathy Wylde. The Partnership Plaza financial package includes $2.5 million in city capital funds and another $2.5 million in risk capital from the Partnership's Investment Fund. And once again, as with New Homes, the federal government, with more than a nudge from a New Yorker in a key spot, is providing critical support. This time the New Yorker is Andrew Cuomo — the son of long-time Governor Mario Cuomo, and a man with political aspirations of his own. As HUD Assistant Secretary for Community Planning and Development, Cuomo steered a $4.6 million "economic development initiatives" grant and $15 million in federal loan guarantees to New York for Partnership Plaza. (Cuomo was promoted to Secretary of HUD early in President Clinton's second term.) The hope is that the entire package — political and financial — will be sufficient to induce wary bankers who must still provide the bulk of the capital, and prospective retail firms who have stayed away from these neighborhoods, to change their behavior, taking the same sort of risk as the buyers of New Homes.

In November 1996, Mayor Giuliani, Governor Pataki, and New York City Partnership leaders held a press conference announcing a "complete financial package" and promised "construction starts in 1997." If Partnership Plaza does succeed, the re-creation of neighborhoods laid waste in the 1970s will have passed yet another huge milestone.

Prospects — The Daunting 1990s Agenda

In the early 1980s, the Housing Partnership confronted New York's vast stretches of vacant land with an idea: middle-income homeownership. The idea was simple, the execution difficult. Indeed, most knowledgeable New Yorkers gave it little chance to succeed. Although the Partnership overcame the long odds against New Homes in the 80s, its expanded agenda in the 90s is still more daunting. New York's *in rem* housing problem has defeated a multitude of expensive, misguided strategies. And the revival of strong retail trade and other businesses in inner-city neighborhoods is an elusive goal even when housing has made a comeback. Yet, much of the wasted land has been redeemed and a nearly extinct homebuilding industry revived — and new homeowners make the city stronger with their financial and civic investment. Now almost routine, New Homes continues to produce a thousand or more houses annually, on a scale not approached by any other city, even adjusting for New York's size.

In taking up the challenge of job creation and economic development, the Partnership brings a stubborn optimism that a previously insoluble problem will yield to sustained, determined, professionally skillful, and politically sophisticated effort. Where most people would see a forlorn and dispirited neighborhood, the leaders of the Partnership and their allies see resourceful and tenacious neighborhood survivors, eager to engage the tasks of community renewal.

Yet, successful implementation is hardly automatic. The expanded agenda will take years to implement and millions of dollars in private money — in addition to a large commitment of public funds in an era of renewed fiscal stress at all levels of government. There are no shortcuts. And, in the nature of things, some people would not mind seeing the Partnership overreach and fail. "Success in this town is a disease," says Alan Bell, a New Homes developer with the Hudson Companies. "People think it needs to be stamped out."

We shall see. Despite the intrinsic difficulty of the tasks and the sniping of naysayers and skeptics, the Partnership has going for it a laser-like focus on the bottom line of program results and a zestful determination to hammer through — or circumvent — any barrier that stands in the way.

And because of the Housing Partnership's improbable successes in the 1980s, support for the expanded agenda will come more readily. Foundations are more ready to invest their money and prestige in a winning organization. People of talent are more inclined to sign up despite a probable sacrifice of potential earnings. Politicians and business leaders are eager to be visibly involved when they see good things happening. Community groups are hungry for the money and technical support that can help them accomplish what they want to do anyway.

The chances for successful community renewal in New York City are also affected — positively, in my view — by a confluence of national political and social forces that cut against the conventional, pessimistic estimate of the outlook for American cities. The final chapters of this book make the case for a more hopeful prospect.

13

COMMUNITY DEVELOPMENT: THE MAKING OF A NEW URBAN POLICY PARADIGM

Father Louis Gigante, head of the Southeast Bronx Development Corporation (SEBCO), was speaking in 1984 about neighborhood development from his perspective as a community activist. "SEBCO," he said, "started simply as a bunch of people who really were interested in the state of the neighborhood, and wanted to see their neighborhood developed. It lost the battle of the 1960's and early 1970's. By 1975, we were demolished. But we found a way. We found the way through the new programs coming in through the Federal government. Thanks be to God, we were involved from the inception of the Section 8 Program." Gigante went on to list several Section 8 low-income rental projects, adding up to 1,500 apartments, built in the late 1970s. Then the New York state housing agency, which had yet another allocation of HUD Section 8 subsidy available, approached SEBCO about sponsoring more rental projects. Gigante's response was emphatic.

We said: "No! We will do what we can do to rebuild the neighborhood, but with very low and moderate income people only, we can't do it. What would happen is the same thing that happened in the 1960s; we will become a dumping ground for every social agency, and we will cause our neighborhood once again to be rife with tremendous social problems that nobody, except God himself, could contend with."

So we said, we must balance our neighborhood. We love the poor. We are working with the poor. But we have to bring an economic class in that can sustain the neighborhood. So we shifted. Our shift was to reserve certain properties for home-building, long before the New York City Housing Partnership, and long before the City of New York was active in the program. By 1979, I approached the City and said, "Can I have three [city-owned] lots? I want to build three homes." They thought I was crazy. They said, "You will never sell homes up there." I said, "I have already sold them; just let me build the homes."

The city eventually hooked SEBCO into the Section 235 federal homeownership subsidy program, which city officials were struggling to implement. Twenty-four homes were built. "Let me tell you, it was a hassle," said Gigante, what with "all kinds of bureaucratic sign-offs" needed from both city and federal officials. SEBCO, which did the mar-keting and screening of about 300 program applicants, did not cover its costs. The builder also lost money. "I will never do it again this way," said Gigante. Still, it was worth the effort; people who bought the homes "with some trepidation . . . because they were coming back to a devas-tated area of the past" were "doing very well" and helping to stabilize the neighborhood.

When the Housing Partnership was organized, Gigante's SEBCO continued to push homeownership, acting as both community sponsor and nonprofit developer on several projects. Speaking in 1984 to a Hous-ing Partnership conference, Gigante said, "What we are doing with them [the Partnership] is trying to pull this thing off. Believe me, it has been dragging on again due to the bureaucratic problems with the UDAG money." He again stressed the effort to "stabilize" and "balance" the neighborhood, including "even higher-income people — those who are hiding some money and want to live in the neighborhood." Concluding his remarks, he argued that nonprofits like SEBCO ought to be ready to put some of their own money into homeownership programs: "I think if the city is giving subsidies, if the private sector and everybody is pitching in, we all ought to be able to give something back besides simply our hands, our minds and our hearts. If we have some money, we ought to do that to make this thing work, because there is too much land out there that is going to waste. Amen."

Father Gigante's spirited comments — his emphasis on grassroots organizing, his rejection of continued large-scale subsidized rental housing and embrace of homeownership, his call for economically mixed neighborhoods, and his recognition of the interlocking roles of government and the nonprofit sector — serve as a fitting introduction to this chapter on the state of the nation's policy toward major cities.

Researching and telling the Housing Partnership story has pushed me to reconsider the dominant policy paradigm of urban advocates, a paradigm that is fixated on ever-deepening ghetto pathology and calls for the federal government to respond with sweeping initiatives that match the scale of the problem. The best-known proponent of this paradigm is William Julius Wilson, referred to by *New York Times* book reviewer Sean Wilentz as "the most celebrated sociologist in America," and regarded by *Time* magazine as one of "America's 25 most influential people" of 1996. Wilson, the author of *The Truly Disadvantaged* and *When Work Disappears*, is in the forefront of those who assert that the key trends affecting inner-city neighborhoods are all running in the wrong direction.

Wilson's litany has become familiar: Cities have lost the industrial base that provided entry-level jobs for yesterday's unskilled residents and immigrants; the most able and ambitious people have left or are leaving for the suburbs; poverty, particularly black poverty, is increasingly concentrated and isolated in the worst ghettos — cut off from the churches and social networks that once provided positive middle-class role models for the young and offered succor to the needy. Crime, drugs, violence in schools, family disarray, teenage pregnancy rates, homelessness — all are out of control and getting worse.

For the general public, the pathology of inner cities is displayed daily in newspapers and, more vividly, on the evening news. With local television stations adopting the motto — "If it bleeds, it leads" — the ubiquitous minicam and the surveillance camera have given us what Paul S. Grogan, the president of the Local Initiatives Support Corporation, calls "body-bag journalism" — a nightly procession of the dead, the bloodied, and the apprehended crossing the screen. Pessimism about cities dominates public opinion: A February 1997 national survey conducted by the Pew Research Center for the People and the Press found that "only 10 percent of the Pew national sample picked 'getting better'" when asked about the state of America's major cities, "while 48 percent chose 'getting worse.' About 37 percent answered, 'staying the same.'"

It seems small comfort that a wealthy remnant, still hooked by an urban lifestyle, stays in the city, but it walls itself off in fortified enclaves where proximate misery is kept out of sight and, so far as possible, out of mind. Its presence detracts little from a view of the city as politically orphaned, economically crippled, socially destructive, and violent.

As Wilson surveys the urban public policy arena, he presents two basic choices. The first alternative, which he associates with the Republican takeover of Congress in 1994, is to continue the "dramatic retreat from using public policy as a way to fight social inequality" by cutting the social programs that Wilson advocates. This policy of "retreat," as Wilson labels it, relies on "simplistic and pious statements about the need for greater personal responsibility" on the part of poor people, and ignores "inequities in the larger society." It is, in other words, for Wilson a policy of blaming the victim — telling people to "help themselves and not turn to the government for handouts." The second policy alternative is to advance "bold, comprehensive, and thoughtful solutions" of the sort Wilson advances in his most recent book, *When Work Disappears*. But Wilson's prescriptions, like his analysis of ghetto conditions, draw on an old and familiar formula: An activist federal government should lead the way with new or expanded programs in education and child welfare, universal health care, job training, and government-funded, low-wage public service jobs. For example, Wilson calls for re-creating the Depression-era Works Progress Administration (WPA). Wilson's "neo-WPA" would offer sub-minimum-wage jobs to "anyone who wants one," jobs that "could range from filling potholes and painting bridges to serving as nurse's aides, clerks, and cooks."

Wilson does not give his package of proposals much chance for adoption. He writes: "I . . . do not advance proposals that seem acceptable or 'realistic' given the current political climate. Rather, I have chosen to talk about what *ought to be done to address the problems of social in-equality* . . . that threaten the very fabric of society."

Both Wilson's analysis of the urban condition and his outline of policy choices are incomplete. His bleak account of inner city decline simply overlooks the surge of neighborhood rebuilding that has occurred and is occurring across the land, especially since the mid-80s. One could argue that none of this benefits "the truly disadvantaged," but surely a healthier urban economy and an influx of stable working families into previously devastated neighborhoods can at least begin to address two of Wilson's key concerns — job prospects for the unemployed and positive role models for the ghetto underclass. Moreover, the public policies which have stimulated the rebirth of many neighborhoods need to be better understood and deserve support, not as substitutes for social spending, but as the strong contributors that they are to the improved outlook for cities.

Beyond the Anecdotal Success Story

Father Gigante's implausible pitch in 1979 for building new homes among the wreckage of the South Bronx was one of the early challenges to the dominant view of the inner city at that time and since. But Gigante's was only one voice among a growing chorus of community-based activists who all through the 80s and into the 90s have stuck with their battered neighborhoods. They have organized, incorporated, and enlisted allies from among politicians and private sector leaders, and they have begun to see the fruits of their efforts — sometimes dramatically, as in the "Bronx Miracle," and sometimes quietly, in the redemption of a single vacant lot or block. Although the federal government since the early 1980s has had less money to spread around to the cities, necessity has mothered invention in a thousand different places. The result, as LISC's Paul Grogan points out, is much "hidden good news" coming out of cities, news that cuts against the prevailing image of urban despair. What is one to make of these reports?

The New York City Housing Partnership is part of the good news. As a citywide "intermediary" that bridges the gaps between the private sector, government, and community groups, it is clearly a success story on quite a large scale. Several thousand houses in places like the South Bronx, Brooklyn, and Harlem make a major statement about the possi-bilities of neighborhood transformation even in a city as big as New York.

Again, one needs to ask: If cities are increasingly defined as islands of wealth surrounded by seas of misery and depravity, why are thousands of working- and middle-class families eagerly buying new houses in New York City, and why is new ownership housing also catching on in places such as Philadelphia, Baltimore, Chicago, Kansas City, Louisville, and even Detroit?

One possible response is that the Housing Partnership and other examples of urban regeneration are merely anecdotal success stories. After all, in the worst of times and circumstances, there are always the shining exceptions, the small victories won by generous leaders of extraordinary talent, resourcefulness, and drive. They deserve to be recognized, celebrated, written about, perhaps emulated as role models. But other cities, in considering the New York City story, might have reason to be discouraged about their own prospects. How could the New York Partnership have failed, it might be asked, given David Rockefeller's wealth, prestige, connections with the powerful, and willingness to push the right political buttons at critical times?

The answer is that the Partnership might easily have failed, for two reasons. First, the political tensions and bureaucratic complexity of New York are the most extreme of any American city and would have defeated all but the most tenacious implementers. The second reason has to do with timing. The Housing Partnership was seeking to establish itself and its programs in the early 80s, a time when the community development movement was in its beginning stages and when the notion of public-private-nonprofit partnership on a large scale was still novel and largely untested. When the Housing Partnership got started, the broader policy environment was unreceptive to what it was seeking to do. That environment changed in the mid-1980s as local leaders across the country came to reluctantly accept the reality of a diminished federal role in funding urban programs and responded with a burst of homegrown programs that drew on multiple sources of capital and new arrangements for program delivery through established and emerging nonprofit entities. As one such entity, the Housing Partnership made its own contribution to that changed environment and at the same time benefited from it.

"The future of cities under the new fiscal realities," Kathy Wylde has written, "will depend on the successful convergence of the community empowerment and privatization movements, a direction that has already been charted by the nation's community-based housing industry." In this chapter I explore the making of a new urban policy paradigm that helps to explain — beyond the remarkable achievements of gifted individuals — what is providing a nurturing and hopeful climate for neighborhood preservation and renewal. There is, I have concluded, more going on in cities than the occasional good-news story here and there. Rather, I identify a confluence of forces — some political, some demographic, some market-driven, some planned, some accidental — that are working in favor of cities and offering hope for places brought low by economic dislocation, abandonment, and social anguish.

Without taking away one jot from the admirable achievements recounted in this book, I also argue that a new paradigm for community development was already taking shape and helping to create a context within which the Housing Partnership and other local initiatives elsewhere could successfully advance an agenda of neighborhood rebuilding and renewal.

As elements of the paradigm, I propose the following:

(1)   The Community Reinvestment Act (CRA), a 1977 law which requires banks to serve the credit needs — business and residential — of their service areas, including low- and moderate-income neighborhoods;

(2)   The dramatic rise of nonprofit community development corporations (CDCs), which combine advocacy and development skills to lead neighborhood improvement efforts;

(3)   The emergence of national "intermediaries" — private sector consortia of banks, corporations, and foundations, such as the Local Initiatives Support Corporation — which funnel private investment and technical support to local CDCs;

(4)   The low-income housing tax credit, enacted in 1986, which provides large incentives for corporations to invest in low-income rental housing;

(5)   The continued availability to local governments of flexible federal block grant funds — in particular the Community Development Block Grant, enacted in 1974, and the HOME block grant for housing, enacted in 1990;

(6)   Vacant urban land, a legacy of negative economic trends and program failures that is a largely untapped resource for creative re-use;

(7)   The new immigrants, a powerful social and market force
       that is transforming neighborhoods in many cities; and

(8)   The rise of urban homeownership as an affirmation of con-
       fidence and commitment on the part of private investors and
       new homebuyers.

These policies and trends represent an opportunity for cities; they
are a foundation to be defended and built upon. Each of the elements has
been around for awhile; together they are, for the most part, a combination of forces with roots in the 1970s and 1980s. Although not designed
as such by a wise policy guru, they are, in my opinion, largely responsible for the promising signs of urban rebirth in the 1990s. This rebirth is
a long way from being an accomplished fact, and skeptics will say that
the list does not add up to all that much when measured against the conventional estimates of urban prospects. But I would invite them to take
a closer look.

The Community Reinvestment Act

"You realize pretty fast that if there isn't any money flowing into a community it'll die." This was Gail Cincotta speaking with trademark blunt-
ness about her Austin neighborhood in Chicago in the 1960s, a racially
changing neighborhood where banks had stopped lending money for
home improvements and stopped giving mortgages except for those insured by the Federal Housing Administration (FHA). "What we saw
was the whole economic thing," says Cincotta. "The first step is when
the banks and savings and loans refuse to give [conventional] mortgages
or loans for rehabilitation and repairs on the houses. The second step is
when the speculators come in to panic-peddle. They used to be less
sophisticated and just say the blacks were coming. They don't do that
anymore. Now they say, 'This is an FHA area.'" But Cincotta fought
back.

Cincotta, a housewife and mother of six boys, began her career as
a citizen activist by getting involved in neighborhood school issues.
Austin's overcrowded schools had pupils attending in shifts, often in
makeshift mobile classrooms. Soon branching out from the PTA and
school issues, Cincotta also became active in forming block clubs in an
effort to cope with the stress of rapid, unstoppable racial change. Meanwhile, a group of local ministers, interested in preserving some measure
of racial integration, had also called in Tom Gaudette, a Saul Alinski-

trained organizer, to help stitch together a coalition of groups that would focus on common problems, ranging from garbage collection and abandoned cars to beefing up police patrols. After working for a year, Gaudette called a conference of several hundred delegates — black and white — from block clubs and community organizations; the outcome was the formation of Organization for a Better Austin (OBA). Cincotta was elected president.

Although OBA and Cincotta would pursue a broad agenda, it was in housing policy that they would prove to have the most far-reaching influence. A small army of real estate agents, about 300 of them, had invaded Austin and "were making a hell of a lot of money off the racial change." Cincotta's protest strategy mixed cool documentation and hot rhetoric. By slogging through the records of property sales transactions in Austin, she and her group were able to uncover a pattern of real estate agents buying older houses cheap from owners under pressure and then selling them "as is" to black buyers for several times the original sales price. The inflated price would be supported by a compliant FHA appraiser and a mortgage guaranteed by FHA. In effect, the federal government was financing real estate and mortgage banking profiteers at the expense of the neighborhood — both the remnant of white homeowners, like Cincotta, who wanted to stay put and the incoming black residents, who were being cheated by high prices for houses that were often "riddled with code violations."

Cincotta and her supporters fought the system with Alinsky-style techniques. Organization for a Better Austin members tied up local bank offices by opening and closing one-dollar accounts; they also went to bank executives' homes and draped them with red crepe paper to signify the banks' practice of "redlining." The local HUD/FHA director, John Waner, also received many uninvited visits from Cincotta-led delegations — at his home and at his HUD office, where he installed extra security doors in the corridors.

But off the picket line and without her barely needed bullhorn in hand, Cincotta was (and is) a skilled and disarming negotiator in corporate boardrooms and the chambers of government. Branching out from her Austin base, Cincotta formed the Metropolitan Area Housing Alliance in Chicago, a coalition of groups across the city that were also struggling with wrenching neighborhood change. The Alliance extracted lending concessions from banks, pressured HUD to free up more funds for housing rehabilitation, and lobbied Chicago Mayor Richard J. Daley to pass a city ordinance requiring banks with city deposits to make public their lending records. Cincotta was clearly onto something big. She went national.

Neighborhood change and disinvestment were common problems in older cities across the country in the 1960s, and grassroots groups were springing up in protest everywhere. To share the Austin story with groups in other cities, Cincotta organized a national conference to be held in Chicago in March 1972. She hoped that about two or three hundred people would show up, but the attendance turned out to be more than 2,000 delegates from 365 groups in thirty-six states. The Chicago gathering decided to form a national organization called National People's Action, which held its inaugural meeting a month later in Baltimore. Cincotta became the chairman and chief spokesperson for National People's Action (NPA); in 1973 she established an NPA affiliate, the Chicago-based National Training and Information Center, which she has directed continuously since its founding.

National People's Action descended on Washington annually with a couple of thousand delegates. They looked like America — white, black, and brown; men and women; young and old. They spoke bluntly, with a confident and authentic voice. Official Washington began to pay attention.

The core of the NPA legislative agenda was initially quite modest: NPA wanted, of all things, information to be provided by banks on their mortgage lending practices — how much they were lending, to whom, and especially where. Cincotta was granted a hearing before Congressional banking committees to make her case. Senator William Proxmire, the Senate banking committee chairman, liked the idea and invited NPA to work up draft legislation for him to introduce. According to Cincotta, the bill that became the Home Mortgage Disclosure Act of 1975 "was written in a church basement by a whole bunch of folks piecing it together on scratch paper."

It must be said here that the banks never acknowledged the validity of the case brought against them by Cincotta and her movement. They denied "redlining" — arbitrarily denying credit to entire geographical areas without regard to the merits of an individual application. They insisted and would always insist that they did nothing other than apply prudent lending standards to whatever business came in through the door; indeed, they argued, this was their responsibility to their depositors and stockholders, and to the banking regulatory bodies that issued their charter. The banking lobby tried to stop the Home Mortgage Disclosure Act as an unnecessary and meddlesome intrusion that would burden them with costly record-keeping and paper work, but politically, it was an awkward defense: The banks weren't being asked to do anything special, only provide records. And since the facts on bank lending were in dispute, gathering the facts seemed reasonable to Congress.

Passage of the Home Mortgage Disclosure Act gave NPA credibility and momentum. Two years later, in 1977, NPA scored its next legislative victory with passage of the Community Reinvestment Act (CRA), which requires banks and other financial institutions to serve the credit needs of their service areas, including "low- and moderate-income areas." Federal banking regulators must assess an institution's CRA performance as part of their standard supervisory review and assign a rating; this rating is then considered whenever a bank applies for permission to expand through merger, acquisition, or new branches. For banks, the hooker in the Community Reinvestment Act is that it opens the way for outside groups, such as an activist neighborhood organization, to mount a "CRA challenge" against a bank seeking regulatory approval for expansion of its operations.

The banking lobby vigorously opposed CRA for many of the same reasons it opposed the Home Mortgage Disclosure Act — onerous record-keeping requirements, and the implied rebuke it posed to current practices. The banks also objected, with some cause, to the law's vagueness, and to their consequent vulnerability to subjective judgments: None of the key terms in CRA — such as service area, low- and moderate-income communities, credit needs, or satisfactory compliance — are defined.

Ever since CRA's passage in 1977, there has been a running debate over the effectiveness of CRA enforcement. In their heart of hearts, most — though not all — bankers would probably like the law to disappear; they have never stopped complaining about the cost of compliance. Community groups, for their part, have often criticized what they view as weak enforcement; nearly all banks (90 percent) receive a "satisfactory" or better rating from government regulators, and successful CRA challenges have been rare. "Over the years," according to a December 1993 Federal Reserve Bank staff report, "the [regulatory] agencies have sought to deal with these issues by providing increasing guidance about compliance standards; downplaying paperwork requirements to clarify that results, not process, determine an institution's evaluation; instructing examiners to be sensitive to the special burdens on small institutions and improving enforcement techniques. Nevertheless, both institutions and community groups have remained very vocal about their concerns, and the agencies have repeatedly been questioned on their records before congressional hearings."

In 1993 the Clinton administration called for revamping of CRA regulations, a process that took two years and drew over 14,000 public comments. The new regulations, which took effect in 1996, seek to cut back on detailed reporting requirements by emphasizing performance over process; small banks (with less than $250 million in assets) will have special streamlined reporting procedures. Cincotta, still in the thick of community lending politics, applauded the new regulations as signaling an end to eighteen years of confrontation. "The banks thought of us not only as their enemy, but also thought we wanted them to make bad loans." Now, she says, CRA "has blossomed into a spirit of cooperation between banks and the communities."

For all the criticism of timid CRA enforcement, however, community groups have always embraced it fervently and used it effectively as leverage in negotiating investment commitments locally. According to Cincotta, "CRA has resulted in over $35 billion in lending agreements for underserved neighborhoods and has demonstrated that community banking is a safe, sound, and even profitable business." The *Wall Street Journal*, in reporting on its analysis of 1994 mortgage lending, noted a sharp "rise in lending . . . in hard-hit inner-city and rural areas, heavily populated by minorities, that long were underserved by banks and mortgage companies. Indeed, in many cities, low-income and minority borrowers can now find mortgage credit on better terms than affluent whites, Federal Reserve officials say." The wave of bank mergers in the 1990s has prompted banks to make what the *Journal* calls "eye-popping community-lending commitments" such as the $45 billion promised by Wells Fargo in connection with its takeover of First Interstate Bancorp. With whatever mix of corporate motives — public relations, a sense of civic responsibility, pressure from regulators and advocacy groups, even profits — banks have indeed expanded their urban lending, and CRA compliance has been one of the prods. And there is increasing evidence that banks no longer need to be dragged into community lending. "Banks Are Competing to Make Loans in New York City's Poorer Areas," read a *New York Times* headline on July 11, 1994. Banker Jeffrey Denler told the *Times*: "A lot of lenders are looking to other areas [than Manhattan] and finding that loans in neighborhoods they never looked at are just as safe." According to the *Times'* Emily M. Bernstein, "The increased lending in these areas is having a ripple effect, improving the housing stock and generally helping stabilize neighborhoods that had been teetering on the edge of decline."

Without question, the banks' receptivity to community lending has been helped along by the rise of a new kind of banking professional — people who believe in and make their living off CRA-related business, and who build networks of support for CRA within the bank. The new CRA-oriented bankers are more likely to have a degree in planning than an MBA, and have the ability to move easily between executive suites, government agencies, and the storefront offices of community development corporations — foreign and threatening territory for the traditional banker. Many banks, particularly the big ones, have found such people indispensable in steering them through CRA compliance and spotting both the opportunities and pitfalls in community lending.

Although the success of CRA has not protected it from continuing attack — in 1995, some members of Congress labeled CRA an "affirmative action program" ripe for "deregulation" — the law has institutionalized changes in banking practice that are likely to be lasting. As Paul Grogan of the Local Initiatives Support Corporation has observed: "What we've really seen is a credit revolution in the inner city."

Community Development Corporations — "CDCs"

The Community Reinvestment Act was about getting banks to change their behavior by opening their lending windows to credit starved city neighborhoods. The rise of the community development corporation (CDC) is about taking that money and combining it with other sources to achieve physical and economic betterment in a defined neighborhood. CDCs marched into the troubled spaces that had been vacated by public policy confusion and paralysis, and private sector fear and indifference. And, for two decades, as Paul Grogan notes, CDCs "have been quietly building their now prodigious track record."

No one planned the explosive growth in CDCs that occurred in the 1980s; the movement arose more or less spontaneously in response to neighborhood crises and in the face of a national political environment that was unfriendly to city interests. In spirit, the movement has one foot in the Saul Alinsky tradition of combative community organizing and protest and the other in the domain of real estate development and management — where, ultimately, the market rules. It can be a precarious balancing act; nevertheless, CDCs emerged from the 1980s as a significant force, "supported by a web of relationships among public agencies, private funders, corporate givers, and local executive and legislative bodies."

Historically, the CDC movement began in the 1960s; the first organizations were created with direct federal funding under the War on Poverty program. The idea of nonprofit, community-based development attracted the high-profile support of New York Senator Robert Kennedy, who is credited with mobilizing corporate and philanthropic backing for the Bedford-Stuyvesant Restoration Corporation in Brooklyn. "Bed-Stuy" successfully packaged large grants of public and private money and drew on executive talent donated from major New York corporations to compile an impressive record in both housing rehabilitation and economic development. The Bedford-Stuyvesant model prompted replication efforts in several other cities, often with funds from the Ford Foundation, which committed "more than $100 million in grants and program-related investments to a group of these development corporations" in the 1960s and 1970s.

As an organizational type, CDCs defy easy classification. Since the 1960s, they have emerged in all sizes and shapes, from tiny organizations with a desk in the corner of a church basement to well-staffed professional real estate operations. Some CDCs limit their activities to housing, usually rehabilitation; some only do commercial development; some do both. Many CDCs are active in other program areas besides real estate development, including social services, community organizing, home-ownership counseling, and homeless assistance. Despite their diversity, the common thread running through CDCs is that they are locally controlled, typically by a board of neighborhood residents, businesses, and representatives of social institutions (schools, churches, etc.), and that they seek the improvement of a defined territory. Nationally, there is no definitive list of CDCs in existence, although the most informed estimate — by the National Congress for Community Economic Development — is that there are between 2,000 and 2,200 such organizations.

CDCs, whatever their size and sophistication, have set for themselves a daunting task. Real estate development under any circumstances is a complex and risky undertaking, and CDCs must operate in a sector of the market that has been avoided by for-profit players. (Banks dislike risk; hence the importance of CRA.) And because the CDCs' housing clients are typically low- and moderate-income neighborhood residents, CDCs must scramble for subsidies from several different sources to patch together a financing package that works. The CDC organization itself is usually a struggling, hand-to-mouth operation, so there is a never-ending search for money to cover staff salaries, office rent, and other expenses. The chronic money shortage can also paralyze development initiatives if there are no "front-end" funds for property acquisition, proposal writing, and professional fees for architects, engineers, and lawyers. There is an element of "Catch 22" here: CDCs are dependent on money to establish a track record, but the banks, public agencies, and foundations who control grant and loan funds want reasonable assurance of success — and avoidance of embarrassment. (The "intermediaries," as we shall see, would come to play a critical role in helping resolve this dilemma.)

Given this list of impediments, CDCs have nevertheless accomplished a lot. Although complete and definitive production data are not available, the National Congress for Community Economic Development, a CDC advocacy organization, estimates that through 1993 CDCs have been instrumental in providing a total of about 400,000 units of housing, with half of this total being produced between 1988 and 1993, indicating an acceleration in output. Only 6 percent of CDCs produced more than 100 units a year, while 70 percent built fewer than 25 units. Between 1991 and 1993, however, average annual production per organization increased from 26 to 29 units. The National Congress also reports that CDCs have produced 23 million square feet of commercial and industrial space and provided business loans totaling about $200 million.

These aggregate totals are impressive, although not overwhelming. CDCs operate in an environment full of political and financial risks; they cannot be expected to work miracles. Yet, they perform a critical institutional role as a buffer between the raw forces of political and economic change and the aspirations of ordinary people. In the process, they have demonstrated remarkable agility and survival skills, and the stronger ones are racking up concrete achievements in housing and neighborhood improvements on a notable scale. The weaker CDCs will struggle; some will fail and deserve to. But the sector as a whole is likely to show continued staying power.

The Intermediaries

The Urban Institute's Christopher Walker calls the creation of intermediaries "the single most important story of the nonprofit development sector in the 1980s." For good reason: Without them, local community development corporations would have a much harder time surviving; with them, CDCs can not only survive but also be much more productive.

Intermediaries are nonprofit organizations — financially backed by corporate investors and private philanthropy — that operate at the national, state, or citywide level to support neighborhood-based CDCs. They bring investment capital and technical competence to the neighborhood development agenda, but often are a step removed from directly implementing specific projects in the field. Intermediaries also bring a level of involvement that complements that of the local CDCs. The people who sponsor and staff the intermediaries have their hearts in the right place, but they leaven their commitment with a measure of discipline and detachment that may be lacking in the streets and storefronts of the neighborhood. Most important, intermediaries bring credibility and prestige by attracting the leadership and involvement of big names from the corporate, financial, and philanthropic sectors. At bottom, the intermediaries are about reducing risk.

The largest of the national intermediaries is the Local Initiatives Support Corporation (LISC). An initiative of the Ford Foundation and seven corporations, LISC was organized in 1979 with $10 million in capital, half of it from Ford. Since then, LISC — which operates out of thirty-six offices located throughout the country in addition to its New York City headquarters office — has raised more than $2.4 billion from 1,600 different sources, mainly corporations and foundations. Through 1996, LISC support has benefited about 1,400 CDCs who have built or rehabilitated 73,000 units of housing and created 10 million square feet of commercial and industrial space.

Paul Grogan, the president of LISC since 1986 and former director of Boston's neighborhood development agency, characterized several hundred CDC supporters as "crazy people" in remarks to a January 1995 gathering in Chicago of bankers, civic leaders, public officials, and neighborhood development activists. Grogan's epithet was an ironic throwback to an earlier time, when suggestions of mental imbalance had an unkinder bite: Father Gigante had been told he was crazy to push homeownership in the South Bronx, and David Rockefeller was said to be afflicted with "terminal lunacy" for thinking that the Housing Partnership could succeed. After fifteen years, however, LISC's backers can claim to be quite sane: LISC launched a $200 million capital campaign in 1991 and reached its goal in 1995, a year ahead of schedule. Yet, for all of its achievements, LISC's public profile is low; there is a touch of injured regret in the title of its 1994 annual report: "The Hidden Good News."

Three years after the creation of LISC, a second major national intermediary, the Enterprise Foundation, was formed by developer and philanthropist James Rouse in 1982. Rouse, the visionary developer in the 60s of the new community of Columbia, Maryland, again bucked conventional wisdom in the 70s by developing successful inner-city "festival" marketplaces, such as Boston's Quincy Market and Baltimore's Inner Harbor. In the 80s, Rouse directed his energy to raising capital for the sponsorship of low-income housing.

Like LISC, the Enterprise Foundation has become an important player in helping to support local CDCs. Since its formation, Enterprise has raised $1.8 billion in private capital for grants, loans, and equity investments channeled mainly to CDCs. More than 550 CDCs in 150 locations have produced 60,000 units of housing with Enterprise assistance. And in 1991, LISC and Enterprise spearheaded the National Community Development Initiative, a $62.5 million program collaboration among seven foundations and the Prudential Insurance Company that will support nonprofit development in twenty cities.

The success of the two major national intermediaries has helped stimulate the formulation of counterpart intermediaries at the citywide, regional, and state levels. These may be branch offices of the nationals, or organizations — often called "partnerships" — set up by local leadership. A 1994 compilation of such organizations by the National Association of Housing Partnerships lists forty-nine groups in twenty-eight states, a very diverse collection whose "common attribute is that they bring business, government, and communities together to address affordable housing needs, assist community and resident groups and families, and support sound community development." Among the groups, the New York City Housing Partnership is the largest and has the best production record.

Intermediaries in medium-sized and large cities can pool capital and help steer emerging CDCs through complex financial and legal shoals; such help reassures donors and investors nervous about the competence of individual CDCs. Foundations and corporations, confronted with dozens of requests from community organizations with varying track records — including those who are just trying to get started — are increasingly turning to intermediaries to sort through multiple requests and to act as administrators of a lump sum. For example, the Chicago-based MacArthur Foundation in 1988 created the Fund for Community Development, an $11.3 million fund which is administered by the Chicago office of the Local Initiatives Support Corporation and supports twenty-seven community-based nonprofits. (Although this represented the bulk (70 percent) of MacArthur's commitment to nonprofit developers, the foundation continued to make individual grants as well.) Nationally, about two-thirds (64 percent) of foundation grants are being channeled through local intermediaries.

In addition to LISC and Enterprise, a third significant national intermediary is the Neighborhood Reinvestment Corporation, "a congressionally-chartered, public nonprofit established in 1978 with the principal purpose of revitalizing older urban neighborhoods by mobilizing public, private and community resources at the neighborhood level." The Neighborhood Reinvestment Corporation (NRC) receives most of its financial support from a congressional appropriation ($49.9 million in fiscal year 1997), but also raises money from banks, corporations, and foundations. NRC sponsors the creation of counterpart local, neighborhood-based nonprofits, which are governed by boards representing banks, businesses, government agencies, and community organizations. Since the 1970s, NRC's local affiliates, usually called Neighborhood Housing Services, have specialized in helping homeowners of modest incomes to secure loans for home repair and improvements. But in 1993, NRC expanded its efforts by launching a five-year "NeighborWorks Campaign for Home Ownership," a program aimed at helping 10,000 low- and moderate-income families buy homes. Ninety-six local NeighborWorks organizations in thirty-five states have been offering credit counseling to prospective buyers, and working with local real estate agents and lenders to develop special loan products that "are better tailored to meet the special needs of lower-income borrowers." By 1996, the Campaign had assisted 6,529 families to achieve homeownership.

Intermediaries at all levels have without question changed the urban policy landscape. The two forces that prompted their creation were the courageous but often inept efforts of emerging CDCs along with the retreat of the federal government from direct involvement in local project financing. To a considerable degree the intermediaries have come to occupy the program space vacated by the federal government. The federal role, however, remains critical in fostering a procommunity development policy environment. The Community Reinvestment Act is one example; another is the low-income housing tax credit.

The Low-Income Housing Tax Credit

The push and pull of national tax policy have traditionally driven the behavior of the housing construction industry in important ways. When housing production is slumping, tax breaks can give it a prod. If tax inducements are fat enough, builders will build and banks will finance developments even when the market demand for new production may turn out to be weak. Then the government acts to slow things down.

The 1980s version of this familiar policy drama introduced a new twist. The decade began with a bottom-scraping housing production rate of fewer than a million units in 1981. Multi-family construction was especially depressed, at 319,000 units nationwide. That year Congress shortened the depreciation schedules for new apartment buildings to attract investment. The industry responded quickly; apartment construction more than doubled by 1985. In fact, a glut of new apartments hit many local markets, and vacancy rates sailed up. Congress reacted in 1986 by stripping away the 1981 incentives, causing a slowdown. But in the same 1986 legislation, Congress threw a bone to affordable housing advocates: a new low-income housing tax credit that was intended to partially compensate for the death of the Section 8 subsidized rental production program enacted in 1974.

The low-income housing tax credit (LIHTC) helps profitable corporations do well by doing good. Companies that invest in low-income rental housing may take a tax credit (a dollar-for-dollar offset against other taxes) for the entire investment over a ten-year period: A million-dollar investment, for example, would provide an annual credit of $100,000. For five more years, the company may deduct additional amounts for "passive" real estate "losses." Total return on the original investment is 12 to 15 percent annually.

After enactment in 1986, the LIHTC got off to a slow start. Congress gave the tax credit only a three-year life, and the Internal Revenue Service took its time getting out implementing regulations. Many investors, not wanting to get caught in another Congressional change of heart, were cautious. Between 1989 and 1993 the LIHTC was kept alive with

annual extensions until a persistent lobbying effort led Congress to make
LIHTC "permanent." As we shall see, however, LIHTC came under attack in Congress again in 1995 as a form of "corporate welfare."

Despite LIHTC's somewhat precarious political status for many
years, it has achieved success as a production stimulus for rental housing
aimed at its target group: households earning no more than 60 percent of
median income. Since the typical corporation had no idea how to go
about connecting its tax credit investment to a specific housing development, the intermediaries, led by the Local Initiatives Support Corporation and the Enterprise Foundation, immediately leaped into the role as
packagers of the credits for distribution to CDCs developing rental housing. LISC formed a subsidiary in 1987, the National Equity Fund, that
has gathered in $1.2 billion from 117 corporate investors to help finance
over 25,000 homes. Enterprise's subsidiary, the Enterprise Social Investment Corporation, also began in 1987 and has raised $1.4 billion from
165 corporations. All told, the tax credits have attracted $12 billion in
corporate investment in the first ten years since enactment and contributed to the financing of an estimated 750,000 housing units. In any given
year, the number of apartments financed is limited by a national cap on
available tax credits established by Congress; a formula allocates the
total pool of credits to state governments, which are responsible for
suballocating to communities in each state. Annual production nation-
wide since 1993 is estimated to be about 100,000 annually.

When CDCs put together the financing on specific housing development deals, the capital derived from tax credits typically forms one layer of
a much more complex financing package. This is because using the tax
credit by itself usually does not result in rent levels much below $400 to
$450 per month, still too high for a low-income family. To bring rents lower,
CDCs must hunt for subsidies from other sources, such as below-market
interest rate mortgages from state or local housing agencies, philanthropic
grants, and federal block grant funds (which we discuss next).

Why would anyone want to get rid of LIHTC? Here is a program
that attracts private capital, is run by the states, works pretty much as
intended, and has a broad base of political support from major corporations, foundations, mayors and governors, and grassroots community organizations. Critics of the LIHTC, however, cite its relative complexity
and the transaction costs associated with putting together tax credit
deals: Between 20 and 30 percent of an investor's contribution is drained
off to pay the "syndication" fees of lawyers and accountants. Others ob-

ject to the LIHTC as a form of "corporate welfare" that swells the federal deficit: A U.S. Treasury estimate put the revenue loss at about $14.6 billion over a five-year (1995-99) period. The question is whether corporate investors should be permitted a generous return on their money in exchange for helping generate several hundred thousand housing units targeted to low-income families. Despite its imperfections, the low-income housing tax credit has become a critical weapon in the CDC arsenal; its loss would seriously hobble CDC housing production.

CDBG and HOME

For community development corporations, before there were tax credits and intermediaries there was "CDBG" — the Community Development Block Grant program. Enacted in 1974, CDBG was a product of the Nixon version of New Federalism — an amalgam of previous categorical programs, the largest being Urban Renewal and Model Cities. CDBG provided all cities of over 50,000 population with broad-based, flexible entitlement grants that could be spent by mayors for almost any purpose that could be shown to benefit primarily low- and moderate-income city neighborhoods. CDBG could be used for housing rehabilitation, although not for new construction. It could also be used to fund neighborhood-based organizations engaged in community planning and advocacy, and in the actual operation of programs aimed at improving housing, commercial strips, parks, and streetscapes. In addition, social services could be funded by CDBG on a limited basis.

As the CDC movement was gathering momentum in the 1970s, local groups worked aggressively through the political process to gain a share of the cities' CDBG entitlement. City Hall could be wary of groups that appeared to have their own political agenda or to be engaged in posturing against the "power structure"; yet mayors also wanted good-news stories and ribbons to cut in the neighborhoods — and CDBG was a way to build political support among groups that could deliver successful projects. The program's unusual flexibility quickly established CDBG as everyone's favorite urban program. Although it has been fiddled with occasionally and has not grown much from its annual $3-to-$4 billion-dollar range, CDBG is the largest federal neighborhood assistance program, providing $48 billion to 946 entitlement communities since 1974 — and it has survived attempts by the Reagan and Bush administrations to either cut it or fold it into a larger block grant. In many cities CDBG has been a lifeline for the more established CDCs with a moderately strong political constituency; the loss of CDBG would be a severe blow to the CDC movement. Fortunately, its popularity makes it unlikely that that will happen.

In 1990, a second important block grant joined CDBG as a valuable resource for neighborhood rebuilding. This was the HOME (not an acronym) program, a flexible block grant distributed by formula to states and cities, to be used for housing targeted to low- and moderate-income families. The idea for a housing block grant also had a New Federalism origin. In 1982, a presidential commission appointed by President Reagan recommended that a separate "Housing Component" be tacked on to CDBG and that new housing construction be permitted under CDBG itself. Reagan didn't buy it, but the idea re-emerged toward the end of the Reagan administration. Housing advocates had gathered their forces to form a National Housing Task Force, a privately funded group "organized to help set a new national housing agenda." The group's cochairs were developer James Rouse, founder of the Enterprise Foundation, and David Maxwell, then CEO of Fannie Mae. *A Decent Place to Live* — the Task Force's report, issued in 1988 — had as its centerpiece recommendation the creation of a $3 billion housing block grant program, which would allow wide discretion with respect to how the funds could be used. This recommendation was especially significant because it represented the political abandonment by the subsidized housing lobby of federally run rental "production" programs with deep, risk-free federal subsidies attached to each project. The most recent one, Section 8, had been killed during the Reagan administration and would not rise again; the Task Force did not seek to resurrect it in some other form. According to the Task Force, future federal money for housing development should be put into a pot, for state and local officials to allocate as they saw fit. In 1990, after spirited debate, Congress agreed, creating the HOME block grant with a $1.5 billion appropriation.

HOME gives CDCs another source to tap into for housing initiatives. What's more, their claim is explicitly recognized in the legislation itself; jurisdictions receiving HOME funds must set aside at least 15 percent for nonprofit "Community Housing Development Organizations" that have "a history of serving the local community or communities within which housing to be assisted . . . is to be located."

One of the truisms of domestic policy since Ronald Reagan is that the federal government has almost completely pulled out of programs that benefit cities. Ironically, this view suits the political purposes of both conservatives and liberals — conservatives because it signifies "less government" and the end of "failed programs," and liberals because it helps shore up their urban political base and provides a rationale for increased social spending. The reality is, as usual, more complex. Although some urban programs have suffered cuts or elimination, the Community Development Block Grant has been durable and popular. And the HOME program, which is modeled after CDBG, is a very substantial recent addition to the urban program arsenal. Together, the two block grants mesh effectively with housing tax credits and CRA-induced private bank financing. Thus, despite all one hears about the federal government's abandoning the cities, the fact is that Washington is still very much of a player in neighborhood rebuilding.

Vacant Urban Land

Cities have a lot of unused land — the legacy of population decline, abandoned factories, retail businesses gone broke, and derelict housing left behind by departing families. New York City's vast store of vacant land led in the 1970s to the "planned shrinkage" controversy, a debate echoed in the 1990s in Detroit, where city ombudsperson Marie Farrell-Donaldson has proposed "mothballing" nearly deserted areas — fencing them off, landscaping the perimeter, and shutting down city services inside. In Chicago, city planners — who in 1958 had feared the city would run out of all developable land by 1973 — estimated in 1987 that 19.1 square miles of land were vacant, almost half of it in residential areas. A 1990 study done by the Philadelphia Planning Commission identified more than 15,000 vacant lots and 27,000 abandoned buildings. Although no national inventory of urban vacant land exists, the condition is pervasive and plainly visible in almost any city. The main function of such land, apparently, is to act as a repository of society's unwanted debris.

What is to be done? The problem has many causes and took several decades to develop — and it will not be solved quickly. But it is important to get started. The first step is obvious: Cities need to take a comprehensive inventory of their vacant land to determine its location, previous use, and general condition.

The next steps are much trickier, both politically and legally. The goal is, clearly, to get as much land as possible back into private hands and productive use. "But can city governments assemble vacant lands and recycle them smartly?" asks Neal R. Peirce, a writer and consultant on urban affairs. Peirce's answer isn't encouraging. "The record is grim. Burdened with land laws written generations ago, and often unaware of their vacant land inventory, many cities take three to five years to turn over a single parcel." As the New York City Housing Partnership discovered, city government's land disposition machinery is frequently gummed up by bureaucratic turf battles and bungling. But bureaucracy was only part of the problem in New York; the city had real difficulty sorting out its ambivalence about the value of vacant land. On the one hand, the market's judgment seemed to be that a site was worthless and could be given away; on the other hand, the city wanted to believe that an auction would attract interested bidders, providing revenue for city coffers and eventually property tax revenues as well. In addition, politicians in New York and elsewhere always worry about being charged with giving away the city's land to well-connected cronies.

But where vacant land is abundant in largely abandoned former residential areas, it makes no sense for cities to be timid about turning over sites for development if the market is ready. In the Chicago neighborhood of Woodlawn, for example, the population dropped from 81,279 in 1960 to 27,473 in 1990; after the exodus, 70 percent of Woodlawn was vacant land, half of it owned by the city. The *Chicago Tribune* called Woodlawn "a South Side neighborhood whose name is a byword for inner-city decay, middle-class flight, crime and despair." But Chicago is discovering, as New York did a decade earlier, that there is a market for ownership housing in places like Woodlawn. In 1994, a new development called Plaisance Place — the first market-rate new construction in at least forty years — quickly sold out its first eight houses at prices averaging around $140,000. Another twenty-one houses were added in 1995. Several blocks away, the Kenwood Pointe Development broke ground in November 1995 for forty-one new homes; these qualify for a $20,000 city subsidy under the "New Homes for Chicago" program. As in New York, the political cover for conveying land for new housing is provided by a nonprofit development entity which oversees the work of private developers; in the Woodlawn projects, the CDCs involved are the Woodlawn Preservation and Development Corporation and The Woodlawn Organization (TWO). Other cities that are starting to adopt similar strategies include Cleveland, Baltimore, St. Louis, Boston, and Louisville.

Cities need to make a fresh assessment of their vacant land, and of the snarl of laws and regulations that tie up land disposition for years.

Tax-delinquent vacant property should be seized for public land banking. And there are, as Peirce writes, "whiffs of reform." Cleveland, for example, cut delinquent owners' redemption period from five years to two weeks. Rigid requirements for public auction of vacant land also need to be scrutinized. In neighborhoods where competent CDCs are active, it makes much more sense to consult with them about the use of vacant land than to automatically auction it off for a token price to a developer who may just sit on it anyway. As the Pennsylvania Horticultural Society recommended in its 1995 report on Philadelphia's vacant land challenge, CDCs with a "solid record as expert housing rehabilitators should be encouraged to plan for entire neighborhoods around their properties, using the easily available land for more gardens, landscaping, yard and play space, parking for residents and businesses — indeed, to add a measure of suburbia's spaciousness in the inner city."

Putting CDCs at the center of land disposition and management issues is another way for cities to stretch the limited resources available to them. Doing so will probably not remove all strife from the process: Private developers will make their competing claims, and CDCs themselves have been known to fight with each other for turf. But the goal of a community-based land strategy is not the avoidance of controversy; the goal is to establish vacant land as part of the mix of assets and incentives that can be combined creatively at the neighborhood scale. If there is competition between groups and proposals, it is city government's job, finally, to sort them out and make the call.

The Immigration Wave

In the 1980s, immigration to the United States reached a historic high of more than ten million people, and it is likely that the 1990s will break that record. "The immigration wave is changing the nation, and our industry will change with it," says James Johnson, Fannie Mae chairman and CEO. He is correct. Immigration policy is also housing policy and urban policy.

Since 1980, the nation's doors have been opened wider by three important pieces of legislation: the Refugee Act of 1980, the Immigration Reform and Control Act of 1986, and the Immigration Act of 1990. The first law established systematic procedures for admitting refugees and granting permanent asylum to people already in the country. The second law had the dual purpose of legalizing the previous undocumented status of many illegal immigrants and cutting the future influx of illegals by means of better border control and penalties to employers who hire illegals. (The first purpose was achieved, the second not.) The third law increased the annual legal immigration cap by 40 percent, not including refugees and close relatives of U.S. citizens — a large exception. Taken together, these laws contributed to the record inflow of immigrants and will continue to do so unless changed.

Immigration policy since the 1960s has also caused a dramatic shift in the racial and ethnic composition of immigrants. Before 1960, 80 percent of new immigrants came from Europe. By the 1980s, however, more than four-fifths of legal immigrants were coming from Latin America and Asia. The trend continues: In 1993, the top ten countries of origin for immigrants were Mexico, China, the Philippines, Vietnam, the former USSR, Dominican Republic, India, Poland, El Salvador, and the United Kingdom. In addition, the diversity of the countries of origin is growing markedly: In 1990, forty-one different countries provided more than 100,000 immigrants each, compared with twenty-one in 1970.

The scale of recent immigration has become a hot issue. Policies governing legal immigration are complicated by the nation's evident failure to control illegal immigration. The native-born public worries about immigrants taking away their jobs and about the burden of providing health care and schooling to the newcomers; both California and Florida have sued the federal government for reimbursement of the public service costs associated with their large undocumented immigrant populations. Underscoring public anxiety, California voters in 1994 approved Proposition 187, a measure that would take away health, education, and other social services from undocumented immigrants. Although constitutional challenges have prevented Proposition 187's implementation, it is a sign of deep political division on the immigration issue.

There is more to the immigration question, however, than can be encompassed in a thirty-second political advertisement. Policy analysts, as is their wont, have emphasized the complexity of the issue: The multiple policy goals, the need to distinguish between measures to control immigration and measures to deal with immigrants once they arrive, and the difficulties of assessing labor market impacts and quantifying the public costs and benefits associated with immigration. With respect to the last set of issues — those related to economic and fiscal impacts — the Urban Institute's Michael Fix and Jeffrey S. Passel have reviewed the available research, and they conclude in general that "there is no strong evidence that immigration reduces overall availability of jobs," and that the "annual taxes paid by immigrants to all levels of government more than offset the cost of services they received, generating a net annual surplus of $25 billion to $30 billion." These are, of course, aggregate numbers that do not sort out which level of government receives the revenue and which level provides the services. According to Fix and Passel, the federal government is a clear winner; the "state-level impact varies by state"; and "at the local level, the costs of immigrants — and of the native born — exceed taxes paid. The major 'cost' is education of immigrant children." On job creation, they report: "Immigrants create more jobs than they themselves take, and self-employment is higher than among native-born Americans." Also, the use of welfare is low as compared with natives. Finally, if past trends hold, the immediate costs associated with new immigrants will tend to diminish over time: "[B]oth refugee and legal immigrant households that arrived before 1980 currently have higher average incomes than those of native born U.S. citizens."

In liberalizing immigration policy, the federal government was not setting out to reshape American cities and neighborhoods, but that is what is happening in those cities where immigrants are settling in large numbers. About seven out of ten of the 1980s immigrants have settled in just five states: California (36.2 percent), New York/New Jersey (17.5 percent), Texas (8.5 percent), and Florida (7.5 percent). Within these states, immigrants tend to concentrate in the major metropolitan regions, four of which — Miami, Los Angeles, San Francisco, and New York — now have a foreign-born population ranging form 20 to 34 percent of their total population. Another nineteen regions with populations exceeding one million have between 5 and 17 percent foreign-born residents. And since immigration is the principal source of population growth in the United States, these numbers are sure to go up.

Because most immigrants arrive with little more than their hopes and an entrepreneurial spirit, they are drawn to the parts of cities where housing and commercial space are cheapest — to neighborhoods where the current residents are leaving for what they hope are better places elsewhere. As the new arrivals settle in, they seem to bring a jolt of resourcefulness and energy that eluded the best efforts of publicly sponsored redevelopment schemes. Mitchell Sviridoff, a veteran of Ford Foundation-led inner-city improvement programming, describes the process: "Masses of new people arrive each day, uplifting forsaken neighborhoods in ways beyond the expectation of earlier and failed urban redevelopment. They demonstrate, as did the older migrations, that new people possessed of a sturdy work ethic and stable families matter more than buildings.

"As the immigrants filter into drained communities, they refill churches and schools. Retail streets are rejuvenated and boards come off the store windows. Even in the current real estate depression, when prestigious shopping streets experience unprecedented vacancies, one sees few if any for-rent signs in the enclaves of immigrant concentrations."

It is possible, I suppose, to romanticize the immigrant experience — to be mesmerized by colorful, teeming streets so lately drab and neglected. Behind the almost festive facade, the immigrant's lot is often hard: A "sturdy work ethic" may mean exhausting days and nights working for exploitative wages in a restaurant kitchen or garment-making sweatshop — run, more often than not, by one's own countrymen. "Housing" may consist of a vermin-infested cubicle. Immigrants must also bear the emotional strain of trying to build a home in an alien and unsympathetic culture. Yet, even in those places where immigrants live in what social researchers call "concentrated poverty," they show a relatively low incidence of so-called "underclass" characteristics — unemployment, welfare dependency, and teenage pregnancies. Urban Institute researchers Wendy Zimmerman and Mitchell Tobin found "striking differences" when they compared foreign-born and native-born poverty areas in seven cities: "Even though people in 'immigrant' neighborhoods have less education on average than those in 'native' neighborhoods, the former were more likely to be employed and have higher incomes, and much less likely to be in families headed by women or to use welfare." Despite daunting obstacles, most immigrants, it seems, are indeed "making it," often without the government's help.

The new immigrant communities complicate city governance in many ways. In their entrepreneurial activities, they sometimes operate at the margins of legality. They are not immune to street gangs and organized crime. Inter-ethnic rivalries — between immigrant groups, and between immigrants and "natives" — can get nasty when one group seeks to expand its boundaries at the expense of another. These tensions are real and challenging, but they have also constituted the stuff of urban life and politics for at least a century. The net benefits of the immigrants' arrival to previously flagging city neighborhoods have been overwhelmingly positive.

14

URBAN HOMEOWNERSHIP AND THE FUTURE OF CITIES

Homeownership has a special place in the community development paradigm because it represents an affirmation of new confidence in the future of a neighborhood and of a city. Homebuilders, buyers, and banks stay away from places that seem to have no future; they will move in and risk their capital only if they believe the prospects for a neighborhood are good. Although the expansion of urban homeownership is surely no panacea for all of the cities' problems, it does provide a critical market test of how well *other* forces are at work to improve that outlook.

"Nothing spells turnaround in a more profound way . . . than saying, 'I want to make my home here. I want to buy a home here and raise my family here.' Areas like Woodlawn need an influx of new families coming into the community, not as renters but as investors." So says the Reverend Leon Finney, Jr., chairman of The Woodlawn Organization in Chicago, about a neighborhood — like the South Bronx in New York — that has been a legendary symbol of urban disaster. After forty years or more, homeowners are indeed trickling back into Woodlawn, buying CDC-sponsored housing built on vacant city land. Finney puts his finger on what is special about homeowners: They are "investors" laying out thousands of dollars of their own cash and assuming a large debt in an act of commitment to their families and community. New homeowners undercut the dominant stereotype of the city as a place to leave if you are on your way up in the world. Renters are fine people, too, who may also contribute to stable communities; but they do not, literally, buy into a neighborhood's future to the same degree as owners.

In the main homeownership story of this book, the leaders of the New York City Housing Partnership draw upon elements of the new paradigm in significant ways. For example, the Community Reinvestment Act helps apply regulatory pressure on banks to provide mortgage financing that is vital to the Partnership's program. The rise of strong CDCs gives the business-dominated Partnership an entrée into the politically volatile world of neighborhood affairs. The availability of vacant city-owned land is critical to the financial feasibility of Partnership developments. And New York's burgeoning immigrant groups, and their aspirations for homeownership, account for a significant segment of the market for Partnership homes.

Although other cities differ from New York in particular respects, the main elements of the new paradigm are pervasive in urban America. If conditions were right for a surprising expansion of homeownership in New York City, it seems likely that they are also right for furthering homeownership in other cities. Other cities, in fact, might face fewer obstacles. As we have seen in this book, New York City's huge size, racial and ethnic diversity, and political and bureaucratic complexity all contribute to the sheer difficulty of getting anything done. And other cities have the benefit of New York City's experience to draw on.

There are two questions that need to be addressed about the prospects for urban homeownership, however. The first relates to the scale of market demand. Central cities in general have had since the early 1980s a homeownership rate that has held at about 49 percent; the suburban homeownership rate is about 70 percent and the nonmetropolitan rate about 72 percent. Realistically, what are the chances for achieving an upward bump in the urban homeownership rate? The second question relates to policy. The New York City Housing Partnership and other programs of smaller scale depend to varying degrees on a deliberate strategy to promote homeownership with publicly funded inducements such as free land, property tax deferrals, low-interest mortgages, and outright grants to reduce purchase price. Not everyone agrees that this is a responsible use of public subsidies at a time when other housing needs seem to be more urgent. Other critics see homeownership as working against the goal of racially integrated communities. As we shall see, the "market" issues and the "social" issues are often interconnected.

Where will the new urban homebuyers come from? There was a moment — after the mid-1970s Arab oil embargo triggered an "energy crisis" — when some urban experts thought that a "back-to-the-city" movement would draw in suburbanites wanting to cut commuting costs to their downtown jobs. Wishful thinking, as it turned out; the crisis passed, the exodus continued. However, the source of today's demand for ownership is largely a *stay*-in-the-city movement driven by working families of modest income who would rather own than rent for the traditional reasons, tangible and intangible. One indicator of potential demand is the success of "Home-Buying Fairs" sponsored by Fannie Mae: since 1992, these fairs have been held in 23 cities, attracting a total of more than 185,000 people, and eighty to one hundred exhibitors at each fair. Survey research helps to quantify this demand: More than two-thirds of all renter households intend to buy at some time in the future, and three-fourths of these potential buyers expect that some sacrifices (of vacations and new cars, for example) may be necessary to achieve that goal.

Within cities, the potential demand for homes is coming largely from working- and middle-class blacks, Hispanics, and immigrants. An analysis by Varady and Lipman, for example, of ownership demand among renters indicates that many black renters have sufficient income to buy a home, and about four out of ten (38 percent) intend to make that their next move. And Harvard's Joint Center for Housing Studies estimates that an additional 855,000 black households in the nation's forty largest metropolitan areas could become owners if blacks attained the same rate of homeownership as whites in comparable circumstances.

Other research focuses on the homeownership potential among Hispanic, Asian, and other immigrant groups. A 1995 survey commissioned by Fannie Mae found that "[i]mmigrants are strongly committed to achieving homeownership as a symbol of their integration into American life," and that "[i]mmigrants who rent are almost three times more likely than all adult renters to list owning a home as their 'number one priority.'" Because of the scale of immigration — ten million immigrants in the 1980s alone — this drive to own translates into some very big numbers as it hits the housing market. Typically, immigrants enter the urban housing market as renters, and over time, their homeownership rates tend to converge with those in the general population. For example, a study by Nancy McArdle and Kelly Mikelson of the Harvard Joint Center for Housing Studies traced the homeownership rate of young adult (25-34) immigrants in the 1970s. By 1980, 24.2 percent had become owners — 45 percent of the rate among native-born households in their age group. Ten years later, however, the immigrants' rate had gone up to 54.9 percent — or 81 percent of their comparable age group. The conclusion: "The tendency for immigrant homeownership rates to increase rapidly with time in the United States suggests that the immigration surge during the 1980s and 1990s will be a substantial source of homeownership demand."

Data compiled by the *Wall Street Journal* suggest that a sharp upswing in black and Hispanic homebuyers is in fact occurring. Comparing 1993 and 1994 mortgage approvals, the *Journal* reported an increase of 38 percent in approvals for blacks and 31 percent for Hispanics. (The comparable figure for whites was only 12 percent.) For both groups, the number of borrowers was close to a quarter of a million persons in 1994. Banks are clearly targeting minorities with attractive mortgage products — partly as a result of CRA pressures, but also because they sense the profit potential of a historically underserved market. Moreover, the decision by Fannie Mae, announced in 1994, to commit $1 trillion in mortgage financing for 10 million homes by the year 2000, will help maintain the momentum behind the minority homebuying surge.

The challenge for cities is to capture a good share of this emerging homeownership market. At the neighborhood level, CDC leaders are increasingly concerned about attracting or retaining working- and middle-class families who have other options. The old fears of "gentrification" — that well-off people will push out the poor — are fading, largely because there is so much vacant land for development. As Marc A. Weiss, special assistant to HUD Secretary Andrew Cuomo, comments: "This is not the urban renewal days where you're going into neighborhoods and throwing people out of their homes." Margaret Jackson, the chairperson of Community Board 10 in Harlem, remarked in 1984 that gentrification was "not as big a concern as the young people that we are losing out of Harlem. . . . You cannot build a community on just Section 8 [low-income rental] housing." Working with the Housing Partnership, Jackson observed, was one way "to stop the rush out of the City" and to "keep some of our people, our young professionals and our moderate- to middle-income people from leaving. . . . They are growing up; they have gone to school and gotten their degrees; they have gotten their jobs and their raises, and the income in that family has gone up. They have to have a place to live too."

More recently, the Pilsen Resurrection Project, a Chicago CDC operating since 1990 in a Hispanic neighborhood, has been building one- and two-family homes on vacant city-owned land in direct response to the loss of upwardly mobile families to the suburbs. Demand for Resurrection's new homes has forced sales to be determined by lottery. According to The Resurrection Project's (TRP) fifth anniversary report, TRP has been offering homes that are affordable to families earning as little as $17,500 annually, but, in addition, TRP has built larger "move-up" models "that allow [higher- income] working families to buy a home in Pilsen comparable to ones they could find in the suburbs. TRP is actively encouraging economic integration as one component of creating a healthy community." Victor Knight, who heads a Chicago CDC building homes in Woodlawn, a nearly all-black community, echoes the economic integration theme: "'The idea is to have economic integration' — that is, a mixture of economic classes, not just the poor left behind when so much of the inner city's population fled. 'If we can get racial integration, too, fine, but the first thing is economic integration.'"

I find striking in these statements a notion of "community" that clearly includes economic integration but not racial or ethnic integration. When Harlem's Margaret Jackson spoke of keeping "our" young professionals and middle-income families in the community, she was obviously talking about African-Americans. Similarly, leaders in Pilsen seek to build a "healthy community" that is grounded in its Mexican-American heritage. In both cases, the identified threat to the achievement of mixed-income neighborhoods is, of all things, the lure of the *suburbs*. The articulation of this threat by community leaders — coupled with Victor Knight's ho-hum nod to racial integration as a secondary goal — comes as a jarring counterpoint to a generation of policy literature that labels white racism and exclusionary suburbs — "the division of race by place" — as being at the bottom of all urban ills. No one doubts either the existence of racism or the exclusionary policies of many suburbs — but neither seems to be conspicuously on the minds of many emerging community leaders. They are right to be concerned about the appeal of the suburbs. As M. Leanne Lachman and Deborah Brett report: "Middle-class minority households have been leaving the central cities in droves. Nationwide, the African-American suburban population grew 34% during the '80s; for Hispanics, suburban growth was 69% and for Asians, 126%. By contrast, the white suburban population grew by only 9%." Cities and neighborhoods are in a bidding game for these households; for them to compete, they need to offer an attractive product.

Subsidizing Homeownership: The Equity Issue

Cities, especially since 1980, are seeking to respond to middle-income housing demand in order to avoid a dangerous hourglass social structure — with an angry, impoverished underclass on one end and an intimidated, heavily guarded elite on the other. As Cleveland Mayor Michael R. White, who is African-American, puts it: "We can't ultimately end up with a city of all old people and all poor people, because when that happens, they'll call us Detroit and turn the lights out." David Varady, a professor at the University of Cincinnati, has written that there "is increasing consensus among scholars and policy-makers that if central cities are to remain healthy they need to stimulate middle-income housing production by offering incentives" such as land, low interest loans, and property tax breaks. Despite this consensus, Varady expected that his research on specific middle-income programs would show them to be controversial "because of opposition from minority politicians and community activists" as well as from planning professionals committed to the notion of "equity planning," which holds that the poorest citizens should have priority claim on all public resources. However, in conducting case studies of seven cities (Baltimore, Cleveland, Montreal, New York, St. Louis, St. Paul, and Wilmington) where middle-income programs have gotten started, Varady found his hypothesis to be incorrect. Middle income ownership programs have been remarkably *non*controversial and have attracted broad support from minority officials (including black mayors in Cleveland, Baltimore, and New York), as well as from many neighborhood organizations. Citing his interview with Kathy Wylde, Varady notes "that the social justice argument against middle-income housing programmes had become marginalized because of the emergence of a minority middle-class." He then quotes Wylde directly: "If you want [the minority middle-class] to stay [in the city] there has to be a product. The private sector cannot deliver the product without assistance."

The Reverend Arthur Brazier, who chairs The Fund for Community Redevelopment and Revitalization in Chicago, makes a similar point: "I think since the 60s and 70s very little attention was paid to those people and those families who were upwardly mobile and who could make choices. All of the interest was paid toward people with deep subsidies. And since no one was paying attention to the needs of the moderate income residents they left the city."

But opposition to middle-income housing assistance cannot be dismissed quite so quickly. What about the "equity" issue? Any proposal to give additional homeownership incentives — within cities or elsewhere — must contend with criticism from housing policy analysts who would like to confine the issue to a question of how to allocate money from a limited pool of housing subsidy. Many analysts would include in their definition of "subsidy" the substantial tax benefits already enjoyed by owners: the deduction of mortgage interest and property taxes from taxable income, and the ability of older (over 55) owners to write off up to $125,000 of profit gained in the sale of a residence. These benefits — called "tax expenditures" by federal budget-makers — add up to a large number: an estimated $84 billion in 1994. Cutbacks in federal rental subsidies have helped draw attention to these incentives. Burchell and Listokin, for example, state that HUD's subsidized rental housing outlays in 1993 were only "about one-third the federal tax contribution to homeownership. Yet the tax deductibility, except in arcane tax accounting, is hardly recognized as the major housing assistance that it is, perhaps because it largely benefits the upper classes, whereas the other subsidies benefit the poor." This leads some analysts to recommend cutting the homeowner tax breaks — especially for the richest owners, who benefit the most — and redirecting the savings to fund housing for poor renters and the homeless.

On the other side, proponents of homeowner tax benefits disagree that such benefits are properly classified as an outright subsidy; they assert that expanding homeownership is a broadly desirable social and economic goal that has been explicit national policy for generations. The purpose of benefits attached to homeownership, therefore, is to encourage behavior that serves the general welfare. So far, this line of argument has carried the day politically.

When the homeowner subsidy debate moves specifically into an urban context, the equity issue is in some respects sharpened. The new generation of urban homeownership programs like New York's, in addition to tapping the usual federal incentives, also tacks on such local features as low-cost public land, property tax relief, reduced-interest mortgages, or outright grants to reduce purchase price. How can such benefits to middle-income homebuyers be justified when there are so many poor people still paying high rents for wretched housing or sleeping under viaducts?

This is a vexing question, but I believe the answer lies in the testimony of several community leaders previously cited. For example, when Harlem's Margaret Jackson speaks of stopping "the rush out of the City" of young black professionals, when the South Bronx's Father Gigante says "No!" to still more low-income rental housing, and when Woodlawn's Reverend Finney says "nothing spells turnaround in a more profound way" than homeownership, they are clearly not debating the relative merits of owner versus rental housing subsidies. Rather, they are putting the issue in the context in which I think it belongs — in the economic, social, and spatial realities of their neighborhoods. What matters to them is the creation of a "healthy community," one that includes a mix of housing types and income groups.

Despite the completely valid claim of poor renters for public support, housing policy is not a simple matter of allocating shares from a finite pool of subsidy dollars. As Anne B. Shlay of Temple University writes, housing policy has "many layers." In the context of community economic development, she argues, housing is "a large investment typically requiring outside financing" that brings capital into a community; it is a "consumption item [that] may operate as a local economic stimulus. . . . Finally, housing policy may be used to promote local ownership and control of property. . . . Housing policy may therefore be a part of a creative strategy for enhancing the well-being of individuals and communities." In this broader policy context, the new generation of urban homeownership programs stands up to scrutiny very well indeed.

A Shorter Way Home

New urban homeowners have a personal financial stake in their property, and by extension in their neighborhood and community. They represent a measure of stability. If nothing else, their investment makes them less likely to move away; but more likely, a financial stake in and emotional commitment to one's own place go hand-in-hand. As Doug Dylla, the coordinator of the Neighborhood Reinvestment Corporation's Neighbor-Works Campaign, writes: "The willingness to invest — as evidenced by a homeowner's commitment, a lender's confidence, and insurance agent's belief in an acceptable level of risk . . . [makes] a powerful statement . . . about a neighborhood being worthy of attention and investment."

Moreover, from a land use standpoint, home construction is an attractive and productive use of idle land. As high-quality, low-density neighborhoods begin to appear on previously derelict land sites, the before-and-after contrast creates surprise, excitement, and a sense of promise. These days, the transformation brings out the news cameras and feature writers; it might, in time, become commonplace.

Cities need to awaken to the potential for expanding homeownership. Cities with small, tentative programs should seek to enlarge them; cities with no program should test the waters. Although it is axiomatic that local real estate markets differ, the tendency to underestimate the demand for new homes — dramatically illustrated in New York City — is much more of a danger than overestimation.

But New York City's story also shows that programs do not fall into place and thrive automatically. Although no one program model can insure success, in New York, the high-profile leadership and commitment of Mayor Ed Koch and David Rockefeller, and the creation of the city-wide nonprofit Housing Partnership led by Kathy Wylde, were critical in attracting the participation of banks, homebuilders, and community groups; in brokering competing and conflicting interests; while, at the same time, keeping the focus unrelentingly on the bottom line of home production. For New York and the Housing Partnership, the process was long, complex, and often contentious; there were no shortcuts. For other cities, however, New York's experience can point toward a shorter way home.

Appendix A

NYC Housing Partnership Projects

NYC Housing Partnership Homeownership Programs (as of June 1997)			
Total Projects	*# Projects*	*# Units*	*Bank Loan*
Completed	118	10,092	$652,390,788
Under Construction	40	2,547	$190,582,473
With Bank Commitments	16	882	$ 42,559,405
Total	174	13,521	$885,532,666
Bronx	*# Projects*	*# Units*	*Bank Loan*
Completed	44	4,308	$269,961,195
Under Construction	13	739	$ 48,545,590
With Bank Commitments	7	114	$ 3,698,570
Total	64	5,161	$322,205,355
Brooklyn	*# Projects*	*# Units*	*Bank Loan*
Completed	44	3,221	$213,932,210
Under Construction	16	1,004	$ 72,978,792
With Bank Commitments	5	539	$ 34,832,525
Total	65	4,764	$321,743,527
Manhattan	*# Projects*	*# Units*	*Bank Loan*
Completed	5	835	$ 66,099,047
Under Construction	1	80	$ 6,767,964
With Bank Commitments	3	184	$ 4,028,310
Total	9	1,099	$ 76,895,321
Queens	*# Projects*	*# Units*	*Bank Loan*
Completed	15	923	$ 62,990,251
Under Construction	7	429	$ 35,595,651
With Bank Commitments	1	45	$ —
Total	23	1,397	$98,585,902
Staten Island	*# Projects*	*# Units*	*Bank Loan*
Completed	10	805	$ 39,408,085
Under Construction	3	295	$ 26,694,476
With Bank Commitments	—	—	—
Total	13	1,100	$ 66,102,561

NYC Housing Partnership Neighborhood Entrepreneurs Programs (as of June 1997)		
Total Projects	*# Projects*	*# Residential Units*	*# Commercial Units*
Completed	46	589	11
Under Rehabilitation	143	1,599	67
With Bank Commitments	42	229	18
Total	231	2,417	96
Bronx	*# Projects*	*# Residential Units*	*# Commercial Units*
Completed	7	115	1
Under Rehabilitation	18	352	9
With Bank Commitments	—	—	—
Total	25	467	10
Brooklyn	*# Projects*	*# Residential Units*	*# Commercial Units*
Completed	15	90	2
Under Rehabilitation	72	551	21
With Bank Commitments	40	187	18
Total	127	828	41
Manhattan	*# Projects*	*# Residential Units*	*# Commercial Units*
Completed	24	384	8
Under Construction	53	696	37
With Bank Commitments	2	42	—
Total	79	1,122	45

NYC HOUSING PARTNERSHIP HOUSING ACTIVITY BY BOROUGH

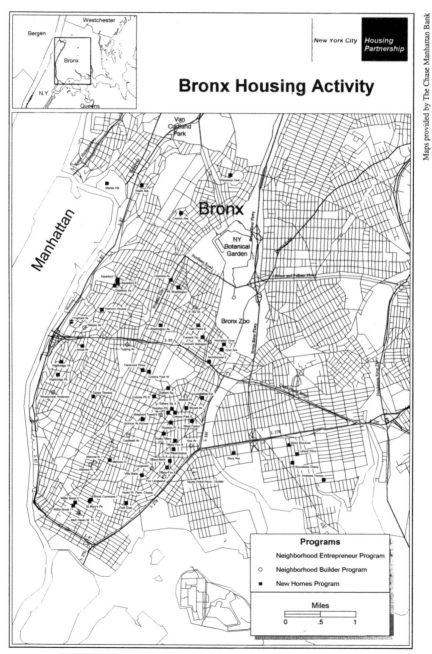

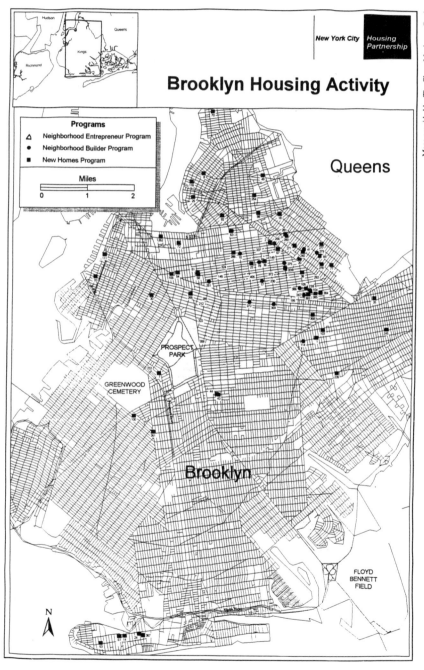

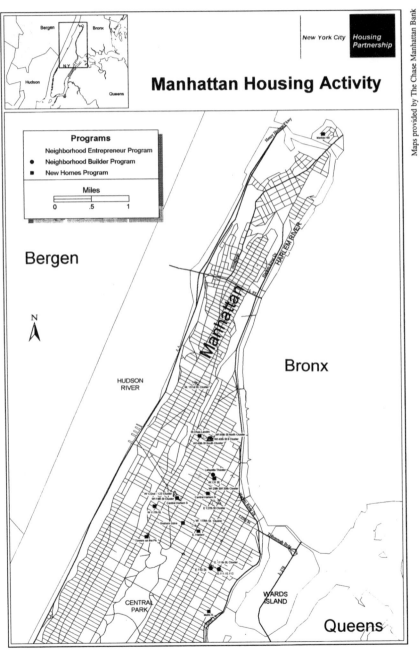

Maps provided by The Chase Manhattan Bank

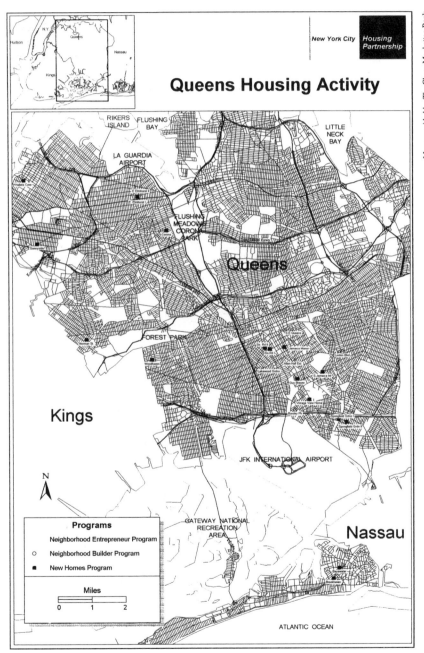

Maps provided by The Chase Manhattan Bank

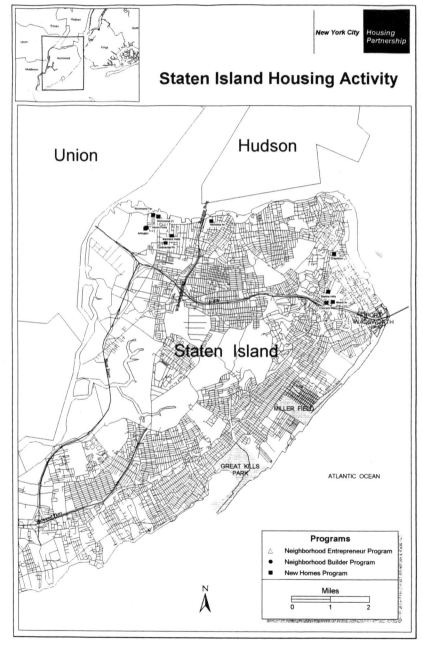

Appendix **C**

NYC Housing Partnership Development Process

Note: This chronology does not include site selection and selection of the developer.

1. The NYC Department of Housing Preservation and Development (HPD) mails designation letter to Developer which identifies initial requirements.

2. Housing Partnership/Developer hold initial meetings to discuss partnership program.

3. HPD/Partnership/Developer hold planning meeting to discuss site conditions and other related development issues.

4. HPD/Partnership provides Developer with the required Disclosure Statements (VENDEX) to be filled and returned to HPD Project Manager within two weeks of receipt.

5. Partnership in conjunction with the Developer, identifies technical assistance needs and schedules implementation (for Neighborhood Builders only).

6. Developer submits pre-development Seed Loan budget for Partnership's review and approval(for Neighborhood Builders only).

7. Developer prepares and submits preliminary pre-construction development schedule to Partnership within two (2) weeks of planning meeting. (Three (3) weeks for the Neighborhood Builders only.)

8. Developer submits original insurance certificate to HPD Project Manager for License Agreement, copy to Partnership.

9. HPD prepares License Agreement between it and the Partnership.

10. Partnership prepares to Sub-license Agreement and the Partnership.

11. Developer, with input from Partnership, chooses development team. (Contracts must be received and approved for Neighborhood Builders only.)

12. Developer prepares and submits finalized pre-construction development schedule to Partnership and HPD.

13. Neighborhood Builders submit seed loan budget to the partnership.

14.   Developer order surveys, borings, and title report.

15.   Developer files for tentative tax lot numbers at the City Surveyors Office.

16.   Developer obtains street addresses from Borough President's Office.

17.   Developer submits preliminary project package to Partnership for review. Partnership submits project package to HPD. (See list of Builder's requirements.)

18.   HPD prepares (with assistance from Developer's architect) Environmental Assessment Form and submits the package for environmental approvals to the state

19.   HPD schedules meeting between Developer, Partnership, and Community Planning Board to review preliminary plans.

20.   HPD orders appraisal.

21.   HPD presents the project package to the City Council for UDAAP approval and calendars for City Council/Mayoral hearings.

22.   HPD prepares Article XVI Loan Agreement with Community Sponsor to review plans and discuss design and marketing issues.

23.   Partnership, Developer and HPD meet with Community Sponsor to review plans and discuss design and marketing issues.

24.   Developer provides Partnership and HPD with final plans and specifications.

25.   Developer submits application to lender for construction financing after Partnership and HPD.

26.   Partnership obtains information from Developer for application to Affordable Housing Corporation (AHC) for State Subsidy. (See list of Builders requirements for AHC application.)

27.   Developer submits building application to HPD for signature as owner of the property and HPD attached fee deferral letter.

28.   Developer submits building plans to the Department of Buildings and obtains job numbers.

29.   HPD, Developer, Architect, and Partnership meet with DEP for pre-filing meeting to discuss Site Connection proposal (if necessary).

30. Developer notifies HPD of completed sewer application (Site Connection Proposal/SD1 and 2) for letter of expedite (optional).

31. Developer submits sewer application to DEP's Bureau of Sewers.

32. Developer notifies HPD of completed Builder's Pavement Plan for letter of expedite/fee waiver.

33. Developer submits Builder's Pavement Plan to the Department of Transportation.

34. City Council approves project, i.e., land use. Land Disposition Agreement (LDA) submitted to Mayoral Hearing for approval of business terms and authorization to convey property.

35. Developer submits sales information (floor plans, features, house prices, renderings) to Partnership and Community Sponsor) for preparation and approval of marketing material.

36. Developer submits information to obtain CPS-1/No Action Letter from Attorney General's Office (AG) if project is a condominium or Homeowner Association (HOA).

37. HPD receives necessary environmental approvals.

38. Developer obtains CPS-1/No Action Letter (if necessary).

39. Developer secures bank commitment.

40. Partnership submits application to AHC.

41. Partnership/Lender submits application to SONYMA (for Neighborhood Builders or GRAND-designated projects only).

42. Developer prepares Offering Plan and submits draft to Partnership if project is co-op or condominium.

43. Developer, Partnership, and Community Sponsor enter into marketing services agreement.

44. Developer/Community Sponsor begins outreach and marketing.

45. All parts participate in the preparation and review of closing documents (see summary of Legal Documents related to Partnership Projects)

46. AHC (and SONYMA for Neighborhood Builders or Grand designated projects only) approves projects.

47. Developer secures DOB, DEP, and DOT approvals on construction related applications.

48. Partnership submits requisition to AHC for subsidy.

49. Developer submits Insurance Certificate to Partnership in accordance with Site Development Agreement (SDA).

50. All parties participate in construction loan closing.

51. Developer submits Purchase Agreement and Deed to Partnership and HPD for approval.

52. Developer begins construction.

53. Developer and Community Sponsor enter into sales contracts and refer to purchases to bank for mortgage process.

54. Developer secures Permanent Certificates of Occupancy.

55. Developer contacts Partnership for pre-closing inspection of homes.

56. Developer/Community Sponsor conducts pre-closing workshops with buyers.

57. Developer conducts pre-closing walk-through with individual buyer.

58. All parties participate in individual homeowner closings.

59. Developer/Community Sponsor conduct post-closing educational workshops.

NOTES

Chapter 1. A Groundbreaking in Brooklyn

1   WINDSOR TERRACE GROUNDBREAKING: Pictures and news accounts in the December 9, 1983, *New York Times*, *New York Post*, *New York Daily News*, and *Newsday*. Names of purchasers were taken from a list of Windsor Terrace purchasers in Housing Partnership files.

2   "SOMETHING NEW IS GOING TO BE GROWING IN BROOKLYN": WCBS-TV news broadcast, December 8, 1983.

      QUOTATION FROM SUSAN MOTLEY: Interview with Motley.

      "WHEN WE ANNOUNCED THE HOUSING PARTNERSHIP": Conference transcript, "New Homes for New York Neighborhoods" (New York City Housing Partnership, October 15, 1984), p. 11.

      "YOU WANT TO BUILD *WHAT*?": Interview with David Daly.

3   "THE LEVELS OF COMPLEXITY": George Sternlieb and James W. Hughes, *Housing and Economic Reality: New York City, 1976* (Center for Urban Policy Research, Rutgers — The State University of New Jersey, 1976), p. 35.

      "NEW YORK MAY BE THE MOST DIFFICULT CITY": John Ellis and Associates, *The Partnership Cost Study of Affordable Housing Projects* (New York City Housing Partnership, June 1988), p. 1.

      "IN A CITY AS COMPLICATED AS NEW YORK": Edward C. Sullivan, quoted in Kit Lively, "Reformer or Autocrat?" *Chronicle of Higher Education*, December 1, 1993, p. A26.

4   "WHAT IS BARELY HINTED AT": Saul Bellow, "New York: World-Famous Impossibility," in *It All Adds Up* (Viking, 1994), p. 217. Bellow's essay on New York was first published in the *New York Times Book Review*, December 6, 1970.

MAYOR KOCH AND MOTHER TERESA: This account is drawn from Philip K. Howard, *The Death of Common Sense* (Random House, 1992), pp. 3-4.

5   "CONSTELLATION OF . . . STRUCTURES": Peter D. Salins and Gerard C. S. Mildner, *Scarcity by Design* (Harvard University Press, 1992), p. 37.

"IN THE WORLD OF NEW YORK POLITICS": Salins and Mildner, p. 68.

"THERE'S NO BALANCE LEFT": Interview with R. Randy Lee.

7   "IT TAKES A MINIMUM OF THREE YEARS": Edward J. Logue, Speech to the Citizens Housing and Planning Council, *The Assessor*, April 5, 1985, p. 7.

"IF YOU HAD TOLD ME FIVE YEARS AGO": Conference transcript, "New Homes for New York Neighborhoods," p. 35.

8   REAGAN TOLD A NEW YORK CITY PARTNERSHIP MEETING: New York City Partnership, *Annual Report, 1981*, p. 1.

AN "URBAN SUMMIT" "CALLED FOR INCREASED PUBLIC AND PRIVATE PARTNERSHIPS": The Urban Summit, press release, November 13, 1990.

THE TERM "NEW PARTNERSHIP": Used by Speaker Gingrich and President Clinton in separate appearances addressing the National Governors Association, MacNeil/Lehrer Newshour (PBS), January 31, 1995, author's notes.

9   THE "RE-INVENTING GOVERNMENT" MOVEMENT: See David Osborne and Ted Gaebler, *Reinventing Government: How the Entrepreneurial Spirit Is Transforming the Public Sector* (Addison-Wesley, 1992).

"PUBLIC-PRIVATE PARTNERSHIP" AS A "EUPHEMISTIC" TERM: David J. Ricker, "Plan of Study for the Ph.D. in Public Policy Analysis," University of Illinois at Chicago, October 1996 p. 7. Ricker is director of affordable housing programs for Cook County, Illinois.

10   "IN THE NORTH I HAVE DAVID ROCKEFELLER": Edward I. Koch, *Politics* (Simon and Schuster, 1985), p. 169.

"NOT A BAD LINE": Ibid., p. 169.

11   "I LEAN FORWARD AND I SAY TO HIM": Koch, Ibid., p. 113.

"WE DID NOT GET OFF TO THE BEST START": Interview with David Rockefeller.

AN INCIDENT EARLY IN THE MAYOR'S FIRST TERM: Recounted by Koch in *Mayor!* (Simon and Schuster, 1984), p. 68, and *Citizen Koch* (St. Martin's Press, 1992), p. 148.

14   THE "DANGER OF LOSING OUR CAPACITY TO DREAM BIG DREAMS": David Rockefeller, "Vision and Vicissitude," Remarks to the Citizens Housing and Planning Council of New York (New York City Partnership, May 3, 1984), p. 2.

Chapter 2. Postwar New York:
The Radiant City Meets Jane Jacobs

15   "SO SHOT THROUGH WITH ABSURDITIES": Editorial, *New York Times*, January 5, 1977.

"ONE OF THE MOST IMAGINATIVE PROJECTS": Rockefeller, "Vision and Vicissitude," pp. 9-10.

"WESTWAY REPRESENTS CHANGE": Ibid., p. 10.

ROCKEFELLER CHARACTERIZED ITS LOSS AS "TRAGIC": Interview with David Rockefeller.

16   "HOW MANY OF US": Rockefeller, "Vision and Vicissitude," p. 1.

"THE WAR CAST A GLOBAL PERSPECTIVE": Joel Schwartz, *The New York Approach* (Ohio State University Press, 1993), p. 303.

17   OVER A THOUSAND BUILDINGS: Robert A. Caro, *The Power Broker* (New York: Vintage Books, 1975), p. 7.

"MEGALOMANIACAL SCALE" OF CO-OP CITY: Richard Plunz, *A History of Housing in New York City* (Columbia University Press, 1990), p. 286.

"LOOK AT HIS RECORD!": Caro, p. 737.

AN "INSPIRED CAPITALIST": Schwartz, p. 305.

"PROFESSIONAL CERTITUDES SEEMED EASIER": Dean Macris, "Planning in San Francisco," *Planning and Public Policy*, Spring/Fall 1994, 1-2.

18   MOSES WAS RESPONSIBLE: Caro, p. 20.

"THE CITY WAS UTTERLY UNABLE": Caro, p. 21.

19   "THE RUTHLESS, OVERSIMPLIFIED, PSEUDO-CITY PLANNING": Jane Jacobs, *The Death and Life of Great American Cities* (Vintage Books, 1961), p. 402.

"SAVAGES VENERATING MAGICAL FETISHES": Ibid., p. 90.

20   "PHYSICAL, SOCIAL, AND ECONOMIC CONTINUITIES": Ibid., p. 121.

WITHIN THE PLANNING PROFESSION: See, for example, Norman Krumholz and John Forester, *Making Equity Planning Work: Leadership in the Public Sector* (Temple University Press, 1990).

22   "MOSES ALWAYS HAD THE OPPOSITION": Caro, p. 737.

Chapter 3. New York: City on the Ropes

23   SOME OF THE CHILLING NUMBERS: George Sternlieb and James W. Hughes, *Post-Industrial America: Metropolitan Decline and Inter-Regional Job Shifts* (Center For Urban Policy Research, Rutgers — The State University of New Jersey, 1976), pp. 119-21.

24   "A FEW YEARS AGO": Nathan Glazer, "Introduction," in Economics Department of First National City Bank, *Profile of a City* (McGraw-Hill, 1972), p. 2.

"I MUST PLEAD GUILTY": Sternlieb and Hughes, *Post-Industrial America*, p. 245.

MAYOR ABE BEAME ... INSISTED: *New York Times*, August 3, 1995.

25   DURING THE 1960S: *Profile of a City*, p. 225

DURING THE SAME PERIOD: Ibid., p. 233.

"NEW YORKERS ARE USED TO HEARING": Ibid., p. 245.

AN ANNUAL RITUAL CALLED "GAPMANSHIP": Ibid., p. 240.

THAT ALL THIS FISCAL BRINKMANSHIP DISGUISED: This account of the New York City fiscal crisis is drawn largely from Charles J. Orlebeke, "Saving New York: The Ford Administration and the New York City Fiscal Crisis," in *Gerald R. Ford and the Politics of Post-Watergate America*, ed. Bernard J. Firestone and Alexej Ugrinsky (Greenwood Press, 1993), pp. 359-85.

28   "FORD TO CITY: DROP DEAD": The *New York Daily News* headline seems to have acquired a permanent place in the political lore of New York City-federal government relations. As the headline writer's hyperbole has been embellished over the years, it is now widely believed that Ford actually said "Drop dead." See for example, Adrienne Windhoff-Heretier, *City of the Poor, City of the Rich* (Walter de Gruyter, 1992), p. 31, which states that "at the apex of the fiscal crisis President Ford, unmoved by the City's desperate pleading for financial help, was reported to have said, 'Drop dead, New York.'"

29   "THE FUTURE WE HAVE SKETCHED": Sternlieb and Hughes, *Post-Industrial America*, p. 136.

THE "INTANGIBLE 'NEW YORK' IDEA": Kenneth Lipper, "What Needs to Be Done?" *New York Times Magazine*, December 31, 1989, p. 46. Lipper, a former Deputy Mayor of New York (1983-85), is an investment banker who wrote the novel *Wall Street*.

Chapter 4. After the Crisis: Groping for an Agenda

31   IN THE DEVASTATED NEIGHBORHOODS: The quotations from Frank Kristof and Roger Starr are from the *New York Times*, April 12, 1979.

32   QUOTATION FROM VICTOR MARRERO: *New York Times*, April 12, 1976.

IN EARLY 1976 STARR BEGAN FLOATING THE IDEA: *New York Times*, February 3, 1976.

A VARIANT OF STARR'S IDEA: *New York Times*, March 16, 1976.

33   THE "PLANNED SHRINKAGE" NOTIONS: *New York Times*, March 17, 1976.

IT TURNED OUT TO BE AN EASY AND ENDURING METAPHOR: See, for example, Harold DiRienzo, "Planned Shrinkage — The Final Phase," *City Limits*, April 1989, p. 10.

35   LOGUE PROPOSAL TO FORD ADMINISTRATION: The account of Logue's proposal is based on the author's involvement in the issue while serving as Assistant HUD Secretary for policy development and research in the Ford administration. Quotations are from memoranda and letters in the author's files.

39   LOGUE'S CHARLOTTE STREET DEVELOPMENT: *New York Times*, March 19, 1983.

LOGUE CALLED CHARLOTTE GARDENS: Logue, *The Assessor*, p. 1.

40   "WE WOULD BE HERE FOR A WEEK": Rockefeller, "Vision and Vicissitude," p. 7.

Chapter 5. Moving Toward Partnership

41   WHEN THE CRISIS STRUCK: David Rockefeller, "Ingredients for Successful Partnerships: The New York City Case," in *Public-Private Partnerships: Improving Urban Life*, ed. Perry Davis (The Academy of Political Science, 1986), pp. 122-23.

42   "THE FINANCIAL CRISIS OF 1975": Frank J. Macchiarola, "Managing Partnerships: A CEO's Perspective," in *Public-Private Partnerships: Improving Urban Life*, p. 127.

QUOTATIONS FROM DAVID ROCKEFELLER: Interview with Rockefeller.

43   QUOTATIONS FROM LEWIS RUDIN: Oral history interview with Rudin,
       07.001.1.973, November 29, 1993, Abraham D. Beame Collection, La
       Guardia and Wagner Archives, La Guardia Community College,
       CUNY, pp. 1-2, 11.

       QUOTATIONS FROM DAVID ROCKEFELLER: Interview with Rockefeller.

44   "THE BUSINESS/LABOR WORKING GROUP WAS A WONDERFUL GROUP":
       Rudin, oral history, pp. 17-18.

       QUOTATIONS FROM DAVID ROCKEFELLER: Interview with Rockefeller.

       THE MCKINSEY CONSULTANTS: Macchiarola, p. 127.

45   THE RESULT WAS: Ibid., p. 128

       IT WAS DECIDED THAT THE CHAMBER OF COMMERCE: Interview with
       Rockefeller.

       "TENUOUS BEGINNING": New York City Partnership, *Annual Report
       1981*, p. 2.

       THE CHAMBER'S "WHITE ELEPHANT SALE": Interview with Rockefeller.

       AN ENTITY CALLED "SERVCO": New York City Partnership, *Annual Re-
       port, 1981*, p. 20.

       THE CHAMBER'S BUILDING: Interview with Rockefeller.

       ROCKEFELLER . . . URGED UNION LEADERS: Ibid.

       VAN ARSDALE AND GOTBAUM: Ibid.

47   "I AM STILL AMAZED THAT HE CAME": Ibid.

       ANNOUNCEMENT OF THE HOUSING PARTNERSHIP: "Remarks by David
       Rockefeller at First Annual Partnership Luncheon," January 14, 1982
       (Draft #3), David Rockefeller papers, Rockefeller Financial Service
       Corporation files.

48   THE CITY "WILL MAKE EVERY EFFORT": Department of Housing Preser-
       vation and Development, press release, January 14, 1982, p. 2.

       "MANY DETAILS OF THE PROJECT": *New York Times*, January 15, 1982.

Chapter 6. In Search of a Blueprint

49   DISCUSSION DRAFT OF HOUSING PARTNERSHIP PROPOSAL: "A Program
       to Expand Housing Opportunities for Middle-Income Residents of
       New York City," December 16, 1981, David Rockefeller papers.

53   QUOTATIONS FROM JACK SCHWANDT: Interview with Schwandt.

BACKGROUND ON KATHRYN WYLDE: Interview with Wylde.

WYLDE WAS ... "TO PERFORM A KEY ROLE": Louis Winnick, *New People in Old Neighborhoods: The Role of New Immigrants in Rejuvenating New York's Communities* (Russell Sage Foundation, 1990), p. 102.

54   MONEY FLOWED IN FOR HEAD START: Winnick, pp. 106-7.

HOUSING PARTNERSHIP IMPLEMENTATION PLAN: New York City Housing Partnership Implementation Plan, April 12, 1982, David Rockefeller papers.

56   COMMUNITY PRESERVATION CORPORATION (CPC) ROLE IN HOUSING PARTNERSHIP: Although CPC's board of directors and CEO Michael Lappin decided against incorporation within the Housing Partnership structure, the two entities have sometimes cooperated on specific financing packages.

58   QUOTATION FROM FRANK MACCHIAROLA: Conference transcript, "New Homes for New York Neighborhoods," pp. 77-78.

QUOTATIONS FROM KATHRYN WYLDE: Interview with Wylde.

59   QUOTATION FROM KATHRYN WYLDE: Ibid.

QUOTATION FROM ED KOCH: Conference transcript, "New Homes for New York Neighborhoods," p. 5.

QUOTATION FROM ANTHONY GLIEDMAN: Conference transcript, "New Homes for New York Neighborhoods," p. 42.

ON JULY 25, 1979, KOCH SENT A NOTE: Koch's note is referred to in a memorandum from housing commissioner Nathan Leventhal to Koch, August 23, 1979, David Rockefeller papers. The Leventhal memorandum was appended to the Housing Partnership Implementation Plan as "Exhibit D."

"DESPITE THE MANY SOUND BENEFITS OF A HOME-OWNERSHIP PROGRAM": Memorandum, Nathan Leventhal to Mayor Edward I. Koch, p. D-2.

62   QUOTATION FROM ANTHONY GLIEDMAN: Interview with Gliedman.

63   "THE CITY'S HOMEOWNERSHIP PROGRAM WILL START": Memorandum, Housing Preservation and Development Commissioner Anthony Gliedman to Mayor Edward I. Koch, December 14, 1979, David Rockefeller papers. The Gliedman memorandum was appended to the Housing Partnership Implementation Plan as "Exhibit E."

QUOTATION FROM ALAN WIENER: *New York Times*, February 22, 1980.

"SOME BUILDERS HAVE EXPRESSED DISMAY": *New York Times*, February 22, 1981.

64   "THE 235 EXPERIENCE DEMONSTRATES THE CLEAR NEED": Kathy Wylde, "Report to N.Y.C. Partnership Housing Task Force on New York City Small Homes Production Program," February 8, 1982 (Housing Partnership files, p. 1).

"THERE IS CONSIDERABLE DOUBT": Ibid., pp. 9, 10.

THE SMALL HOMEBUILDER . . . WERE "NOT WELL SUITED": Ibid., p. 10.

65   BUILDERS FAULTED THE CITY'S HOUSING AGENCY: Ibid., p. 8.

Chapter 7. The Money Chase

67   HOUSING PARTNERSHIP INITIAL FUNDING PLAN: Memorandum from Edgar Lampert and Henry Murray to David Rockefeller, J. Paul Lyet, and E. Virgil Conway, April 29, 1982, David Rockefeller papers.

68   GEORGE RONIGER MEETING WITH EDGAR LAMPERT: Memorandum from Edgar Lampert to J. Paul Lyet, June 8, 1982, David Rockefeller papers.

QUOTATION FROM KATHRYN WYLDE: Interview with Wylde.

HOUSING PARTNERSHIP REQUEST TO ROCKEFELLER BROTHERS FUND: Letter, Morris Dantzker to Thomas Wahman, October 8, 1982, David Rockefeller papers.

69   ASTOR FOUNDATION DONATION TO HOUSING PARTNERSHIP: Interview with Kathryn Wylde.

DAVID ROCKEFELLER LETTER TO SAMUEL PIERCE: David Rockefeller papers.

70   QUOTATION FROM WARREN LINDQUIST: Interview with Lindquist.

71   "THEY COULD HAVE SAID NO TO A LOT OF THINGS": *New York Times*, February 13, 1983.

73   "THE SCOPE OF SERVICES TO BE PROVIDED": Letter, Anthony Gliedman to Samuel Pierce, October 1, 1982, David Rockefeller papers.

HUD WAS "HOPING TO MAKE NEW YORK CITY": *New York Times*, October 24, 1982.

74   HUD WAS PAYING ABOUT THREE-FOURTHS: Memorandum from Kathy Wylde to Jim Brignati and Steve Bogart, May 13, 1985.

MUCH OF THE BALANCE NEEDED: Memorandum from Kathy Wylde to Frank Macchiarola, March 20, 1984.

75   DAVID STOCKMAN'S OPPOSITION TO UDAG: David A. Stockman, *The Triumph of Politics: Why the Reagan Revolution Failed* (Harper and Row, 1986), pp. 142-43.

BACKGROUND ON URBAN DEVELOPMENT ACTION GRANTS: Michael Rich, "UDAG, Economic Development, and the Death and Life of American Cities," *Economic Development Quarterly*, Vol. 6, No. 2 (May 1992): pp. 150-72.

76   NOVEMBER 11, 1982, PARTNERSHIP BOARD MEETING WITH MAYOR KOCH: Memorandum to file by Jack Davies, David Rockefeller papers.

ROCKEFELLER'S PITCH TO THE FORD FOUNDATION: Memorandum, Jack Davies to David Rockefeller and Mayor Edward I. Koch, February 4, 1983, David Rockefeller papers.

QUOTATIONS FROM KATHRYN WYLDE ON FORD FOUNDATION MEETING: Interview with Wylde.

77   QUOTATIONS FROM THOMAS WAYMAN ON TRUST FUND IDEA: Memorandum, Thomas Wayman to David Rockefeller, February 7, 1984, Housing Partnership files.

78   QUOTATIONS FROM KATHRYN WYLDE ON THE CREATION OF A HOUSING TRUST FUND: Memorandum, Kathryn Wylde to Anthony Gliedman, Ron Marino, and Charles Reiss, July 9, 1984, Housing Partnership files.

"HELPING THE CITY ESTABLISH A HOUSING TRUST FUND": Memorandum, Kathryn Wylde to Anthony Gliedman, August 13, 1984, Housing Partnership files.

Chapter 8. The Elusive UDAG

79   QUOTATIONS FROM STANLEY NEWMAN ON HOUSING PARTNERSHIP'S UDAG PROPOSAL: Conference transcript, "New Homes for New York Neighborhoods," pp. 94-95.

81   QUOTATIONS FROM DAVID DALY: Interview with Daly.

HOUSING PARTNERSHIP NEGOTIATIONS WITH HUD ON UDAG GRANT: Kathryn Wylde laid out the chronology of Housing Partnership-HUD negotiations in a memorandum to the Housing Partnership board, "New Homes Progress Report," June 11, 1984, Housing Partnership files.

82   "MAY HAS BEEN A WATERSHED MONTH FOR THE PROGRAM": Ibid., p. 3.

84   "A COOKIE-CUTTER OPERATION": Interview with Kathryn Wylde.

85   "IT WAS A VERY SPECULATIVE DEAL": Interview with Steven Brown.

ANOTHER "DEAR SAM" LETTER: Letter, David Rockefeller to Samuel Pierce, May 13, 1985, Housing Partnership files.

QUOTATION FROM DEBORAH WRIGHT: Interview with Wright.

86   PROJECT FEE ISSUE: Memorandum, Kathryn Wylde to Frank Mac-chiarola, October 31, 1983, Housing Partnership files. Also, interview with Wylde.

89   "A STATE 'HOUSING UDAG'": Memorandum, Kathryn Wylde to William Ellinghaus, Stan Smith, Donna Smith, and Frank Macchiarola, March 12, 1985, Housing Partnership files.

      "AFTER MEETINGS YESTERDAY": Memorandum, Kathryn Wylde to Housing Partnership Board, March 19, 1985, Housing Partnership files.

90   QUOTATION FROM BERNIE MCGARRY: Interview with McGarry.

      QUOTATION FROM DAVID ROCKEFELLER: Interview with Rockefeller.

      "YOUR EFFORTS AND THOSE OF DAVID ROCKEFELLER": Letter, Mario Cuomo to William Ellinghaus, May 1, 1985, Housing Partnership files.

91   QUOTATIONS FROM DAVID ROCKEFELLER: Interview with Rockefeller.

      SIMILARITY BETWEEN NEW STATE HOUSING PROGRAM AND UDAG: Memorandum, Kathy Wylde to Tony Gliedman, Ron Marino, Jose Cit-ron, and Michel Aronson, November 26, 1985, Housing Partnership files.

Chapter 9. Getting to Production: Ceremonies and Realities

93   BEDFORD-STUYVESANT GROUNDBREAKING: This account is based on author's notes taken at the ceremony, June 27, 1993.

96   HARLEM RIBBON-CUTTING CEREMONY: This account is based on author's notes taken at the ceremony, July 9, 1994.

98   MID-1997 HOUSING PRODUCTION NUMBER: New York City Housing part-nership Production Report, Appendix A.

      MID-1986 HOUSING PRODUCTION NUMBERS: Memorandum, Connie Reese to Kathy Wylde, July 31, 1987, Housing Partnership files.

      QUOTATIONS FROM HAROLD BLUESTONE: Interview with Bluestone.

100   BY MID-1983 WYLDE HAD PUT TOGETHER: Memorandum, Kathryn Wylde to Anthony Gliedman, June 15, 1983.

      ANOTHER TWO DOZEN BUILDING SITES WERE TARGETED: "New Homes Program Project Construction Schedule," December 31, 1983, Hous-ing Partnership files.

"A WATERSHED MONTH FOR THE PROGRAM": Memorandum, Kathryn Wylde to Housing Partnership Board, June 11, 1984, p. 3, Housing Partnership files.

101 "NEW HOMES STATUS REPORT": Memorandum, Kathryn Wylde to Anthony Gliedman, August 13, 1984, Housing Partnership files.

102 QUOTATION FROM ALVIN PREISS: Conference transcript, "New Homes for New York Neighborhoods, p. 18.

QUOTATIONS FROM CHARLES REISS: Conference transcript, "New Homes for New York Neighborhoods, pp. 66-69.

104 "AT PRESENT, MORE THAN 30 SITES": Memorandum, Kathryn Wylde to Virgil Conway, January 16, 1985, Housing Partnership files.

105 QUOTATIONS FROM TONY GLIEDMAN: Interview with Gliedman.

106 1982 LIST OF PROPOSED HOUSING PARTNERSHIP SITES: Kathryn Wylde, "New York City Partnership Implementation Plan for Small Homes Production Program," July 30, 1982, Housing Partnership files.

THE CITY'S SHIFTING POSITION ON PARTNERSHIP SITES: Memorandum, Kathryn Wylde to Frank Macchiarola and Edgar Lampert, March 8, 1983, Housing Partnership files.

"WE HAVE HAD DIFFICULTY IN SECURING SITES": Kathryn Wylde, "Program Initiatives with the Public Sector as of April 30, 1983," Housing Partnership files.

107 QUOTATION FROM KATHRYN WYLDE: Memorandum, Wylde to Macchiarola and Lampert.

108 MAY 1985 REPORT ON PROPOSED HOUSING PARTNERSHIP SITES: Memorandum, Kathryn Wylde to Ron Marino, Jose Citron, and Jessica Williamson, "New Homes Program Status Report," May 6, 1985, Housing Partnership files. Subsequent quotations on specific sites are from this report.

109 ARLINGTON SITE DEVELOPER PROBLEM: Memorandum, Kathryn Wylde to Frank Macchiarola, May 22, 1985, Housing Partnership files.

111 TALLY OF HOUSING PARTNERSHIP PRODUCTION THROUGH JUNE 30, 1987: Memorandum, Connie Reese to Kathy Wylde, July 31, 1987, Housing Partnership files.

WAS THE PARTNERSHIP'S PROBLEM . . . ? . . . WYLDE'S JUDGMENT: Memorandum, Kathryn Wylde to Frank Macchiarola, "The Need for a Reaffirmation of the City's Commitment to the Housing Partnership and the New Homes Program," October 1, 1985, Housing Partnership files.

115   WYLDE HAD "EXPECTED 1985 TO BE A BANNER YEAR": Memorandum, Kathryn Wylde to First Deputy Mayor Stanley Brezenoff, April 11, 1986, Housing Partnership files.

Chapter 10. The Koch Housing Plan: Reaching for New "Partners"

118   IN 1976, GOVERNOR HUGH CAREY: Hugh L. Carey, "State of the State Message, *Public Papers of Governor Hugh L. Carey, 1975* (State of New York, Executive Chamber), p. 21.

DECEMBER 1985 KOCH CHALLENGE TO MAJOR DEVELOPERS: Bonnie Brower, *Missing the Mark: Subsidized Housing for the Privileged, Displacing the Poor* (The Association for Neighborhood & Housing Development, Inc., and the Housing Justice Campaign, August 1989), p. 32.

119   QUOTATION FROM KATHRYN WYLDE: Memorandum, Wylde to Ronald Shelp, October 20, 1988, Housing Partnership files.

THE PROPOSAL WAS "HAILED BY BOTH DEVELOPERS AND THE CITY": Cited in Jim Sleeper, "Days of the Developers — Boom and Bust with Ed Koch," *Dissent*, Vol. 34, Fall 1987: 445-46; no date given.

THE HOUSING PARTNERSHIP . . . ASSISTED REBNY: Memorandum, Kathryn Wylde to Ronald Shelp, October 20, 1988, Housing Partnership files.

120   "ANOTHER POSITIVE EVENT IS THE DECISION OF THE CITY": Memorandum, Kathryn Wylde to Frank Macchiarola, Housing Partnership files.

MAYOR'S ANNOUNCEMENT OF $4.2 BILLION HOUSING PROGRAM: *New York Times*, April 30, 1986.

"NEW YORK'S . . . HOUSING INITIATIVE": Kathryn Wylde, Gale Kaufman, Jody Kass, and Karen Sunnarborg, *Building in Partnership: A Blueprint for Urban Housing Programs* (New York City Housing Partnership, November 1994), p. 5.

121   QUOTATION FROM MEREDITH KANE: Interview with Kane.

QUOTATIONS FROM MAYOR KOCH: *New York Times*, January 11, 1986.

DONALD MANES SCANDAL AND SUICIDE: For a chronology, see *New York Times*, March 14, 1986.

122   STANLEY FRIEDMAN INVOLVEMENT IN SCANDAL: *New York Times*, April 11, 1986.

QUOTATIONS FROM MAYOR KOCH: *New York Times*, February 25, 1986.

123   MAYOR'S CONTRACT REVIEW COMMITTEE BACKLOG: *New York Times*, August 13, 1986.

124   QUOTATIONS FROM MEREDITH KANE: Interview with Kane.

125   QUOTATION FROM KATHRYN WYLDE: Interview with Wylde.

QUOTATION FROM JODY KASS: Interview with Kass.

QUOTATIONS FROM MAYOR KOCH: *New York Times*, August 13, 1986.

QUOTATION FROM DAVID ROCKEFELLER: Memorandum, Kathryn Wylde to Frank Macchiarola, May 27, 1986, Housing Partnership files.

MACCHIAROLA'S "DEAR ED" COVER NOTE: Letter, Frank Macchiarola to Mayor Koch, May 30, 1986, Housing Partnership files.

126   CITY'S REJOINDER ON HIGH CONSTRUCTION COSTS: Memorandum, Susan Wagner and Stuart Klein to Robert Esnard, June 20, 1986, Housing Partnership files.

WYLDE'S DRAFT POSITION PAPER FOR NEW YORK BUILDING CONGRESS: "Housing Production: Let's Get Back in the Business," New York Building Congress, August 1981, p. 15, Rockefeller Family Associates files.

QUOTATIONS FROM KATHRYN WYLDE: Memorandum, Wylde to Macchiarola, May 27, 1986, Housing Partnership files.

128   QUOTATIONS FROM WAGNER AND KLEIN: Memorandum, Susan Wagner and Stuart Klein to Robert Esnard, June 20, 1986, Housing Partnership files.

KATHRYN WYLDE COMMENTS ON WAGNER/KLEIN MEMORANDUM: Memorandum, Wylde to Macchiarola, July 1, 1986, Housing Partnership files.

129   QUOTATION FROM KATHRYN WYLDE: Memorandum, Wylde to Ronald Shelp, October 20, 1988, Housing Partnership files.

130   HOUSING PARTNERSHIP AS A "BOUTIQUE" OPERATION: Memorandum, Kathryn Wylde to Mark Willis, October 21, 1986, Housing Partnership files. Wylde argued that "[c]ity investment in boutique projects stimulates development and preservation of substantially more housing than the subsidized units themselves."

DANGER OF CITY'S DEPENDENCE ON HOUSING PARTNERSHIP: Interview with Mark Willis.

TIBBETT GARDEN PROBLEMS: Interview with Kathryn Wylde. Also, Sleeper, "Days of the Developers — Boom and Bust with Ed Koch," pp. 446-48.

131   QUOTATION FROM KATHRYN WYLDE: Memorandum, Wylde to Ronald
        Shelp, October 20, 1988, Housing Partnership files.

        QUOTATION FROM ABE BIDERMAN: Interview with Biderman.

        QUOTATION FROM GEORGE STERNLIEB: Jim Sleeper, "Days of the De-
        velopers — Boom and Bust with Ed Koch," p. 446.

Chapter 11. Production Breakthrough

133   QUOTATIONS FROM MEREDITH KANE: Interview with Kane.

134   QUOTATIONS FROM JERRY SALAMA: Interview with Salama.

        QUOTATION FROM KAREN SUNNARBORG: Interview with Sunnarborg.

135   QUOTATIONS FROM ABE BIDERMAN: Interview with Biderman.

        CHARACTERIZATION OF DAVID DINKINS: *New York Times*, September 13,
        1989.

        ABE BIDERMAN AS A "BRILLIANT TACTICIAN": Interview with former
        HPD official.

136   A $500 MILLION COMMITMENT TO " . . . AFFORDABLE HOMEOWNERSHIP":
        Ten-Year Housing Plan — Fiscal Years 1989-1998, City of New York,
        1988.

137   "WHERE ARE THE HOUSES?": Memorandum, Kathryn Wylde to Housing
        Partnership Board, June 11, 1984, Housing Partnership files.

        QUOTATION FROM FORMER HPD OFFICIAL: Interview.

138   QUOTATION FROM MARK WILLIS: Interview with Willis.

        QUOTATION FROM KAREN SUNNARBORG: Interview with Sunnarborg.

        QUOTATION FROM FORMER HPD OFFICIAL: Interview.

        QUOTATION FROM KATHRYN WYLDE: Interview with Wylde.

139   KATHRYN WYLDE LETTER TO *NEW YORK DAILY NEWS*: Letter, Wylde to
        Robert Laird, April 1, 1986, Housing Partnership files.

140   NEW HOMEOWNER MARY BOSWELL: Interview with Boswell.

        NEW HOMEOWNERS ELSA AND GEORGE ORTIZ: Interview with the Or-
        tizes.

141   NEW HOMEOWNER MARYANNE MANOUSAKIS: Interview with Ma-
        nousakis.

        NEW HOMEOWNERS DORIS BEMBURY: Interview with Bembury.

143   THE NEHEMIAH PLAN: For background, see Samuel Freedman, *Upon
        This Rock* (Harper Collins, 1993), pp. 307-44.

144   EBC'S CLAIM TO HAVE RAISED $12 MILLION: Ibid., p. 337.

EBC ANNOUNCEMENT OF PLANS FOR 5,000 TOWN HOUSES: *New York Times*, June 30, 1982.

QUOTATION FROM ALAN OSER: *New York Times*, April 16, 1989.

QUOTATION FROM RICHARD PLUNZ: Plunz, *History of Housing in New York City*, pp. 331-32. Some observers of the Nehemiah program note that over the years, Nehemiah owners have given their homes individual touches — landscaping, porches, wrought iron fencing, and the like — that soften the otherwise bleak facade. See, for example, Zane Yost, "Affordable by Design," in *The City as a Human Environment*, ed. Duane G. Levine and Arthur C. Upton (Praeger, 1994), p. 15; see also Howard Husock, *Repairing the Ladder: Toward a New Housing Policy Paradigm* (Reason Foundation, July 1996), p. 42.

COST AND PRICE OF NEHEMIAH HOMES: Michael Gecan, "From Graveyard to Hope and Beyond — East Brooklyn's EBC-IAF Nehemiah Plan," in *CUPREPORT* (Center for Urban Policy and Research, Rutgers — the State University of New Jersey), Summer 1993: 6.

145   PER-UNIT COST OF HOUSING PARTNERSHIP HOMES: John Ellis and Associates, *The Partnership Cost Study*.

NEHEMIAH WILL NOT BUILD UNLESS: Gecan, "From Graveyard to Hope," p. 6.

IT "MUST HAVE MONEY POWER": Ibid.

146   QUOTATION FROM KATHRYN WYLDE: *New York Times*, September 27, 1987.

I. D. ROBBINS ON BUILDING 200,000 NEHEMIAH HOMES: Plunz, p. 333.

ROBBINS DISMISSING WYLDE'S THESIS: *New York Times*, September 27, 1987.

I. D. ROBBINS: "WE'RE DOING GOD'S WORK": Ibid.

QUOTATION FROM GROCERY STORE OWNER: Plunz, p. 334.

147   CONTENTION BETWEEN NEHEMIAH AND OTHER NONPROFIT GROUPS: *New York Times*, October 6, 1992.

QUOTATION FROM CONGRESSMAN SCHUMER: Conference transcript, "New Homes for New York Neighborhoods," p. 154.

QUOTATION FROM KATHY WYLDE: Letter, Wylde to Congressman Charles Schumer, January 22, 1985, Housing Partnership files.

PRODUCTION UNDER NEHEMIAH PROGRAM: James E. Wallace, "Financing Affordable Housing in the United States," *Housing Policy Debate*, Vol. 6, Issue 4 (1995): 802-03.

148   QUOTATION FROM INDUSTRIAL AREAS FOUNDATION: Industrial Areas Foundation, *IAF 50 Years*, 1990, p. 5.

Chapter 12. Beyond Housing: Expanding the Partnership Agenda

149   QUOTATION FROM KATHRYN WYLDE: Interview with Wylde.

       QUOTATION FROM MAYOR DINKINS: From Dinkins' comments at a Bedford-Stuyvesant ground breaking ceremony for Housing Partnership homes, June 27, 1993 (author's notes).

150   QUOTATION ON $100 MILLION INVESTMENT FUND: New York City Partnership, *An Investment in New York City*, February 1995, p. 3.

151   "THE CLASSIC 'CATCH 22' SCENARIO": Community Partnership Development Corporation, *Mainstreaming Minority Builders*, 1993, p. 2.

       WYLDE PROPOSAL FOR MINORITY BUSINESS DEMONSTRATION: Memorandum, Wylde to Frank Macchiarola and others, June 27, 1984, Housing Partnership files.

153   WYLDE PROPOSAL FOR A MINORITY-RUN SPIN-OFF ENTITY: Memorandum, Wylde to Ellen Strauss, September 21, 1987, Housing Partnership files.

       PROPOSAL FOR A COMMUNITY PARTNERSHIP DEVELOPMENT CORPORATION: Memorandum, Kathryn Wylde to Ida Schmertz, Michael Orban, Jack Davies, and Chris Kennen, December 28, 1987, Housing Partnership files.

154   JAMES D. ROBINSON III ROLE IN SWAYING MAYOR KOCH: Interview with Kathryn Wylde.

       HOUSING PARTNERSHIP'S AUGUST 1988 PROPOSAL: Memorandum, Kathryn Wylde to Mark Willis, August 19, 1988, Housing Partnership files.

155   QUOTATION FROM FRED WILPON: Interview with Wilpon.

       QUOTATIONS FROM DEBORAH WRIGHT: Interview with Wright.

156   DEVELOPERS' $500,000 "BACKSTOP" POOL FOR NEIGHBORHOOD BUILDER PROJECTS: Interview with Kathryn Wylde; also, Elsie Crum, *Building Minority Entrepreneurship: An Evaluation of the Neighborhood Builder Program*, New York City Housing Partnership, 1993.

Lawrence Silverstein is quoted but not identified in Crum's report on p. 18.

157   SONYMA ROLE IN NEIGHBORHOOD BUILDERS CONSTRUCTION LOAN GUARANTEE: Interview with Kathryn Wylde.

QUOTATION FROM NEIGHBORHOOD BUILDERS EVALUATION: Elsie Crum, p. 18.

URBAN DEVELOPMENT CORPORATION "MINORITY REVOLVING LOAN PROGRAM": *Mainstreaming Minority Builders*, p. 16, and Elsie Crum, pp. 20-21.

158   QUOTATION FROM DEBORAH WRIGHT: Interview with Wright.

THE "CENTRAL PRINCIPLE OF THE PROGRAM": *Mainstreaming Minority Builders*, p. 14.

DATA ON NEIGHBORHOOD BUILDERS PRODUCTION: Elsie Crum, pp. 23-25, 33-34.

159   "EVERYBODY LIKES LES": Interview with Deborah Wright.

"I'LL NEVER DO ANOTHER MODULAR": Interview with Les Levi.

160   MEETING WITH MT. CARMEL MINISTERS: Account is based on author's observation of the meeting.

LEVI'S FINANCIAL DIFFICULTIES: Interviews with Kathryn Wylde and Steven Brown.

161   *NEW YORK TIMES* FEATURE ON LES LEVI: *New York Times*, November 16, 1992.

QUOTATIONS FROM LES LEVI: Interview with Levi.

QUOTATION FROM STEVEN BROWN: Interview with Brown.

162   "ECONOMIC DEVELOPMENT HAS NOT KEPT PACE": Kathryn Wylde, "The Contribution of Public-Private Partnerships to New York's Assisted Housing Industry," paper prepared for the Center for Real Estate and Urban Policy, New York University School of Law, March 28, 1996, p. 15.

THE *IN REM* HOUSING PROBLEM: Salins and Mildner, pp. 100-103; and New York City Housing Partnership, "Funding Proposal in Support of the Neighborhood Entrepreneurs Program" May 15, 1994, pp. 1-5.

163   "WE FOUND [THAT] NOTHING GOOD HAPPENED": Interview with Anthony Gliedman.

164   "LEAVING MANY VIOLATIONS UNCORRECTED": Wylde et al., *Building in Partnership*; p. 48.

OTHER POMP OWNERS: Kim Nauer, "Soft Sell," *City Limits*, April 1995: 9.

THIS SECOND APPROACH: *Building in Partnership*, p. 48.

165 QUOTATION FROM DEBORAH WRIGHT: Interview with Wright. In 1996, Wright left her position at HPD to become president and CEO of the Upper Manhattan Empowerment Zone Development Corporation.

HPD HAD "IGNORED THE ASPIRATIONS OF LOCAL RESIDENTS": "Funding Proposal in Support of the Neighborhood Entrepreneurs program," May 15, 1994, p. 4.

"NEIGHBORHOODS WHERE THE CITY'S CONTROL OF RESIDENTIAL PROPERTY": Ibid., p. 3.

166 NONPROFIT GROUPS ARE NEEDED "TO SERVE AS AGENTS OF THE PARTNERSHIP": New York City Housing Partnership, Neighborhood Entrepreneurs Program, *Interim Report*, July 1995, p. 4.

"THE EASIEST STUFF TO REHABILITATE": *New York Times*, September 24, 1994.

"WHAT HAPPENS WHEN THE CITY": Ibid.

167 QUOTATIONS FROM GEORGE CALVERT: Interview with Calvert.

168 THE EMPLOYMENT PILOT: Neighborhood Entrepreneurs Program, *Interim Report*, pp. 11-12.

NEW YORK TIMES EDITORIAL ON NEW YORK CITY INVESTMENT FUND: "New York City's Pot of Gold," August 24, 1994.

QUOTATIONS FROM INVESTMENT FUND BROCHURE: New York City Partnership, *An Investment in New York City*, February 1995, pp. 3, 8.

169 "AT LEAST 250,000 SQUARE FEET OF RETAIL SPACE": *HPD Pipeline*, Newsletter of the Department of Housing Preservation and Development, September 1995, p. 1.

QUOTATION FROM RICHARD SCHWARTZ: *HPD Pipeline*, p. 1.

"THEY HAVE HAD TWENTY YEARS": Interview with Kathy Wylde.

PARTNERSHIP PLAZA FINANCIAL PACKAGE INCLUDES: Henry R. Kravis, letter, "To Our Investors," January 2, 1997, p. 2.

"A COMPLETE FINANCIAL PACKAGE": [CHUCK TO SUPPLY]

171 "SUCCESS IN THIS TOWN IS A DISEASE": Interview with Alan Bell.

Chapter 13. Community Development: The Making of a New Urban Policy Paradigm

173   QUOTATION FROM FATHER LOUIS GIGANTE: Conference transcript, "New Homes for New York Neighborhoods," pp. 58-60.

175   "THE MOST CELEBRATED SOCIOLOGIST IN AMERICA": Sean Wilentz, "Jobless and Hopeless," *New York Times Book Review*, September 29, 1996, p. 7.

ONE OF "AMERICA'S 25 MOST INFLUENTIAL PEOPLE": *Time Magazine*, June 17, 1996.

BOOKS BY WILLIAM JULIUS WILSON: *The Truly Disadvantaged* (The University of Chicago Press, 1987) and *When Work Disappears* (Alfred A. Knopf, 1996).

176   "IF IT BLEEDS, IT LEADS": Cheryl Lavin, "Violence at 10 — Fast, cheap and easy to produce, local TV news taps our darkest fears," *Chicago Tribune*, April 4, 1997. Lavin is quoting Jack Bowen, chairman of a media consulting firm.

"BODY-BAG JOURNALISM": Paul Grogan, remarks to Chicago Neighborhood Development Awards meeting, January 31, 1995 (author's notes).

THE "DRAMATIC RETREAT FROM USING PUBLIC POLICY": William Julius Wilson, *When Work Disappears*, pp. 208-9.

WILSON'S "NEO-WPA": Ibid., p. 231.

"I . . . DO NOT ADVANCE PROPOSALS": Ibid., p. 209.

177   "BRONX MIRACLE": Title of *New York Times* editorial, March 12, 1995.

"HIDDEN GOOD NEWS": Paul Grogan, remarks to Chicago Neighborhood Development Awards meeting. "The Hidden Good News" is also the title of the 1994 annual report of the Local Initiatives Support Corporation.

178   NEW OWNERSHIP HOUSING [IS] ALSO CATCHING ON: For descriptions of ownership housing programs in several cities (including New York), see U.S. Department of Housing and Urban Development, *New American Neighborhoods* (June 1996). Also, *New York Times*, July 5, 1997.

A NEW URBAN POLICY PARADIGM: The term "new urban policy paradigm" was suggested by Richard P. Nathan. Nathan and colleagues at the Urban Neighborhoods Study Group (Nelson A. Rockefeller Institute of Government, State University of New York), outlined a "new policy paradigm" in a paper prepared for the 1994 Annual Meeting of the Association of Public Policy and Management: "Minority Work-ing- and Middle-Class Neighborhoods in New York: Case Studies of Other New Yorks," October 1994.

A FEBRUARY 1997 NATIONAL SURVEY: Local Initiatives Support Corpo-ration and Center for National Policy, *Life in the City* (1997), p. 6.

"THE FUTURE OF CITIES": Kathryn Wylde, "The Contribution of Public-Private Partnerships to New York's Assisted Housing Industry," p. 16.

180   "YOU REALIZE PRETTY FAST": Julie Johnson, "Gale Cincotta: Putting Pressure on the Banks," *The Neighborhood Works*, December 1993/January 1994: 16.

"WHAT WE SAW WAS THE WHOLE ECONOMIC THING": Brian Boyer, *Cities Destroyed for Cash* (Follett, 1973), pp. 180-81.

181   REAL ESTATE AGENTS ". . . WERE MAKING A HELL OF A LOT OF MONEY": Boyer, Ibid., p. 180.

"RIDDLED WITH CODE VIOLATIONS": Ibid., p. 181.

ORGANIZATION FOR A BETTER AUSTIN MEMBERS: Julie Johnson, "Gale Cincotta," p. 16.

THE LOCAL HUD/FHA DIRECTOR: Boyer, p. 182.

182   "WAS WRITTEN IN A CHURCH BASEMENT": Julie Johnson, "Gale Cin-cotta," p. 16.

183   VAGUENESS OF KEY TERMS IN CRA: Memorandum, Staff to Board of Governors of the Federal Reserve System, December 7, 1993 (author's files).

COMMUNITY GROUPS, FOR THEIR PART: Ibid., p. 6.

"OVER THE YEARS": Ibid., pp. 6-7.

184   CLINTON ADMINISTRATION REVAMPING OF CRA: "The New CRA," *Profitwise* (Community Affairs Newsletter of Federal Reserve Bank of Chicago), Summer 1995: 1-3.

"THE BANKS THOUGHT OF US": "Responses to the New CRA," Ibid., p. 4.

"CRA HAS RESULTED IN OVER $35 BILLION": Ibid.

QUOTATIONS FROM *WALL STREET JOURNAL*: February 13, 1996.

185   QUOTATION FROM PAUL GROGAN: *New York Times*, October 4, 1996.

CDCS "HAVE BEEN QUIETLY BUILDING": "President's Letter," *A Partner-ship of Progress* (LISC 1996 Annual Report), p. 2.

186   "SUPPORTED BY A WEB OF RELATIONSHIPS": Christopher Walker, "Nonprofit Housing Development: Status, Trends, and Prospects," *Housing Policy Debate*, Volume 4, Issue 3: 403.

FORD FOUNDATION SUPPORT OF COMMUNITY DEVELOPMENT CORPORATIONS: Mitchell Sviridoff, "The Seeds of Urban Revival," *Public Interest*, Winter 1994: 94.

CHARACTERISTICS AND NUMBER OF CDCS: National Congress for Community Economic Development, *Tying It All Together*, 1995: 19.

THE CDCS' DAUNTING TASK: See Walker, "Nonprofit Housing Development," pp. 385-93; Robert Giloth, James Tickell, Charles Orlebeke, and Patricia Wright, *Choices Ahead: CDCs and Real Estate Production in Chicago* (Nathalie P. Voorhees Center for Neighborhood and Community Improvement, May 1992), pp. 1-8.

187   ACCOMPLISHMENTS OF CDCS: National Congress for Community Economic Development, *Tying It All Together*, pp. 1-2.

188   "THE SINGLE MOST IMPORTANT STORY": Walker, "Nonprofit Housing Development," p. 393.

DATA ON LOCAL INITIATIVES SUPPORT CORPORATION: *A Partnership of Progress*, 1996 Annual Report of the Local Initiatives Support Corporation, p. 10.

CDC SUPPORTERS AS "CRAZY PEOPLE": Paul Grogan, remarks to Chicago Neighborhood Development Awards meeting.

189   DATA ON THE ENTERPRISE FOUNDATION: The Enterprise Foundation, Fact Sheet, December 1995.

A VERY DIVERSE COLLECTION WHOSE "COMMON ATTRIBUTE": National Association of Housing Partnerships, Preface to *A Catalogue of Local Housing Partnerships*, 1994.

190   MACARTHUR FOUNDATION'S FUND FOR COMMUNITY DEVELOPMENT: Robert Giloth et al., *Choices Ahead*, p. 1.

NATIONALLY, ABOUT TWO-THIRDS: Walker, "Nonprofit Housing Development," p. 396.

"A CONGRESSIONALLY-SPONSORED PUBLIC NONPROFIT": Neighborhood Reinvestment Corporation, *Affordable Homeownership: Making It Happen*, October 1991, p. 1.

191   RETURN ON INVESTMENT OF THE LOW-INCOME HOUSING TAX CREDIT: *Wall Street Journal*, November 29, 1995.

192   LOW-INCOME HOUSING TAX CREDIT AS A FORM OF "CORPORATE WELFARE": *Chicago Tribune*, December 20, 1995.

ESTIMATE OF LIHTC-INDUCED HOUSING PRODUCTION: *Wall Street Journal*, November 29, 1995.

193   U.S. TREASURY ESTIMATE OF REVENUE LOSS CAUSED BY LIHTC: James
        E. Wallace, "Financing Affordable Housing in the U.S.," *Housing Policy Debate*, Vol. 6, Issue 4 (1995): 796-97.

        LOSS OF LIHTC WOULD HOBBLE CDC PRODUCTION: Langley C. Keyes,
        Alex Schwartz, Avis C. Vidal, and Rachel G. Bratt, "Networks and
        Nonprofits: Opportunities and Challenges in an Era of Federal Devolution," *Housing Policy Debate*, Vol. 7, Issue 2 (1996): 223.

        THE CDC MOVEMENT AND CDBG: Edward G. Goetz, "Local Government
        Support for Nonprofit Housing," *Urban Affairs Quarterly*, Vol. 27, No.
        3 (1992): 425-26.

        CDBG IS THE LARGEST FEDERAL NEIGHBORHOOD ASSISTANCE PRO-
        GRAM: Richard P. Nathan, "The 'Nonprofitization Movement' as a
        Form of Devolution," prepared for the New Partnership Project, September 25, 1996, pp. 24-29.

194   "COMMUNITY HOUSING DEVELOPMENT ORGANIZATIONS" THAT HAVE "A
        HISTORY OF SERVING": Low Income Housing Information Service,
        Overview Summary of the National Affordable Housing Act of 1990
        (1991), p. 29.

195   DETROIT PROPOSAL TO "MOTHBALL" NEARLY DESERTED AREAS: Penn-
        sylvania Horticultural Society, *Urban Vacant Land: Issues and Recommendations*, (September 1995), p. 53.

        ESTIMATE OF VACANT LAND IN CHICAGO: Department of Planning, City
        of Chicago, *Vacant Land in Chicago* (1987), p. 2.

        VACANT LAND IN PHILADELPHIA: Pennsylvania Horticultural Society,
        Urban Vacant Land, p. 13.

196   QUOTATIONS FROM NEIL PEIRCE: Neil R. Peirce, "Vacant Urban Land —
        Hidden Treasure? *National Journal*, December 9, 1995, p. 3053.

        WOODLAWN — "A BYWORD FOR INNER-CITY DECAY": *Chicago Tribune*,
        December 27, 1994.

        NEW HOME CONSTRUCTION IN WOODLAWN: *Chicago Sun-Times*, November 24, 1995.

197   "WHIFFS OF REFORM" (CLEVELAND): Neal R. Peirce, "Vacant Urban
        Land," p. 3053.

        CDCS WITH A "SOLID RECORD": Ibid.

        QUOTATION FROM JAMES JOHNSON: Fannie Mae Office of Housing Research, *Housing Research News*, June 1995, p. 1.

THREE LAWS AFFECTING IMMIGRATION RATES: Patrick A. Simmons and Isaac F. Megbolugbe, "Catching the New Wave: Recent Immigration to the United States" (Fannie Mae Office of Housing Research, March 1995), pp. 2-3.

198   CHANGES IN NATIONAL ORIGINS OF IMMIGRANTS: Simmons and Megbolugbe, "Catching the New Wave," pp. 8-9, and Urban Institute, "A Sourcebook for the Immigration Debate," *Policy and Research Report*, Summer 1994, p. 20.

ECONOMIC AND FISCAL IMPACTS OF IMMIGRATION: Urban Institute, "A Sourcebook," p. 21.

199   ABOUT SEVEN OUT OF TEN: Simmons and Megbolugbe, "Catching the New Wave," p. v.

CONCENTRATION OF IMMIGRANTS IN CITIES: Kermit Daniel; "Immigrants, Poverty Place Severe Burdens on Urban Areas," *Real Estate Research Bulletin*, Wharton School of the University of Pennsylvania, Fall 1994, p. 1.

"MASSES OF NEW PEOPLE ARRIVE EACH DAY": Mitchell Sviridoff, "The Seeds of Urban Revival," p. 90.

200   "STRIKING DIFFERENCES" BETWEEN FOREIGN-BORN AND NATIVE-BORN POVERTY AREAS: Urban Institute, "A Sourcebook," p. 22.

Chapter 14. Urban Homeownership and the Future of Cities

201   "NOTHING SPELLS TURNAROUND IN A MORE PROFOUND WAY": Quotation from the Reverend Leon Finney, Jr., in the *Chicago Tribune*, November 25, 1995.

202   HOMEOWNERSHIP RATES IN CITIES, SUBURBS, AND NONMETROPOLITAN AREAS: U.S. Department of Housing and Urban Development, *U.S. Housing Market Conditions*, November 1996, p. 80.

203   SURVEY RESEARCH OF RENTERS' INTENTION TO BUY HOMES: David P. Varady and Barbara J. Lipman, "What Are Renters Really Like? Results From a National Survey," *Housing Policy Debate*, Vol. 5, Issue 4 (1994): 499.

ESTIMATE OF POTENTIAL FOR BLACK HOMEOWNERSHIP: *Chicago Sun-Times*, July 7, 1995.

"IMMIGRANTS ARE STRONGLY COMMITTED TO HOMEOWNERSHIP": James A. Johnson, "What Immigrants Want," *Wall Street Journal*, June 20, 1995.

204   HARVARD JOINT CENTER STUDY OF IMMIGRANT HOMEBUYING TRENDS:
       Patrick A. Simmons, "Catching the New Wave," Fannie Mae Office of
       Housing Research, *Housing Research News*, June 1995, p. 5.

       DATA COMPILED BY THE *WALL STREET JOURNAL* ON BLACK AND HISPANIC
       HOMEBUYERS: *Wall Street Journal*, February 13, 1996.

       THE DECISION BY FANNIE MAE: Fannie Mae, "Showing America a New
       Way Home," March 15, 1994, p. 1.

       QUOTATION FROM MARC A. WEISS: *New York Times*, July 5, 1997.

       QUOTATIONS FROM MARGARET JACKSON: Conference transcript, "New
       Homes for New York Neighborhoods," pp. 81, 88.

205   ECONOMIC INTEGRATION GOAL IN PILSEN NEIGHBORHOOD OF CHICAGO:
       The Resurrection Project, *Fifth Anniversary Report*,(1995) p. 4.

       QUOTATION FROM VICTOR KNIGHT: *Chicago Tribune*, December 27,
       1994.

       "THE DIVISION OF RACE BY PLACE": Robert W. Burchell and David Lis-
       tokin, "Influences on United States Housing Policy," *Housing Policy
       Debate*, Vol. 6, Issue 3 (1995): 564.

206   "MIDDLE-CLASS MINORITY HOUSEHOLDS": M. Leann Lachman and De-
       borah Brett, *Commentary* (Schroeder Real Estate Associates, Autumn
       1995), p. 15.

       QUOTATION FROM MICHAEL R. WHITE: David P. Varady, "Middle-Income
       Housing Programmes in American Cities," *Urban Studies*, Vol. 31, No.
       8 (1994), p. 1363.

       QUOTATIONS FROM DAVID VARADY: Ibid., pp. 1345, 1348.

207   QUOTATION FROM REVEREND ARTHUR BRAZIER: Kristin Ostberg, "Here
       Comes the Neighborhood," *Chicago Reader*, April 26, 1996, p. 26.

       HOMEOWNER BENEFITS AS "TAX EXPENDITURES": *The Challenges Fac-
       ing Federal Rental Assistance Programs* (Congressional Budget Of-
       fice, December 1994), p. 2.

       "ABOUT ONE-THIRD THE FEDERAL TAX CONTRIBUTION TO HOMEOWNER-
       SHIP": Burchell and Listokin, "Influences on United States Housing
       Policy," p. 597. The mortgage interest tax deduction has also been
       caught up in the broader issue of federal tax reform. Some proponents
       of the so-called "flat tax," such as one-time presidential contender
       Steve Forbes and House Republican leader Dick Armey, would wipe
       out the deduction as part of a radical simplification of the federal tax
       code. They claim that the economic benefits of filing one's tax return
       "on a postcard" would be so wonderful that homeowners and home-

buyers would actually be better off with the flat tax. Other political leaders who say they like the flat tax idea would spare the mortgage interest deduction because of its great popularity as a homeownership incentive. In addition, the formidable real estate lobby, especially the National Association of Home Builders and the National Association of Realtors, fights any encroachment on the deduction; during the 1996 Republican presidential primary season — when Forbes was still in the race — the real estate lobby bought television ads claiming that abolishing the deduction would rank with termites and tornadoes as "famous American home wreckers." Neil R. Peirce, "Mortgage Deduction: Its Moment of Truth?" *Nation's Cities Weekly*, March 4, 1996, p.7.

208   HOUSING POLICY HAS "MANY LAYERS": Anne B. Shlay, "Housing in the Broader Context in the United States," *Housing Policy Debate*, Vol. 6, Issue 3 (1995), pp. 706, 708.

209   "THE WILLINGNESS TO INVEST": Doug Dylla, "Reclaiming the American Dream," *Stone Soup*, Vol. 14, No. 3 (Spring 1996), p. 6.

INDEX